Information and Communication Technologies in Society

I0004800

With new information and communication technologies now an integral part of society, it has been claimed that we are in a period of almost revolutionary social change. Computers are a universal tool in all leading economic nations, and increasingly becoming so in poorer countries. The Internet is a tool of daily life for hundreds of millions, while third-generation mobile phones will soon be the norm. New, less hierarchical networks of communication are being developed, and new goods and services are proliferating. Services and information can be acquired virtually instantly.

However, this book refutes simplistic assumptions about the effects of these developments on society. It offers a range of empirical chapters that question the extent to which new technologies have actually changed society. The chapters range from qualitative studies of new users to analysis of quantitative longitudinal data and large-scale international comparative surveys. Together they cover a range of issues, such as recent trends in take-up, migration of skilled people, the economic impact of broadband, the digital divide, environmental implications, and issues to do with work, such as employability or the role of telework. It also seeks to answer major questions of welfare, such as the effect of the new technologies on social capital and on quality of life, and the relationship of the new developments with gender equality.

The book argues that the changes it identifies are the result of a complex interaction of social and technological change that is producing widespread but mostly *weak* changes when viewed close up and over short timescales. We should therefore re-think the simple macro-economic model that supposes that increased quality of life or any other social benefits will *automatically* follow from technical innovation.

Ben Anderson is Deputy Director of Chimera, a research institute of the University of Essex, UK, and is also a visiting researcher at the University of Essex's Institute for Social and Economic Research. **Malcolm Brynin** is a sociologist at the Institute for Social and Economic Research at the University of Essex, primarily interested in research on education skills and technology. **Jonathan Gershuny** is Professor of Sociology at Oxford University. **Yoel Raban** is a Senior Research Fellow at the Interdisciplinary Center for Technology Analysis and Forecasting (ICTAF) in Tel Aviv University.

Routledge studies in innovation, organization and technology

Information and Communication Technologies in Society

E-living in a digital Europe

Edited by Ben Anderson,
Malcolm Brynin, Jonathan Gershuny
and Yoel Raban

LONDON AND NEW YORK

First published 2007
by Routledge
2 Park Square, Milton Park, Abingdon, Oxon OX14 4RN

Simultaneously published in the USA and Canada
by Routledge
711 Third Ave, New York, NY 10017

Routledge is an imprint of the Taylor & Francis Group, an informa business

Typeset in Garamond by Wearset Ltd, Boldon, Tyne and Wear

British Library Cataloguing in Publication Data
A catalogue record for this book is available from the British Library

Library of Congress Cataloging in Publication Data
A catalog record for this book has been requested

ISBN10: 0-415-38384-6 (hbk)
ISBN10: 0-203-96823-9 (ebk)

ISBN13: 978-0-415-38384-4 (hbk)
ISBN13: 978-0-203-96823-9 (ebk)
ISBN13: 978-0-415-64853-0 (pbk)

Contents

1   Introduction

Malcolm Brynin, Ben Anderson and Yoel Raban

Who can doubt that new technologies, especially information and communication technologies (ICTs), are now an integral part of a society profoundly
different from that which has gone before? Computers are a universal tool
in all leading economic nations and increasingly so in the poorer countries.
The Internet is a tool of daily life for hundreds of millions, while third-
generation mobile phones will soon be the norm. New, less hierarchical networks of communication are being developed and new goods and services are
proliferating. Services and information can be acquired virtually instantly.
For some time it has been asserted that we are, or soon will be, in a period of
revolutionary social and economic change as fundamental as the Industrial
Revolution (Drucker, 1969; Bell, 1973; Dutton *et al.*, 1999; Castells, 2000).

Much analysis of the social importance of new technology examines the
effects of technological innovation in people's everyday lives. Does the new
technology lead to a qualitative shift in the way we run our lives – making it
more efficient, more fulfilling, richer or, of course, possibly the reverse of all
of these? But the findings of some research hint at a more fundamental social
change, of the emergence of a new form of society where the new technologies
are held to variously erode, create, rework, but alternatively simply *transform*,
for good or ill (and sometimes simultaneously), the way people perform many
important aspects of their lives (Kraut *et al.*, 1998, 2002; Franzen, 2000,
2003; Nie, 2001; Wellman *et al.*, 2001; Gershuny, 2003). Each finding is
implicitly treated as the tip of a hidden iceberg. What is hidden is the future.

However, radical change is unlikely, and not only because of the deflation
of the dot-com bubble. The parallel with the Industrial Revolution (and
indeed the label 'revolution') is unconvincing on numerous counts – as,
indeed, we were forewarned (Trabner, 1986; Schnaars, 1989). In a particularly well-argued critique, May (2001) suggests that there are four linked
tenets of the 'revolution':

* social revolution,
* transformation of economic relations,
* changes in political practices and the communities involved,
* terminal decline of the state and its authority.

May finds little evidence to support any of these general tenets. We also need to distinguish between form and substance. This argument resonates with Gershuny's assertion that, as technology changes, our lives carry on in familiar ways; what changes is the means through which this happens (Gershuny, 1978, 1983).

In addition to conceptual or meta-analyses such as May's, a growing body of empirically based journal articles and books have sought to provide a measured response to the rise of the new ICTs. These include Wellman and Haythornthwaite's collection (2002) and also that of Kraut *et al.* (2006). In the main, these collections have sounded a note of evidence-based caution. As with May, they conclude from the data to hand that it is clear enough that changes are happening, but it is not at all clear what the threads of causality are and what their future significance might be.

So why do we care about change and effects?

There are perhaps three major reasons to be interested in the social side of ICT-related change, which continues to engage the minds and resources of a wide range of researchers. One, which is also the most direct, is the continuing need to test the possibility that we are on the cusp of, or perhaps embedded within, a major social and economic transition. We have cast doubt upon this idea above, but the possibility is both fascinating and important, and cannot be lightly dismissed. Even where fundamental change is unlikely, we can help to map and test the significance of the myriad of small ICT-related changes. Part of the rationale for this book is to help address this issue both substantively, through a range of research results, and methodologically, through the demonstration of the kinds of data and analysis required.

Academic work does not operate in a social vacuum. Many researchers act as independent advisors to, and auditors of, policy-makers and NGOs. Some of the chapters in this book are written by authors who have these twin aims in mind. A second rationale for research in this area, and in particular for this book, is therefore that policy-makers and non-governmental organisations throughout the world need to understand the sorts of changes that are occurring in society, but which are not necessarily visible in or through official statistics. Readers might be familiar with policy initiatives from Chile to the USA or South Korea, or with the United Nations/International Telecommunications Union sponsored World Summit on the Information Society.[1] Also at the supranational level the European Commission has established the e-Europe and i2010 initiatives, which are explicitly about harnessing the potential of ICTs to help achieve policy objectives of social cohesion, inclusion and economic growth (CEC, 2005). Clearly, in order to proceed in an evidence-based manner, such policy initiatives need to be based on analyses of what social benefits ensue for whom and from what kinds of ICTs.

Commercial actors also have a need to understand the same processes, for instance to see how their markets and their supply chains are changing as

ICTs become embedded, but more especially where their business is selling ICT products and services. While academics do not often ally themselves to such goals, it seems obvious to us that there are overlaps between them. Even if social scientists are rarely privy to the vast amount of commercial data that exist on the social demand for new technologies, services or brands, and despite the gulf in analytical goals between academic and commercial researchers, both are inevitably interested in the impact of social divisions on ICT take-up and usage. The typology in the literature on diffusion between innovators and laggards, for instance, directly reflects this joint interest. Commercial interests wish to locate those who will both buy a new idea and stick with it (and tell others about it), putting into their assessments of how to find such people whatever information they might have on income, preferences and prices. The social scientist has the same underlying interest, but will use this or related information to say something about more social processes. Thus, for instance, research on social exclusion from the benefits of ICTs is simply the obverse of the commercial interest in social inclusion.

Malleable technologies

The introduction of any new good or service is often carried out with considerable uncertainty over the target group and the match between its needs and the affordances of the product. It is not surprising, therefore, that early commercial and policy expectations are often misplaced (Anderson *et al.*, 2003). Unforeseen outcomes are a part of the process of technological change. The increase in firepower in seventeenth-century armies led to 'limited' warfare where attempts were made to reduce casualties. Thus, while new technology may drive much industrial change, it often does so in unplanned and unpredictable ways (Form *et al.*, 1988; McLoughlin and Clark, 1994: 22–33; Kling, 1996). McLoughlin and Clark (1994) stress the adaptive, and even accidental, side of technological development. No technologists, policy-makers or investors can wave a magic wand to make people do things suddenly very differently. People have needs, constraints and preferences that determine which innovations succeed or fail. Technology cannot have effect unless there is social room for it to do so. People accept the technologies they want at the same time as they experiment with and adapt them to their needs. The meaning of the technology itself may change through use, whether at work (Robinson, 1993) or in the domestic setting – creating what Bakardjieva calls 'use genres' (Bakardjieva, 2005). This also makes prediction especially complex.

In the case of the new ICTs, the problem is even greater as many new technologies are malleable and multi-functional. In contrast to older technologies such as the television or the telephone, new ICTs are often platforms for many different types of service. Thus the mobile phone was a simple instrument built on the familiar functions of the fixed-line telephone, but is now more complex. The home computer is a platform providing quite disparate functions, which therefore attracts a range of often distinct interests and could have a range of individual level social benefits that cannot be meaningfully aggregated. The Internet is a delivery mechanism for a complex bundling of services and functions. Thus, while it might be possible to analyse and predict the demand for social benefits of specific services, it is extremely hard to predict the take-up of new technologies of the sort that form the subject of this book. There is simply unlikely ever to be a single 'killer technology' at this level.

We can demonstrate this, if in rather simple form, through analysis of the 1998–2001 *Home-OnLine* dataset of British households. We do this by summarising the results of a large number of logistic regressions where usage of a technology or service, or willingness to innovate, is the dependent variable, and a range of variables such as age, family, education, work, preferences (e.g. in respect of the telephone – labelled 'telephonic' in the table), division of household labour and time-use as measured by a time-use diary) form the explanatory variables. The results indicate a general tendency (which has, in turn, been assessed subjectively rather than through some computational method). The outcome is therefore similar to the kinds of profiles and segmentation models generated by commercial or market research using cluster analyses. However, what we present below are not profiles but bundles of profiles. The characteristics associated with usage of a technology need not occur in one person, and are often extremely unlikely to, whilst some characteristics are of households rather than of individuals.

Table 1.1a shows the results for three forms of ICT usage. The first, the number of purchases made in a period of time over the Internet, shows access to a fledgling technology. The second, the size of phone bills, demonstrates consumption of a mature technology. Computer usage, in the middle

Table 1.1a Factors predicting usage and uptake of goods and services

	Internet purchases	*Computer usage*	*Phone bills*
Demographics	Young male	Young	Young male
Education	High/medium	High	High or low
Family	Couples/children	Children	Children
Chores	No	–	Housework
Family beliefs	–	Illiberal	Liberal
Shopping	Equal/shared	Equal/unshared	Unequal
Telephonic	–	–	High
Newspaper	Quality	Quality	Quality
Leisure activity	Indoor	Cinema etc.	Outdoor/social
Income	Own pay	Both	Household
Work time	–	–	–
Leisure time	N/A	–	Cinema etc.
Social time	N/A	No	No
ICT time	N/A	Little TV	Telework

column, is somewhere in between. These 'profiles' are in some respects quite different. Although users or high users of all three are likely to be young and male, and also in some sort of family relationship, education is not always a consistent predictor. The distribution of household tasks varies across the profiles, as do beliefs relating to the family and work (for instance, whether women should work). Attitudes to phone usage are only notably high where phone bills are high. Leisure activities vary considerably, and while income is related to usage, in one case only own pay from work counts, in another total household income, and in the third, both of them. Perhaps the most powerful relationship is between phone usage and the use of a computer for work at home (telework) – a clear case of a functional relationship.

Table 1.1b looks at a specific example of computer usage in the third column – of games (measured through the diary). It can be seen that the profile is quite different from that of general computer usage since it describes young men with low incomes and few interests, still living with their parents. When we move to questions which specifically ask about the willingness to try new products (see also Diduca *et al.*, this volume, Chapter 7), there is no real gender difference and education is not high, which makes these people stand out: in particular, they are quite different from those who are willing to try new technologies – who are young, male and have few apparent other interests.

Do these differences represent different points on the diffusion curve or, rather, a different bundle of preferences and constraints in each case? Both

Table 1.1b Factors predicting usage and update of goods and services (cont.)

	Tries new technology	*Tries new products*	*PC games*
Demographics	Young male	Young	Young male
Education	High	Medium	Medium
Family	Single	–	Children
Chores	–	Housework	–
Family beliefs	–	–	–
Shopping	–	Unequal	Self
Telephonic	–	No	–
Newspaper	None	Midbrow	None
Leisure activity	–	Social	–
Income	–	Own pay	Negative
Work time	Low	High	Low
Leisure time	–	No hobbies	No hobbies
Social time	No	Yes	No
ICT time	PC	PC	Internet

Source: Home-OnLine Survey, UK Data Archive.

Note
For cells marked N/A, requiring time measures, analysis was not possible as a result of the diary sample being significantly smaller than the full sample.

might be a factor. That is, it is possible that when (or if) the Internet is as widespread as the fixed-line telephone, then high usage on one will be similar to high usage on another. However, this is unlikely to be the case. The difference between high users of television and of the telephone already indicates this. The choices people face, dictated by what the technologies can do, are between complex clusters of preferences. This leads to very considerable uncertainty on the part of consumers, investors and social scientists; one of the most significant reasons for this is the increasing malleability of the technologies in which we are interested. How can we either predict the take-up of, say, a future generation of computers or understand what social role they play, when different groups use these for different purposes, and while these purposes simultaneously change? There is no single process of change, but a stream of changes.

This has implications for both the way we conceptualise and analyse change and the applicability of our results. It suggests that we cannot simply analyse the demand for, or social benefits or disbenefits of, the Internet or the mobile telephone. Rather, we need to ask questions about different kinds of uses of different kinds of services. We should not expect to see many 'effects' of Internet adoption because the uses to which the services will be put may vary widely across a population and over time. Instead we should focus at a lower level, on ICT-mediated activities such as online shopping, interpersonal communication (via text, phone calls, voice mail, email, instant messaging, chat, etc.), or job and health information foraging. As editors we have encouraged some contributors to this book to pose their questions and frame their analysis at this level.

How do we know what causes change?

With this as background, we must now consider the extent to which causal explanations of the role of ICTs in social and economic change are possible. After all, if policy-makers or commercial actors want to ground their decisions not only on evidence but on some real sense of underlying social processes, they need some explanatory model that can help them to take decisions and reduce, or at least be forewarned about, otherwise unanticipated effects. In this instance a model based on association (e.g. 'those with Internet access have more social capital') is not sufficient. We need to know if using particular Internet-delivered services makes any real difference. Or is it simply that those with greater social resources are more likely to adopt the Internet simply because they are more wealthy and better educated?

However, causality is not something we can necessarily pick out conceptually, let alone empirically. If we view technological change in terms of its social construction rather than in terms of its social effects alone, then we can especially see that the causal flow is often multi-pathed and even multi-directional. Analytically, we have to say it is not clear how far down these paths we should go. They make causal analysis very difficult. In actor network theory, for instance, technological outcomes are the result of a series of 'translations' of technology design, implementation and use. Technology is 'performative' rather than given (Latour, 1986, 2000). Even more radically, Grint and Woolgar argue that we can interpret all technology in social terms (in much the same way, perhaps, that Marx viewed capital as the final form of all the labour that goes into its construction). Even a bullet already in its trajectory has a social rather than a technological meaning. We have to go even further back in the causal process to find not a cause, let alone an original cause, but yet more causality to unravel. Grint and Woolgar liken the quest for ultimate causation to stripping away layer after layer of an onion, only to find 'there is nothing at the centre' (1995: 164).

What then is the 'stopping rule'? The relationships at the heart of the discussion of the social significance of technological change are certainly complex. But that does not mean that they should be viewed as endlessly recursive or regressive, so we forever chase our own tails. This problem is certainly acknowledged. Grint and Woolgar, for instance, argue that technical phenomena are 'constituted (rather than ... shaped, affected etc.) by social processes' (Grint and Woolgar, 1995: 51). Cause and effect here become indistinguishable. Each apparent effect is a cause in some further process. This is analytically neat but empirically insecure. The relationship between the technological and the social becomes opaque, even somewhat mysterious, almost personal to the analyst. It is no wonder that Grint and Woolgar call their own method 'hard work' (1995: 114).

It also makes it very difficult to develop a general theory of social change related to technology. This paradoxically returns us to the quest for effects. At some point technologies or products and service come into the social domain through the market or through policy/NGO interventions. Whilst we always need to consider the social nature of their development and the increasingly tight loop between use (consumption) and design, we need, at specific points in time, to isolate how people are affected by technological change, even if our view of the section of the causal chain we are analysing would differ if we could examine a longer stretch. Ultimately, after all, the chain is infinite. Probably none of the analysts discussed above, who have helped to unravel the social meaning of technology, would object to the simple idea, for instance, that technology is a mediator and sometimes intensifier of existing social processes. This is a limited research aim.

Even here we need to be precise about the level at which we expect change to occur. In the introduction to the volume by Kraut *et al.* (2006), the analytical problem is viewed as one of being sure what level you are dealing with. The most basic is where we analyse technology as a tool and expect only limited behavioural changes, for instance through substituting one tool for another to achieve the same goal. However, new technologies might be associated with new goals, which form a broader level of effects. If we can additionally observe changes in welfare outcomes, we again move to a more extensive level. Finally, if the summation of these changes induces or interacts with some overall change in society, we are at the broadest of all levels.

The fundamental issue then becomes not, for instance, whether we can genuinely infer from a small qualitative analysis that the Internet or any other technology is making society closer, but whether the micro-level effects we see aggregate into societal-level effects. As we have already suggested, most analysts (including ourselves) like to think that what we find is only the tip of the social iceberg. But in practice the relationship between the micro and the macro, between the small and the large, is often indeterminate. At the very least, the whole is generally less than the sum of its parts. But also, the sum might itself take a long time to work out. In the relatively few years for which we generally have relevant data, the social phenomena of interest are often difficult to observe effectively. In 2030 and with the benefit of hindsight, we may be able to discern a cumulative, aggregate change and thus be able to argue more cogently about revolution or evolution, but in the here and now this is less certain. We need to think very carefully about the methods we use to measure change and to ascribe causality.

How is this to be done?

When we are looking for causal relationships, we can do this in the aggregate (e.g. national level) or through micro-level techniques. The former takes averages and sees how these relate to each other. While comparing national averages obscures the micro-level variation that occurs below that level, research of this sort is at least avoiding possibly unwarranted inferences from micro-level to macro-level change. The chapters in this book by Dutton, Shepherd and di Genarro, by Rothgang and Schmidt, and by Dehio and Graskamp, are examples of the aggregate approach. Most of the rest of the analysis presented in the book is at the micro level, primarily of the individual or household.

This might be qualitative or quantitative, and we have examples of each here. Both have different things to offer, but both also have some overlapping problems. These relate to the above discussion of whether or not we really can separate out cause from effect. There has been a great deal of statistical effort designed to overcome these problems. We take as an example the case of the computer wage premium that has developed within economics, starting with Krueger (1993). What is the actual relationship between the computer and the user? Does the premium derive from the machine itself, from its software, from the skills it requires, or from the processes for which it is typically used? DiNardo and Pischke (1997), Entorf and Kramarz (1997) and Borghans and ter Weel (2004) argue that the effect comes from the individual qualities of the workers who use the computers. These are simply different types of people from those who do not use computers at work. The cause of any pay effects of computer usage might really be these individual and occupational differences. We need a way around the problem, and the most attractive is to use longitudinal data where individuals are repeatedly measured over time to control for individual characteristics prior to, for example, being given a PC at work, and for things that are not measured at all (unmeasured heterogeneity). Some of the datasets that underpin the chapters of this book provide just this kind of data, albeit not over long periods – for instance, Home-OnLine (Britain) has three waves, e-Living (six European countries) only two. But with such data, it might be possible to see if there are social changes associated with technological change such as the increased use of e-commerce or of switching to broadband from narrowband Internet access.

If we return to the sociological approach discussed above, as we cannot easily distinguish the social from the technological, we cannot ever unravel a 'pure' effect of technology. Nevertheless, even if we partially accept that cause and effect are conflated, we cannot leave it like that. We need a method to ensure that, as far as the relationships in which we are interested can be unravelled, this is done correctly. This applies to any form of analysis, but here we give an example of a common problem with regression techniques, which are prominent in this book. We gain by using these because we nearly always do this in a multivariate form that enables us to produce a precise figure for the statistical effect of one factor on another (or an association between them if we are uncertain of a casual relationship), while controlling for the effects of many other factors. The trouble is that we usually only have part of the picture. We might have information on pay and computer usage at work, and also on gender, education and occupation, which comprise the things we mainly wish to control for. But we often know nothing about, say, motivation. What if computer users earn more not because they use computers or because they are, say, male, better educated and in professional jobs, but because, apart from all that, they are simply more highly motivated? In this case we cannot be sure of our causal relationships.

Very broadly, there seem to be four main approaches to this problem. The first is just to pack the equation with as many control variables as possible (if the data exist), in the hope that the remaining variation associated with the factor or factors of central interest is at least partially controlled. Some chapters in this book take this approach.

Second, assumptions can be made about the conditions under which these problems should occur. For instance, the analysis of the effects of computers on wages is problematic, but we need not assume that this is an issue for gender differences, so we can perhaps legitimately describe the gendering of the apparent computer effect even if we do not fully understand the nature of the causal relationship.

A third approach is to use statistical techniques that deal with variation in the dependent variable which is not given directly by the variables of interest, for instance latent class analysis, fixed effects, or some two-stage regression process. Each has its own purpose and requirements, but the latter might be formidable. Fixed effects analysis, for instance, requires panel data, whilst two-stage analysis requires a variable which is an effective instrument and this is often not available. Also, not all analysts are familiar with the techniques on offer and, indeed, no chapters in this volume use any of these more complex techniques.

Finally, we can make clear in the discussion of the results that we are uncertain of the causal relationship. Many of the chapters in this book take this approach. For example using the e-Living data, Sofer and Raban (this volume, Chapter 6) have information on usage (for instance of the Internet), personal characteristics such as age and education, and data on competing leisure or technology usage, such as the amount of time spent watching television. Ideally a statistical solution would be found that either controls for the multiple inter-relationships between these (for instance, TV viewers have specific characteristics that affect the likelihood of using the Internet), or explicitly maps the causal relationships. Instead, the authors make certain assumptions that are important in helping us to understand the nature of the problem. One, for instance, is that usage of a particular technology is not determined by, nor determines, other specific usages. Rather, it follows its own path, which we can try to delineate. It might often be better to make such assumptions (if they are reasonable!) rather than to rely on complex statistical techniques.

The social and economic importance of the new ICTs

Much of what we have written above implies that we need analysis, and overviews of research, that combines more than one approach. The emphasis in published work is often primarily from one angle, whether broadly sociological, social psychological or economic. We believe that these aspects are all different sides of the same coinage, even if each offers a very particular type of insight. In this book we have chapters that look at the social and sociological side, but from the economic angle we include work on the relationship between computers and wages (as an indicator of productivity), while on the commercial side we have inputs on the take-up of broadband and on the growth of ICTs in business-to-business operations.

What sorts of effects can these multiple approaches give an insight into? The literature commonly refers to effects that describe how people relate to each other, how they achieve functional goals, whether the patterns of their lives change – especially through the substitution of one activity through another – and how they work. The first of these has been extensively covered elsewhere, especially in books where the predominant ethos is either social–psychological (e.g. Kraut *et al.*, 2006) or sociological (e.g. Wellman and Haythornthwaite, 2002). None of our chapters are specifically on the issue of networking. However, three chapters investigate the possibility that the new ICTs enhance social capital (Ling, Anderson, and Heres and Thomas). The main conclusion that can perhaps be drawn from these is that the case for an ICT effect is not strong. The studies by Ling, and by Heres and Thomas, indicate that there may be some interactions between ICTs and bonding as well as bridging capital. In the case of bonding capital, which stems from strong ties with similar others, Ling's work shows the way in which mobile phones and email are used to maintain informal social networks. In the case of bridging capital, which stems from weak ties with dissimilar others, Heres and Thomas show that even when a range of socio-demographic factors are controlled for, those who engage in civic activities are much more likely to be Internet users than those who do not participate. Whilst neither chapter makes strong claims about causal relationships, we could suggest that either increased ICT usage increases social activity levels (perhaps by facilitating arrangements), or that the socially active need ICTs to help manage their lives – or, indeed, that both are occurring simultaneously. Anderson examines potential ICT effects on life satisfaction, finding generally little causal link between the two.

The question of the achievement of functional goals is mostly considered here on the basis of what particular types of people might wish and expect. Dutton and colleagues use an international comparative dataset to show how use and non-use may be re-configuring access to people, information and services where participation in this process may be becoming an issue of choice as well as of exclusion through social stratification. This is echoed by DiDuca, Partridge and Heres who look at the question of the functionality of ICTs for older people. They show that lower use of the Internet among the elderly is a result of lack of knowledge about the technology rather than mere technophobia – older people who are users are no different from other users. They suggest several means of encouraging Internet use among older people, such as through public service delivery, and through health services. Livingstone and Bober analyse Internet use by young people. Children gain valued social status by their Internet experience and particularly enjoy new opportunities for communications opened by the Internet. In other words, children add a value of their own to the use of the new ICTs. Sofer and Raban discuss in their chapter the gender gaps in ICT access and usage, and note that, at least in the e-Living sample, gender gaps in ICT usage are still to be found. However, one of the strongest determinants of this is workforce participation (which links well with the message of some other chapters). Implicitly, an increase in the participation rates of women will contribute to reducing the gendered gap. The authors point to a gap in the intensity of home Internet usage, associated mainly with more negative attitudes towards computers and the Internet, but overall it is difficult to believe that the gender differences in ICT access and use are anything more than superficial. The technologies may be functional in different ways for men and women (Boneva and Kraut, 2002) but in overall terms probably equally functional. Such social distinctions also appear in the chapter by Bakardjieva, who addresses how people become a part of the social network of Internet users in Bulgaria, where usage is in its infancy and where the costs of access are high relative to income. Here we see, though, that the standard emphasis on social exclusion breaks down. Now, not only is there no clear gap between Bulgarians and people in richer countries, as professionals in Eastern Europe see it as important to be part of the international community, but within Bulgaria illicit provision of and access to services extends the network amongst those who would otherwise be excluded.

Substitution effects are a central part of the modern research effort because these say something directly about the social role of ICTs. If the Internet replaces social life (Kraut *et al.*, 1998; Nie, 2001), then the social effect is clearly negative. But, as Heres and Thomas note in their chapter, perhaps the Internet complements traditional social behaviour. The chapter by Gershuny specifically tackles this issue through the use of panel data to show that people with specific characteristics select into technology uses, rather than being affected by them, and can therefore on the basis of probability be recognised as users *in advance* by these characteristics. The social underpins the technology, not vice versa. Raban in his chapter of trends in usage similarly finds rather weak relationships in the e-Living sample between the daily time spent at home on the Internet and the frequency of several leisure activities (sports, cinema, restaurants, reading and friends' visits). For most leisure activities, increased Internet usage time hardly affects leisure frequency. Similar issues of substitution and the effects of switching to broadband Internet access are discussed in Anderson and Raban, showing that whilst 'broadband for all' may lead to more time being spent online, it may not make much difference to other aspects of everyday life.

To these effects we can add changes that relate not to social life or consumption, but to work. This is important because a very large part of people's active time is spent at work, and so the aspirations and expectations we derive from it, especially through the adequate utilisation of skills, is often fundamental to people's well-being. Whilst some of the most far-reaching effects of the new technologies occur through organisational change, income from work helps to determine consumption levels, and this in turn has major implications for the demand for new technologies and associated services. In addition, income enables people to spend more on traditional services such as house cleaning, gardening or home improvements (Gershuny, 2000), which releases time for hobbies, or further work which could increase ICT usage and demand.

One element in this network of relationships is the effects of IT usage or skills on wages; if these are positive, an aggregate effect on national productivity (and wealth) is implied through their summation. Alternatively, employers might also introduce computers not only to replace workers but to replace their skills. Much work with computers might therefore be monotonous, uncreative and poorly paid, leading to a decrease in wealth. Thus analysis has to look out for potential distributional outcomes as well as average effects. Brynin's chapter locates the argument not in terms of productivity but of the gendering of technology, an issue of long-standing interest (Cockburn, 1983), finding that women have gained in general from computers, but also that some women have gained substantially more than others.

The use of a computer is a crude indicator of a technological work process. There are computers for complex and for simple tasks. Using the Dutch dataset, Telepanel, Steijn and Tijdens look at the distribution of usage in terms of three indicators – complexity (especially technical), diversity (of functions or software) and intensity (indicating hours of usage). They find that women are likely to use computers more intensively than men, but also in less complex and diverse ways. Thus, there remains a gender bias in the use of computers at work. The work of Steijn and Tijdens is not explicitly about gender, however. More generally, they argue that we can see a clear distribution in the potential welfare outcomes in terms of quality of the work experience.

Overall work-based effects are perhaps amongst the strongest found in this book, although here too selection issues are at stake. Haddon and Brynin's chapter looks at this with respect to telework, which is often held to be a potential factor in changing the relationship between work and home. It is well known that telework remains a very marginal form of work, but this chapter also argues that its use reflects traditional work patterns and social divisions, rather than adding to them. Nevertheless, improving the quality of life in society, for instance through the encouragement of telework, is one of the key objectives of some governments. However, Anderson and Yttri show that this is difficult to achieve. Not only is there considerable churn to and from traditional forms of work, but switching workstyles seems to have no positive effect on either job satisfaction or overall quality of life. Indeed, in some cases the effect is negative.

Economic effects are, of course, much broader than this, and this is captured by the studies in this book that work at the macro level. Implicit in some of the chapters just discussed is the distribution and utilisation of skills. This has important welfare implications which increasingly span the entire globe. When rich countries lack these skills, at least in sufficient numbers, they often seek to import them. People in poorer countries have at the same time a constant incentive to migrate. The 'brain drain' is an inevitable result. The clearest and most controversial source of this is in the field of medical care, with increasing reliance on (rather weak) bi-lateral agreements between governments to limit this. Yet governments, nongovernmental institutions and private companies in poorer countries invest in other skills which are also prone to loss abroad. ICT professionals figure in this, almost to the same extent as health professionals. Here the moral dimension is perhaps less straightforward – after all, the individuals who choose to migrate have also invested in their skills. Nevertheless, the welfare loss to the originating country could be considerable. Rothgang and Schmidt tackle this difficult subject here in an innovative piece of work that examines the determinants of high-skilled migration into OECD countries and, through analysis of the impact of international demand for skills on the expansion of education in poorer countries, some of the welfare effects. Is there a straight transfer of welfare from poor to rich country, or is it more complex than that?

Even after the subsiding of the Internet bubble, the new ICT developments are clearly big business. One way of looking at this is to examine the share of GDP growth taken up by the new ICTs (OECD, 2003) or, alternatively, the aggregate effects on productivity associated with it (e.g. Black and Lynch, 2001). A further approach to the assessment of the impact of the new ICTs is to measure the share of e-commerce in the world's GDP. Dehio and Graskamp undertake this in their chapter. Looking at 2001, right after the dissipation of the bubble, this share amounted to only 1 or 2 per cent, but they argue that this is expected to rise to 8 per cent in 2010.

Of course the computerisation in the workplace discussed above need not be simply about getting the job done, although this is paramount, but may also be about reducing environmental costs, especially where incentivised by shareholder pressure or tax and legislation regimes. Alakeson and Goodman provide a range of insights into sustainable business practices through the lens of corporate social responsibility. Like Pasquini and Viccario, they highlight the potential benefits of increased dematerialisation whether it be of business transactions (Alakeson) or music consumption (Pasquini), but also note that such benefits are often erased by subsequent rebound effects where people, for perfectly rational reasons, choose to re-materialise digital material.

This wide-ranging discussion of the economic effects of change in ICT development, from aggregate economic indicators, through the effects on the wages and work processes of different social groups, to international flows of skills, denotes distinctive changes in the distribution of social outcomes of various kinds. As our discussion of the direct social effect implies, it is possibly through such economic changes that we will for the first time be able to observe and measure the social effects of the new technologies. This is not to say that social effects that are non-economic in origin are likely to be unimportant, but that they are inherently harder to measure. In setting economically oriented studies alongside the studies of social processes in this book, we hope that readers can build on this more integrated view of ICTs and social change.

Conclusion

If there is one word that perhaps simply encapsulates the changes we have described, it is speed. The things we do – obtain or provide information, communicate with people, buy things, use services – are done or obtained faster than ever before. Perhaps, in the case of the new ICTs, speed generates a qualitative change in so far as more can be done, more intensively, and perhaps both more freely and knowingly than before (though Marx commented to the effect that the development of the modern press ushered in an age not of instant knowledge but of instant rumour). Writers on postmodernism such as Harvey (1997) have argued that it is the ability to cut and paste life that now makes things so different. According to this view, the new technologies allow the shifting of functions and uses to fit in with personal inclinations. Technologies have lost their bullying, uncompromising nature. Perhaps here we can begin to see how technology is merging with a new social way of doing things. Nevertheless, many of the processes we and others have described touch most people's lives either not at all or at best tangentially.

Our claim is not that there are no social effects of the new technologies. Rather, they are *widespread but weak*. It is also quite clear that, for a long time now, ICTs have combined and delivered final services in ways that alter social patterns (Gershuny, 1983). This also applies to many other household appliances. In respect of information and communications, it applies to telephony, television and even newspapers and books. Yet all these things existed before the new ICTs, which therefore simply intensify and mediate much the same sort of content that has always come through the mass media. Are these new ways of doing things leading to quantitative and qualitative shifts? With the best evidence available, much of which is captured in this book, it still seems too early to tell.

As a result, the chapters in this volume are rightly cautious about making causal inferences and major claims. Rather, most authors see a complex interaction or co-evolution of social and technological change that is producing widespread but weak changes when viewed close up and over short timescales. This book is one assessment of these changes, with a focus, although not completely so, on Europe. Our emphasis on both the social and the economic illustrates the complexity of phenomena that we and the contributors to this volume study. As this introduction has implied, and each chapter will show, this complexity also requires sophisticated data and methods to be able to say anything meaningful, and these are neither cheap to acquire nor easy to apply. We hope that this volume contributes both to the development of these methods and also to the development of more nuanced understandings of the relationships between ICTs and socioeconomic change.

However the book's strongest message must be that we should carefully re-think the simple macro-economic model which supposes that increased quality of life, social cohesion and so forth will automatically follow from ICT innovations and supply-side interventions. Again, we need a more nuanced view. The small effects are certainly occurring. It remains to be seen whether these will merge into some big effect.

Acknowledgements

Some of the research reported here was funded by the European Commission funded Framework 5 project e-Living (IST-2000-25409).

Note

1 See www.itu.int/wsis/.

References

Anderson, B., Gale, C., Gower, A.P. *et al.* (2003) Digital living – people centred innovation and strategy. *Btexact Communications Technology Series*, 5, 199–226.

Anderson, B. and Tracey, K. (2001) Digital living: the 'impact' or otherwise of the Internet on everyday life. *American Behavioral Scientist*, 45, 457–476.

Bakardjieva, M. (2005) *Internet Society: the Internet in Everyday Life*, London, Sage.

Bell, D. (1973) *The Coming of Post-Industrial Society*, Harmondsworth, Penguin.

Black, S. and Lynch, L. (2001) How to compete: the impact of workplace practices and information technology on productivity. *The Review of Economics and Statistics* 83(3), 434–445.

Boneva, B. and Kraut, R. (2002) Email, gender, and personal relationships. In Wellman, B. and Haythornthwaite, C. (eds) *The Internet in Everyday Life*, Oxford, Blackwell, pp. 372–403.

Borghans, L. and ter Weel, B. (2004) Are computer skills the new basic skills? The returns to computer, writing and math skills in Britain. *Labour Economics*, 11, 85–98.

Castells, M. (2000) *The Rise of the Network Society*, London, Blackwells.

CEC (2005) Working together for growth and jobs: a new start for the Lisbon Strategy. *Communication to the Spring European Council.* Brussels, Commission of the European Communities.

Cockburn, C. (1983) *Brothers: Male Dominance and Technological Change*, London, Pluto Press.

DiNardo, J.E. and Pischke, J.S. (1997) The returns to computer use revisited: have pencils changed the wage structure too? *Quarterly Journal of Economics*, 112, 291–303.

Drucker, P.F. (1969) *The Age of Discontinuity: Guidelines to our Changing Society*, New York, Harper & Row.

Dutton, W.H., Peltu, M. and Bruce, M. (1999) *Society on the Line: Information Politics in the Digital Age*, Oxford, Oxford University Press.

Entorf, H. and Kramarz, F. (1997) Does unmeasured ability explain the higher wages of new technology workers? *European Economic Review*, 41, 1489–1509.

Form, W., Kaufman, R., Parcel, T. and Wallace, M. (1988) The impact of technology on work organization and work outcomes: a conceptual framework and research agenda. In Farkas, G. and England, P. (eds) *Industries, Firms, and Jobs.* New York, Plenum Press.

Franzen, A. (2000) Does the Internet make us lonely? *European Sociological Review*, 16, 427–438.

Franzen, A. (2003) Social capital and the Internet: evidence from Swiss panel data. *Kyklos*, 56, 341–360.

Gershuny, J. (1978) *After Industrial Society? The Emerging Self-service Economy*, London, Macmillan.

Gershuny, J. (1983) *Social Innovation and the Division of Labour*, Oxford, Oxford University Press.

Gershuny, J. (2000) *Changing Times: Work and Leisure in Postindustrial Society*, Oxford, Oxford University Press.

Gershuny, J. (2003) Web use and net nerds: a neo-functionalist analysis of the impact of information technology in the home. *Social Forces*, 82, 141–168.

Grint, K. and Woolgar, S. (1995) On some failures of nerve in constructivist and feminist analyses of technology. In Grint, K. and Gill, R. (eds) *The Gender–Technology Relation: Contemporary Theory and Research*, London, Taylor and Francis.

Harvey, D. (1997) *The Condition of Postmodernity: an Enquiry into the Origins of Cultural Change*, Oxford, Basil Blackwell.

Kling, R. (1996) Computerization at work. In Kling, R. (ed.) *Computerization and Controversy: Value Conflicts and Social Choices*, San Diego, Academic Press.

Kraut, R., Brynin, M. and Keisler, S. (2006) *New Technologies at Home*, Oxford, Oxford University Press.

Kraut, R., Kiesler, S., Boneva, B., Cummings, J., Helgeson, V. and Crawford, A. (2002) Internet paradox revisited. *Journal of Social Issues*, 58, 49–74.

Kraut, R., Patterson, M., Lundmark, V., Kiesler, S., Mukopadhyay, T. and Scherlis, W. (1998) Internet paradox: a social technology that reduces social involvement and psychological well-being? *American Psychologist*, 53, 1017–1031.

Krueger, A.B. (1993) How computers have changed the wage structure: evidence from microdata, 1984–1989. *Quarterly Journal of Economics*, 108, 33–60.

Latour, B. (1986) The powers of association. In Law, J. (ed.) *Power, Action and Belief: a New Sociology of Knowledge?* London, Routledge.

Latour, B. (2000) Technology is society made durable. In Grint, K. (ed.) *Work and Society: a Reader*, Cambridge, Polity Press.

McLoughlin, I. and Clark, J. (1994) *Technological Change at Work*, Buckingham, Open University Press.

May, C. (2001) *The Information Society: a Sceptical View*, London, Polity Press.

Nie, N. (2001) Sociability, interpersonal relations, and the Internet. *American Behavioural Scientist*, 45, 420–435.

OECD (2003) *ICT and Economic Growth: Evidence from OECD Countries, Industries and Firms*, Paris, Organisation for Economic Co-operation and Development.

Robinson, M. (1993) Design for unanticipated use. In De Michelis, G., Simone, C. and Schmidt, K. (eds) *ECSCW '93: 3rd European Conference on Computer-supported Cooperative Work*, Milan, Dordrecht, London, Kluwer Academic Publishers.

Schnaars, S.P. (1989) *Megamistakes: Forecasting and the Myth of Rapid Technological Change*, New York, London, Free Press; Collier Macmillan.

Trabner, M. (ed.) (1986) *The Myth of the Information Revolution: Social and Ethical Implications of Communication Technology*, London, Sage.

Wellman, B., Haase, A.Q., Witte, J. and Hampton, K. (2001) Does the Internet increase, decrease, or supplement social capital? Social networks, participation, and community commitment. *American Behavioral Scientist*, 45, 436–455.

Wellman, B. and Haythornthwaite, C.A. (2002) *The Internet in Everyday Life*, Oxford, Blackwell.

2 Trends in ICTs

Yoel Raban

In this chapter we explain and interpret the major forces influencing the processes of residential adoption and usage of ICTs in six countries (UK, Italy, Germany, Norway, Bulgaria and Israel). In the analysis we focus on the Internet as the main enabler of the information revolution and treat other ICTs such as mobile phones, digital TV and personal computers as access devices.

The uptake of the Internet by households has been studied by many scholars (see Kridel *et al.*, 1999, for example). However, explaining determinants of Internet usage and its impact on our daily life is still a challenge. More than fifteen years after the Internet has started penetrating residential markets, relatively little is known about the characteristics of usage and about the impact of usage on other daily activities.

Our main aim in this chapter is to test the place the Internet has in people's lives. We do this, first, by distinguishing two aspects of take-up – usage and intensity of usage – and, second, through examining the extent to which Internet activity appears to be a substitute for other daily, and more traditional, activities. We argue that the Internet has different levels of impact on people's lives, with intensive users being quite different from other users, while substitution effects are rather limited. The overall implication is that in terms of everyday, general usage, the Internet has a limited social space.

In the following sections, therefore, we analyse Internet uptake, usage and impact in the e-Living sample. Internet uptake is explained by demographics and computer 'literacy'. We produce a graph of Internet diffusion for each country and demonstrate its relationship to the level of computer literacy. We then analyse the determinants of Internet usage intensity. Usage intensity is measured by both duration and depth of use. We explain the variability of both measures by several possible predictors. The last section deals with the impact of daily Internet usage on the frequency of several leisure activities in order to test whether Internet usage substitutes for more traditional leisure time.

The e-Living survey data

The research reported here uses two waves of a longitudinal ICT-focused household panel survey, 'e-Living'. The survey recruited a single adult in 1,750 households in each of the UK, Norway, Germany, Italy, Bulgaria and Israel in 2001. The wave-one sample was recruited and weighted for non-response to provide a representative population sample in each country. Households were selected using a form of stratified random sampling and individuals within households were selected using the first birthday rule. Computer aided telephone interviewing (CATI) was used in all countries except Bulgaria where the low penetration of fixed-line telephony mean that face-to-face (PAPI) interviewing was used. This is reflected in the overall wave-one response rates.

The e-Living wave-two survey attempted to re-interview these respondents in late 2002 using the same methods (CATI in all but Bulgaria), even if they had moved, and it also sought to interview their partners if present. In addition, an extra survey instrument was introduced at wave two. This was a twenty-four hour time-use diary derived from a method developed by Kestnbaum *et al.* (2002) which asked the respondents to recall their sequential activities starting from 0:01 the previous morning through to 11:59 the previous evening.

Overall longitudinal response rates are shown in Table 2.1. As we can see, between 60 per cent (Israel) and 83 per cent (Bulgaria) of wave-one respondents were re-interviewed at wave two, of whom nearly all completed the twenty-four hour time-use diary, except in Israel. A reasonable sample of partners was also achieved, of whom most also completed the time-use diary, again with the notable exception of Israel.

The surveys covered a wide range of socio-demographics, including age and household structure, qualification levels, employment types and structures as well as detailed items on ICT ownership and usage. In addition, it

Table 2.1 e-Living response rates wave one–two

	UK	Italy	Germany	Norway	Bulgaria	Israel
W 1 achieved	1,760	1,762	1,756	1,753	1,750	1,751
W 1 response rate	36%	42%	43%	35%	77%	39%
W 2 achieved	1,153	1,153	1,160	1,216	1,457	1,061
W 2 response as % of wave one achieved	66%	65%	66%	69%	83%	60%
W 2 respondents diary completed	1,137	1,149	1,159	1,215	1,454	1,052
W 2 partners in hh	445	335	433	511	870	630
W 2 partners interviewed	373	316	400	438	870	311
W 2 partner response rate	84%	94%	92%	86%	100%	49%
W 2 partners' diary completed	363	317	400	438	868	310

contained a number of items that captured proxies for social capital indicators and for subjective quality of life.

Internet uptake

The share of PC households in the e-Living sample ranges from 68 per cent
in Norway to 45 per cent in Italy, but only 8 per cent in Bulgaria. The share
of households with Internet access lags slightly with 58 per cent in Norway,
36 per cent in Italy, and 5 per cent in Bulgaria. The penetration of mobile
phones in the e-Living sample is already quite high, reaching close to 80 per
cent in most countries, with the exception of Bulgaria (17 per cent). Digital
TV shows much slower penetration rates, ranging from 39 per cent of
households in Israel to 5 per cent in Italy (and none in Bulgaria, where
digital TV services were not offered at the time).

Internet diffusion

The diffusion of the Internet has already been studied by several scholars.
Most diffusion studies focus on explaining the differences in Internet uptake
between countries (for example, Dholakia *et al.*, 2003 or Beilock and Dimitrova, 2003). A smaller number of studies try to explain the differences in
Internet uptake between individuals (Rappoport *et al.*, 2002). Personal-level
analysis ideally requires longitudinal data on individual choices, rather than
aggregate country level data.

A detailed analysis of PC use in the e-Living panel survey is described in
Raban *et al.* (2002). Education, age and income are important predictors of
PC use. Work status is positively related to PC use, since PC skills are often
both needed and acquired in the workplace. It was also found that there was
no significant increase in PC usage (the percentage of individuals using PCs)
in most countries over the period of the panel, which might indicate some
sort of upper limit of willingness to use a home PC.

PC use can therefore be predicted by a combination of demographics such
as age, education, income and work status. We would expect Internet usage
to be similarly explained. Indeed, Internet uptake is closely related to PC
use. The correlation between the two variables in both waves ranges between
0.63 and 0.77 in the six countries studied.

Figure 2.1 shows Internet use diffusion in the six countries in the
e-Living project. The diffusion is based on respondents' experience with the
Internet, which was converted into the year of Internet adoption. This is a
measure of the actual rate of past adoption. It does not measure the net
yearly rate of adoption, since it does not include Internet drop-outs. We can
see that the rate of Internet adoption is slowing in most countries, and even
stops altogether in Norway, as it approaches the barrier of maximum current
PC use. In some countries (Israel, Italy and Germany) there seems to be a
certain upturn in the pace of Internet adoption in 2002, which may be a

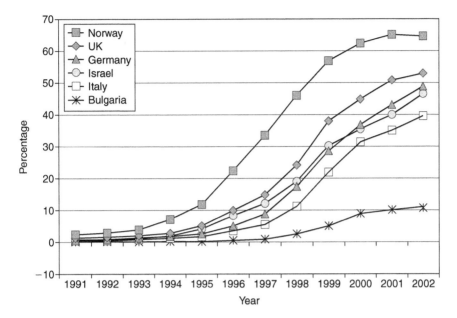

Figure 2.1 Internet use diffusion.

result of new broadband offerings. The pattern of sales slowdown followed by sales growth is known in the marketing literature as a 'saddle'. It can be explained by moving from an early market to the main market (Goldberg *et al.*, 2002), or in our case moving from narrowband to broadband.

This phenomenon is captured by the positive effects of year 2002 dummy variables depicted in Table 2.2. The purpose of this table is to examine factors that might influence the diffusion rates we see in Figure 2.1. It shows logit regression coefficients of Internet use in e-Living's 2001 and 2002 data. Age is a strong predictor of Internet use, while a certain gender gap is visible in most countries. Above all, though, the table confirms other research as well as the PC effect discussed above, in showing the substantial impact on take-up of income and education, though work status surprisingly has a negative coefficient in the UK and Germany.

The use of a PC is the most significant predictor of Internet use, but since it is so dominant, we decided to exclude it from the regression. Digital TV was not used for Internet access during 2001 and 2002 – the percentage of respondents indicating such usage is negligible. Mobile phones were already used for Internet access during this period, but there are no signs in the e-Living sample of any significant use of alternative access modes. The mobile phone is not used as an alternative to the PC. Respondents that used the Internet mostly on a mobile phone accounted for less than 1 per cent in 2001 and 2002.

Table 2.2 Internet use (0, 1) logit regression coefficients

	UK	Italy	Germany	Norway	Bulgaria	Israel
Age	−0.05***	−0.06***	−0.07***	−0.06***	−0.07***	−0.05***
Work status (0, 1)	−0.38*	0.39**	−0.29*	1.01***	0.35	0.39**
Marital status (0, 1)	−0.12	−0.48***	0.10	0.18	−0.82***	−0.78***
High school education	0.78***	1.50***	0.94***	0.88***	1.95	1.24**
Higher education	2.03***	3.09***	1.47***	1.96***	3.29**	2.26***
Male	0.08	0.47**	0.65***	0.59***	−0.00	0.60***
Low income group	−1.27***	−1.02***	−0.52	−0.14	−1.17*	−1.09***
High income group	0.72**	0.93***	0.91***	−0.30*	0.96***	1.90***
2002 dummy	0.26	0.18	0.27*	0.16	0.09	0.36**
Constant	1.81***	0.41	2.02***	1.53***	−1.73	−0.41
R^2	0.29	0.26	0.30	0.31	0.32	0.24
N	1,397	1,389	1,513	1,937	2,547	1,426

Note
* $p < 0.05$, ** $p < 0.01$, *** $p < 0.001$.

Internet drop-outs

Internet drop-outs are a relatively new phenomenon in the research literature. Lenhart (2003) finds that the Internet population in the US is fluid and shifting. A total of 20 per cent of non-users use the Internet indirectly with the help of another family member, 17 per cent are Internet drop-outs and 24 per cent are 'truly disconnected'. Drop-outs stopped using the Internet because of having problems with their computers or Internet connections, or simply because they did not like the Internet (though two-thirds of them said they think they will return to the Internet some day). Katz and Aspden (1998) find that the main reasons for leaving the Internet are: loss of Internet access, lack of interest, problems with use and high costs.

The SIBIS benchmarking project (2003) also measured drop-out rates in the EU.[1] In the EU, drop-out rates in 2002 (per cent of population) range from 3.3 per cent in France to 13.7 per cent in Sweden, compared to 20 per cent in the USA. Drop-out rates are lower in Germany (3.9 per cent), Italy (2.8 per cent), but higher in the UK (12.2 per cent).

The pattern of new Internet adopters and drop-outs in e-Living between 2001 and 2002 differs across countries. We see higher rates of both adopters and drop-outs in Bulgaria (each around 40 per cent of users in 2001), and lower rates in Norway (around 9 per cent). In Norway, the net change in 2002 is already negative (-0.9 per cent).

The intensity of Internet use

There is a difference between people who do and do not use computers, and between people who do and do not use the Internet. We have shown, for instance, a clear relationship between take-up and education and income. But users also vary in their characteristics, and if we wish to understand the potential impact of usage on people's lives we have also to examine the factors that are associated with *intensity* of usage. We will first examine how intensively the Internet is used, and why; and then at how this appears to influence other behaviour.

Measures of intensity

The most basic measure of usage intensity is time spent on the Internet. The more people spend time on Internet applications in a typical day, the more they are willing to 'pay' for the Internet in terms of other daily activities. The daily time people spend on the Internet is a partial measure of the success of Internet applications, or the success of the 'online' world created by the Internet. This online world may compete with the 'offline' world on almost all fronts. Activities such as working, learning, communicating, shopping, all have online applications, which may compete or complement traditional ways of doing things.

Research on diffusion of innovations has traditionally focused mainly on the adoption phase of new technologies, but in recent years we have seen more studies on the degree of new technologies usage, sometimes called 'use diffusion' in the marketing literature. There are several studies focusing on use diffusion in the case of the home PC and the Internet. Internet usage intensity can be studied by focusing on the time people spend on the Internet, or by focusing on the choice of belonging to a certain usage-intensity group (high, medium or low usage). Emmanouilides and Hammond (2000), for example, used a discrete choice methodology to study determinants of active versus lapsed usage of the Internet. They find that the main predictors of active Internet use are the time since first use (pioneers are more likely to be active users), location of use (social use at home) and the specific services used (information services). Shih and Venkatesh (2004) look at PC and Internet usage in two dimensions – variety (number of applications) and rate (usage time). They classify usage into four groups – intense use (high variety and high rate), low use (low variety and low rate), experimental use (high variety and low rate) and specialised use (low variety and high rate). A similar grouping appears in Flacher (2003), which is based on time spent visiting a category of web pages, and the number of pages visited in that category.

We used a similar approach, based on two dimensions – namely, daily minutes of use and number of online activities. The number of online activities is based on the question regarding activities used by respondents in the last three months: shopping, banking, library services, travel information, education, medical assistance, information about the environment, music downloading and information about jobs. The number of activities, which we call 'depth of use', is simply the sum of the activities used by respondents in the last three months.

Usage-intensity determinants

When we observe the average daily time e-Living respondents spent on Internet activities, we see striking differences between countries. Users spend thirteen minutes a day on the Internet in Norway, twenty-seven minutes in Italy, twenty-three minutes in the UK, eighteen minutes in Germany, and forty-eight minutes in Israel. Another interesting finding is that usage intensity has not increased between 2001 and 2002, with the exception of Bulgaria.

Before we turn to the statistical analysis, we have to make several assumptions concerning the relationships between the different usage intensity measures. Attitudes towards computers and the Internet play a key role in determining usage intensity. They are measured by the level of agreement to several questions, such as 'the Internet is a mystery to me'. Once formed, positive attitudes towards computers and the Internet are relatively stable, gradually moving upwards as positive Internet experiences increase. Attitudes are developed over time through a learning process affected by reference group influences, past experience and personality (Assael, 1981). We assume that positive attitudes towards the Internet have a positive impact on both usage time and depth of use. However, we also assume that current usage does not influence current attitudes. The latter are formed instead over time by past Internet experience. In other words, there is a lagged influence of current use on attitudes. We also assume that usage time is determined primarily by depth of use and does not directly affect it. Once we decide what Internet activities are important to us, usage time is derived from that decision. When we are involved in more Internet activities, we tend to spend more time on the Internet, since the experience is habit forming. Once habits are formed, it becomes difficult to change them. The results of these assumptions are that attitudes, usage time and depth of use are not determined together.

The results of the regressions are described in Table 2.3 and Table 2.4. We use ordinary least squares (OLS) to estimate the effects of the several variables on Internet usage time. In these regressions we use an index measuring attitudes towards computers and the Internet. This is computed by adding positive measures and subtracting negative ones. As expected, we see a significant positive impact of attitudes and of depth of use on usage time. Another important predictor of usage time is email activity, measured by the number of emails sent per day. Engaging in email correspondence is a time-consuming activity. It is also associated with being active in more online activities, which is shown in Table 2.4.

Interestingly, the impact of age on Internet usage time is not significant. Age determines usage, but not intensity. One could expect younger people to be more intense users than older people, as is the case with mobile usage.

Table 2.3 Standardised coefficients of OLS regression with Internet usage time (log form) as dependent variable

	UK	Italy	Germany	Norway	Israel
Positive attitudes index	0.26***	0.16***	0.18***	0.20***	0.30***
Number of online activities	0.21***	0.14***	0.24***	0.20***	0.20***
TV watching time per day	0.21***	0.10**	0.15**	0.13***	0.12**
Age	−0.03	−0.01	−0.07*	−0.05	0.03
Work status (0, 1)	−0.03	−0.11**	−0.08*	−0.05	−0.06
Marital status (0, 1)	−0.06	−0.15**	−0.08*	−0.10***	−0.15**
Emails sent per day	0.18***	0.21***	0.17***	0.16***	0.16***
Male	0.08**	0.15***	0.10**	0.15***	0.05
ISDN or faster (0, 1)	0.08**	0.02	0.05	0.09***	0.12**
Time (2002 = 1)	0.04	−0.03	−0.03	−0.11***	−0.09**
R^2	0.31	0.23	0.27	0.27	0.31
N	862	576	790	1,218	528

Table 2.4 Standardised coefficients of OLS regression with number of online activities as dependent variable

	UK	Italy	Germany	Norway	Israel
Positive attitudes index	0.27***	0.14***	0.26***	0.18***	0.21***
Internet years of experience	0.12**	0.26***	0.17***	0.15***	0.12**
Age	−0.09**	−0.11**	−0.15***	−0.15***	−0.11*
Emails sent per day	0.22***	0.20***	0.15***	0.19***	0.14**
High school (0, 1)	0.10*	−0.23	0.05	0.10	0.38*
Higher education (0, 1)	0.17***	−0.34	0.10*	0.18**	0.45*
Time (2002 = 1)	0.02	0.02	−0.07*	−0.08**	0.20***
R^2	0.23	0.17	0.21	0.20	0.18
N	759	598	788	1,256	537

It should be noted that children and teens were not sampled in the e-Living survey. This is not the case for Internet usage time. However, age is a significant predictor of the other intensity measure, the number of online activities, shown in Table 2.4.

As in the usage time regression, we find positive attitudes towards computers and the Internet to be a significant predictor of depth of Internet use. Another important determinant of depth of use is Internet experience. The number of online activities seems to increase gradually as Internet experience advances over time.

We can see some differences in the impact of several predictors on the two intensity measures. Attitudes towards PCs and the Internet are an important driver of both usage time and depth of use. Age, on the other hand, has a more striking impact on depth of use and hardly affects usage time. Email activities impact on both intensity measures, reflecting the importance of the Internet for social interactions. TV watching time is only positively associated with Internet usage time, suggesting that the two media types may complement each other. This could also point to a certain lifestyle where individuals who are intense Internet users may also be heavy TV viewers.

The impact of Internet usage intensity on leisure

These substitution effects have been the subject of some important research. Several conflicting studies deal with the relationship between Internet use and social and leisure activities. Nie and Hillygus (2002) find that home Internet use has a negative impact on time spent with family and friends. On the other hand, Gershuny (2002) finds that there is no significant loss of social activity of Internet users and that the use of the Web complements social activities rather than substitutes them. Both studies use time diaries, although the first uses cross-sectional data and the second uses panel data, which are more suitable for detecting individual changes and causal forces over time.

In order to study the impact of intense Internet usage on leisure activities in the e-Living sample, we used a leisure index. Six leisure activities were included in the e-Living questionnaire – sports, theatre/cinema, eating/drinking out, reading, group activities and friends' visits. We measured the frequency of engaging in each activity by an eight-level scale (ranging from 'never' to 'most days'). The leisure index is computed as the average per respondent of the six leisure activities. The leisure index was regressed on a set of demographic variables and Internet intensity usage variables, including both waves. We can now check whether an increase over time (between 2001 and 2002) in Internet usage has an impact on leisure frequency. It should be noted that since we only have two waves in the e-Living sample, evidence of substitution effects can still be negligible. In fact, by regressing the leisure index on Internet usage time, we capture both substitution effects and differences in lifestyle between individuals in a cross-section. This is due to the fact that we have two large cross-sections for 2001 and 2002. Within a cross-section, there could be a certain correlation between usage time and the leisure frequency index, which could be negative or positive. This correlation can indicate differences in lifestyles. When we combine the data from both waves, we may get some temporal impact, which can point to substitution effects.

As depicted in Table 2.5, Internet usage time has *no* significant impact on the leisure index in all countries, except for Italy, where usage time has a positive relationship with leisure frequency. It seems that Internet usage intensity still does not have a negative impact on leisure activities. This could be attributed to the relative importance people assign to leisure activities. We should also mention that two waves (2001 and 2002) may not be

Table 2.5 Standardised coefficients of OLS regression with leisure frequency index as dependent variable

	UK	*Italy*	*Germany*	*Norway*	*Israel*
Age	−0.16***	−0.07	−0.18***	−0.16***	−0.02
Number of close friends	0.16***	0.21***	0.20***	0.10**	0.18***
Internet daily usage time	−0.01	0.12**	−0.01	0.02	0.07
Daily time spent watching TV	−0.05	0.01	−0.14***	−0.10**	−0.00
Work status (0, 1)	−0.05	0.05	−0.09**	−0.14***	−0.12*
Marital status (0, 1)	−0.19***	−0.40***	−0.15***	−0.17***	0.24***
High-school education	0.20***	−0.06	0.22***	0.111	0.12
Higher education	0.19**	−0.03	0.26**	0.23***	0.23
Low income group	−0.06	−0.006	−0.07	0.018	0.02
High income group	−0.06	−0.06	−0.15***	−0.03	−0.02
R^2	0.14	0.24	0.20	0.11	0.10
N	642	457	621	1,145	429

enough to track changes in individual behaviour over time. Between 2001 and 2002, Internet usage time did not change much on average. Some patterns of substitution may be tracked for younger people who increased Internet usage drastically, but they are the exception rather than the rule.

Important predictors of leisure frequency are age, personal social networks and marital status. Age has a negative impact on leisure activities – younger people are more active than older people. People with larger social networks tend to be more active in their leisure habits, especially in outdoor activities.

Conclusions

The goal of this chapter has been to test the impact of the Internet in people's lives, first, by seeing if it is possible to predict intensity of usage as well as usage itself. And, second, whether people who use the Internet a lot have a more restricted level of leisure activity than those who do not.

Internet diffusion is slowing

The diffusion of Internet use in the last decade is heavily influenced by one major force – PC use. In the six countries studied, the diffusion curves of Internet adoption seem to converge to certain figures that depict the overall PC usage rates in those countries. The speed at which a certain country approaches the PC use limit depends on several variables, such as income, education and age. The e-Living data shows that PC usage rates are indeed a formidable barrier to Internet use. Between 2001 and 2002, the rate of PC adoption is zero or even negative. It is not surprising that most countries are already very close to the use limit and have almost completely exhausted the potential of Internet adoption.

Usage intensity is still modest

The intensity of usage is an important indicator of the overall success level of the Internet. Most Internet services and applications have traditional offline counterparts. The question is whether the Internet substitutes traditional applications or complements them. If the Internet is a substitute for traditional applications, users should spend more time online and less time offline. In most countries, average daily Internet usage is very moderate, with the exception of Israel. Users spend thirteen minutes a day on the Internet in Norway, twenty-seven minutes in Italy, twenty-three minutes in the UK, eighteen minutes in Germany and forty-eight minutes in Israel. With the exception of Bulgaria, the average daily time of Internet use decreased slightly between 2001 and 2002. We claim that there is another important measure of Internet usage intensity, and it is the depth of use, or the number of online activities, in which Internet users engage. Internet usage time is mainly driven by attitudes and not by age. Positive attitudes towards the Internet are affected by past successful usage and tend to increase current usage intensity. The depth of use, on the other hand, depends on age, as well as on attitudes towards the Internet and on Internet experience. Naturally, the two intensity measures (time and the number of online activities) positively reinforce each other.

Impact of usage intensity is limited

We found out that the average frequency of various leisure activities (sports, cinema, restaurants, reading and friends' visits) is not decreasing with higher Internet usage intensity in all countries. Age, social networks and marital status seem to be stronger predictors of leisure frequency. There is no evidence in the e-Living data to support the substitution hypothesis. We should mention, however, that two waves might not be sufficient to track changes in individual behaviour, especially since Internet usage is still quite modest in most countries.

Note

1 These are aggregated figures based on the question 'Did you once have Internet access in your home?' and therefore not comparable to the e-Living numbers.

Bibliography

Assall, H. (1981) *Consumer Behaviour and Marketing Action*, Boston, MA, PWS-Kent Publishing Company.

Beilock, R. and Dimitrova, D.V. (2003) An exploratory model of inter-country Internet diffusion. *Telecommunications Policy*, 27, 237–252.

Dholakia, N., Dholakia, R.R. and Kshetri, N. (2003) Internet diffusion. In Hossein, B. (ed.) *The Internet Encyclopedia*, New York, Wiley.

Emmanouilides, C. and Hammond, K. (2000) Internet usage: predictors of active users and frequency of use. *Journal of Interactive Marketing*, 14(2), 17–33.

Flacher, D. (2003) A European panel approach to Web users and E-consumers. *STAR Project*, Issue Report, 39.

Gershuny, J. (2002) Web-use and net-nerds: a neo-functionalist analysis of the impact of information technology in the home. ISDER Working Papers 2002-1.

Goldberg, J., Libai, B. and Muller, E. (2002) Riding the saddle: how cross-market communications can create a major slump in sales. *Journal of Marketing*, 66, 1–16.

Lenhart, A. (2003) *The Ever-shifting Internet Population: a New Look at Internet Access and the Digital Divide*. Online, available at: www.pewinternet.org/reports/toc.asp? Report = 88.

Katz, J.E. and Aspden, P. (1998) Internet dropouts in the USA: the invisible group. *Telecommunications Policy*, 22(4/5), 327–339.

Kestenbaum, M., Robinson, J.P., Neustadtl, A. and Alvarez, A. (2002) Information, technology and social time displacement. *IT@Society*, 1(1), 21–37.

Kridel, D.J., Rappoport, P.R. and Taylor, L.D. (1999) An econometric analysis of Internet access. In Loomis, D.G. and Taylor, L.D. (eds) *The Future of the Telecommunications Industry: Forecasting and Demand Analysis*, Norwell, MA, Kluwer Academic Press, pp. 21–42.

Nie, N.H. and Hillygus, D.S. (2002) The impact of Internet use on sociability: time-diary findings. *IT & Society*, 1(1), 1–20.

Raban, Y., Soffer, T., Mihnev, P. and Garnev, K. (2002) *E-living D7.1 – ICT Uptake and Usage: a Cross-Sectional Analysis*. Online, available at: www.eurescom.de/e-living/.

Rappoport, P., Kridel, D., Taylor, L. Duffy-Deno, K. and Alleman, J. (2002) Residential demand for access to the internet. In Madden, G. (ed.) *The International Handbook of Telecommunications Economics: Volume II*. Cheltenham, Edward Elgar Publishers.

SIBIS (2003) *Benchmarking Telecommunication and Access in the Information Society*. Online, available at: www.sibis-eu.org/.

Shih, C. and Venkatesh, A. (2004) Beyond adoption: development and application of use diffusion (UD) model to study household use of computers. *Journal of Marketing*. Online, available at: www.crito.uci.edu/noah/paper/Beyond%20 Adoption.pdf.

3 Digital divides and choices reconfiguring access

National and cross-national patterns of Internet diffusion and use

W.H. Dutton, A. Shepherd and C. di Gennaro

Introduction

The widespread diffusion of the Internet and related ICTs has focused increasing attention on their role in many sectors, including everyday life (Dutton *et al.*, 2004). For many decades before the Internet's inception, however, academics and pundits speculated on the social impact of a networked society (Sackman and Nie, 1970; Dutton *et al.*, 1987; Castells, 1996; Dutton, 1999). In line with debate over technology in general (Mesthene, 1997), expectations have continued to range from optimistic Utopian scenarios that emphasise the positive implications of Internet diffusion for social interaction, civic involvement and social inclusion, to a pessimistic dystopian focus on the potential negative implications of Internet adoption for social isolation, disengagement and social exclusion.

Examining the reality of such impacts has been feasible only since the late 1990s, by which time the Internet and related ICTs had become available to a large and diverse enough proportion of the general public over a sufficient time for meaningful data to be gathered on the technologies' actual use and impact. For example, the World Internet Project (WIP) research programme, a collaborative effort by academic researchers currently in about twenty countries, began in 2000 to undertake surveys to track the use and impact of the Internet over time in many parts of the world.[1] In every member country, WIP researchers conduct sample surveys of Internet use.[2]

To assess the explanatory power of competing perspectives on the Internet in everyday life, this chapter draws on the WIP and one of its national studies – the 2003 Oxford Internet Survey (OxIS) of Internet adoption and use in Britain.[3] At the time of this OxIS study, the WIP covered twelve countries: the USA, Sweden, Britain, Italy, Germany, Spain, Hungary, Japan, South Korea, Taiwan, Macao and Singapore. Internet use ranged from as high as over 70 per cent of the US sample to under 20 per cent of the Hungarian sample (see Figure 3.1).

The first section of this chapter examines the 'digital divides' affecting the Internet's diffusion among different social groups within and across

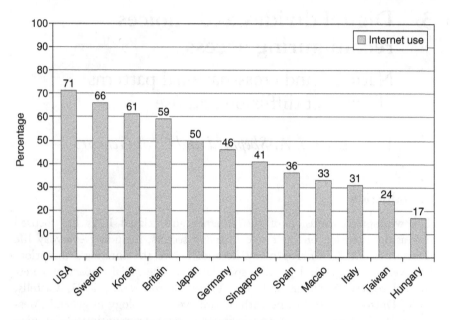

Figure 3.1 Cross-national Internet use *c.*2003 (source: World Internet Project (www.oii.ox.ac.uk/research/?view=wip)).

nations. The second focuses on digital choices – the ways in which people decide to use or not to use the Internet. The third looks at how these 'digital choices' and divides can affect whether or not the Internet systematically supports or undermines social relations in a networked society. The findings provide more complex patterns than those captured by previously dominant dichotomous Utopian–dystopian expectations.

Digital divides: inequalities of Internet access and use

Normalisation vs stratification theories about digital divides

Debate over who will – and who will not – use the Internet has generated much research around the concept of digital divides between differing levels of use among different sections of populations and individuals, within and between countries (Norris, 2001; Katz and Rice, 2002; Bromley, 2004; Chen and Wellman, 2004; Wilhelm, 2004). The main digital divide has been perceived as being between those with and those without access to the Internet. Whether this divide is shrinking or growing, and what difference it makes for individuals and societies, has become one of the central issues around Internet diffusion. Here, we focus on aspects concerned with inequalities in individual access and use.

Views about digital divides range along the Utopian–dystopian spectrum. Cyber-optimists posit a 'normalisation' hypothesis (Norris, 2001), arguing that differences between advantaged and disadvantaged groups in the take-up of the Internet will diminish and even disappear as the Internet disperses more widely. Cyber-pessimists pose what has been called a 'digital divide' or 'stratification' hypothesis (Norris, 2001), based on the expectation that those who do not use the Internet are likely to be those who are already disadvantaged economically and socially, such as low-income groups. Furthermore, since Internet use is a new resource that can help to improve access to information, social networks, services and other resources, non-users' failure to adopt the Internet is expected to reinforce and possibly accentuate their relative economic and social position in society.

The digital divides thesis also argues that differentials in the take-up of the Internet between advantaged and disadvantaged groups are likely to persist, and might even be widened, since advantaged groups can exploit their edge in Internet use to support their relative communicative power in society. Even if Internet use approached that of the entire population, serious divides might remain in the level and nature of Internet use because equal exposure is still likely to accentuate existing 'knowledge gaps' (Comstock *et al.*, 1978: 119; Hargittai, 2002).

Using European data, Norris (2001) tested these normalisation and stratification hypotheses and found evidence for the latter. Looking at cross-national data, Richard Rose (2004) argued that patterns of Internet diffusion have been undermining digital divides, supporting a normalisation thesis. The following sub-sections examine the digital-divide stratification thesis with respect to gender and economic and educational stratification.

Economic stratification

The central issue surrounding the digital divide concerns economic status. Using income as an indicator of economic status, Figure 3.2 supports the stratification hypothesis by showing that the Internet is used more by the highest income quartiles in all twelve countries examined, with little evidence that the difference due to income is less in Asian countries.

Although the income gap is somewhat smaller for the countries with lowest use, it increases as Internet use increases – then diminishes for the highest-use countries, where the Internet begins to reach most of the public. For instance, in high-use countries such as the USA and Sweden, Internet use in the highest income quartile is above 90 per cent, implying that any further increase in use must come from less-affluent groups. It is important to note that mere access to the Internet provides a lowest common indicator, as households can vary more dramatically in their number of computers, modes of access and levels of use. Nonetheless, there is no evidence at present to suggest the normalisation hypothesis applies to the income gap even for this lowest common indicator, and the stratification hypothesis remains a better overall fit.

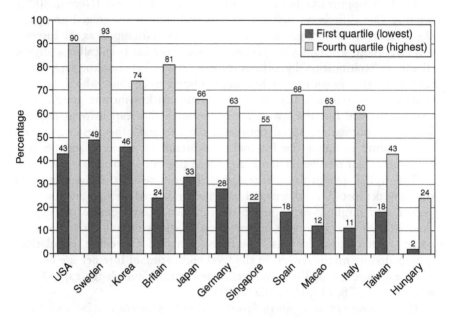

Figure 3.2 Cross-national Internet use by income, *c.*2003 (source: World Internet Project (www.oii.ox.ac.uk/research/?view=wip)).

In the 2003 OxIS survey, respondents were asked for their income. Table 3.1 shows that the online Internet population in Britain remains highly stratified along economic lines, with a disproportionate number of high-income individuals. The gap between richest and poorest users has changed only slightly between 1995 and 2003, from 40 per cent to 30 per cent.

Education-related divides

Education is another indicator of socioeconomic status. However, comparisons of the level of schooling did not demonstrate the same level of persistent stratification as for income, possibly due to the wide exposure to the Internet of nearly all individuals in school, or of school age. The WIP comparative data in Figure 3.3 shows that the gap in Internet use between individuals with the equivalent of an American high school education and those with at least a Bachelor's qualification is lower in nations where Internet use is higher.

The OxIS data show that the online population in Britain was originally much better educated than the general population, but that the difference has diminished over time as Internet diffusion has reached nearly all individuals of school age (see Table 3.1). However, in eleven out of the twelve countries studied, Internet use has remained higher among university gradu-

Table 3.1 Internet use by social group in Britain, 2003

	Percentage of online population in 1995	*Percentage of online population in 1999*	*Percentage of online population in 2003*	*Percentage of overall population*
By income				
Lowest quartile	5	8	8	19
Highest quartile	45	48	38	29
Gap between highest and lowest quartiles	40	40	30	10
By education				
Left school at 16:				
no qualifications	12	15	19	33
Bachelor's or more	39	25	16	11
Gap between bachelor's and no qualifications	27	10	−3	−22
By gender				
Men	59	55	53	49
Women	41	45	47	51
Gap between men and women	18	10	6	2
By age				
25–34 (in 2003)	29	23	22	18
55–64 (in 2003)	11	7	8	12
Gap between 25–34 and 55–64 year olds	18	16	14	6
Percentage of sample online at any point in that year	3	23	62	–

Source: Oxford Internet Survey, 2003 (www.oii.ox.ac.uk/research/?view=oxis).

ates than among high-school graduates. As with gender divides, discussed below, trends within the UK offer some evidence in support of the normalisation hypothesis, but across-system differences continue to demonstrate an education gap that is more supportive of a stratification hypothesis.

Gender divides

A curvilinear pattern has been found in cross-national analyses relating to gender-related use of the Internet (Figure 3.4). This shows smaller differentials in high-use countries, such as the USA and Sweden, and low-use countries, such as Hungary and Taiwan, but greater differences in middle-use nations like Italy and Singapore. There are no major differences in these patterns between Asian and European countries.

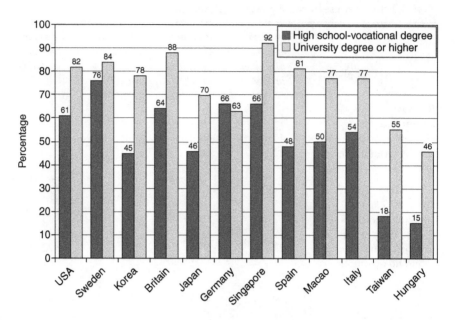

Figure 3.3 Cross-national Internet use by education, *c.*2003 (source: World Internet Project (www.oii.ox.ac.uk/research/?view=wip)).

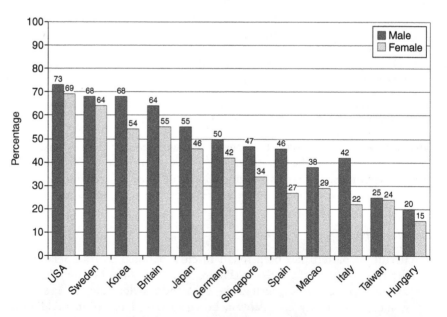

Figure 3.4 Cross-national Internet use by gender, *c.*2003 (source: World Internet Project (www.oii.ox.ac.uk/research/?view=wip)).

In all twelve WIP countries assessed for this study, men use the Internet somewhat more than women, in line with the digital-divide hypothesis. However, high-use countries show diminished gender differences, which lends support to the cyber-optimists' normalisation hypothesis, at least with regard to gender differences.

We investigated changes over time in gender digital divides within Britain by asking people when they first went online. As Table 3.1 above shows, there has been a small increase (from 41 to 47 per cent) in the proportion of women in the online population between 1995 and 2003, and men's participation declined from 59 to 53 per cent. This lends support to the normalisation hypothesis as it shows a slow diminishing of the gender divides. However, gender differences in Internet use persist. For instance, further analyses of the OxIS data indicate that gender differences are more pronounced when the time devoted to Internet use is analysed (Liff and Shepherd, 2004).

Digital divides: summary

For some aspects of digital divides, such as gender and education, the normalisation hypothesis gains some support from the findings reported here of greater equality, both in cross-national and national patterns of diffusion. In most other cases, particularly with income, the evidence for a trend towards converging levels of use is weak or non-existent at the national and cross-national levels, which reinforces digital-divide concerns over stratification.

How users' digital choices shape digital divides

Understanding why some users do not want to go online

Implicit in both the normalisation and stratification arguments is the assumption that all people would benefit from the Internet, and that the prime reasons for not going online are an inability to do so because non-users lack the appropriate financial and/or technical resources. A middle position between optimism and pessimism is the idea that, although divides will never completely disappear, people will not feel they are being excluded if they are unable to do something that they do not actually want to do. If they choose not to use the Internet because they do not see benefits from doing so, should non-use be considered a social issue?

The ability to make such a 'digital choice' incorporates at least two elements. First, people must have sufficient economic resources to go online without sacrificing a great deal in other areas of their life. Second, they must have sufficient technical skill, or opportunity to garner technical skill, to ensure their lack of expertise does not prevent them from going online. If the last two criteria are not met, then this is really a digital divide returning. But if they are met and a person still chooses not to go online, then this is seen to be a voluntary act, albeit possibly based on limited understanding of what the Internet could offer that person.

Herbert Simon's (1955) concept of 'bounded rationality' provides a model of the human behaviour behind such digital choices. Simon argues that people make rational decisions based on the limited amount of knowledge they possess and the likely significant costs of acquiring that knowledge. Making decisions on imperfect information in this way sometimes leads to choices that are different from the ones they would make if they had perfect information.

Why some people stop using the Internet

We gained more insights on the concept of digital choice by looking at the behaviour of past users of the Internet. One group who are unlikely to be excluded from the Internet due to lack of technical ability are past users who have stopped going online.[4] As the Internet is primarily an experience technology, we could ascertain what people with at least the minimum technical ability perceive they gain (or don't gain) from going online by asking past users why they stopped using the Internet and what the consequences were of this decision.

Of all OxIS respondents, 121 (6 per cent) said they were past users, who had been online for an average of 1.4 years prior to going offline. A large majority of these said they lost access to the Internet because they were no longer at the location where they had gone online, typically at work, school or home. This seems to reinforce the digital-divide argument that these people had become excluded from using the Internet. However, the past users also seem to believe that they have not suffered any consequences from not being online, indicating they might have made more effort to get online in their new location if they thought they had more reason to do so.

Other findings suggest many past users are not aware of their communication being limited by not being online. For example, 97 per cent of past users said they had no difficulty getting in touch with other people as a result of not being online, and 98 per cent saw no problems arising when seeking work or changing jobs. This counters the logic of the digital-divide argument that not being online inevitably disadvantages non-users, such as by limiting their social networks.

Further evidence on past users' lack of awareness of the benefits that the Internet can offer came from analysing proxy use in the OxIS sample. This shows that, for past users: 76 per cent had not asked someone to send an email on their behalf in the last year; 75 per cent had not asked anyone to purchase something online on their behalf; and 60 per cent had not asked anyone to find information online on their behalf. Of these, over 90 per cent said they knew someone who would go online or send an email on their behalf.

This again shows that many past users do not feel they have suffered from not having Internet access. It is therefore reasonable to label their being not online as a 'choice', whether or not it is a choice in their best interest.

Skills and technology exclusion

Although past users were likely to have learnt some skills from their use, many still feel they do not have the skills necessary to use the Internet effectively and could not develop them easily. Yet, as shown above, getting around this by asking someone else to go online on their behalf was not a frequently chosen option. Of Internet users, almost half said they learnt to do so without assistance from anyone else, suggesting that basic Internet skills are not hard to acquire. Virtually all (96 per cent) of fourteen-to-sixteen-year-olds surveyed in OxIS use the Internet, with no discernible digital divides based on technical or cognitive ability. This suggests that where people have grown up seeing the Internet as part of everyday life, technical ability does not prevent people from going online. In turn, this implies that a key determinant of Internet use is whether or not the Internet has been incorporated as a useful part of someone's life.

Several questions in the OxIS survey were designed to explore a slightly different version of the technological exclusion argument: that some people have a fear of technology in their everyday lives. For example, people who said they prefer a human cashier to an automatic teller machine (ATM) to get money from a bank could be interpreted as displaying a reluctance to utilise ICTs generally, and not simply the Internet, for everyday purposes. Of the total OxIS sample, the people who said they preferred to use the ATM were more than twice as likely (69 per cent vs 31 per cent) to be Internet users than those who said they preferred a cashier; however, among people below the age of fifty-five, there was only a small difference (75 per cent vs 62 per cent). This points to the potential for technophobic attitudes to be overcome among the young and middle-aged, for whom the Internet has become a common occurrence, and has been largely integrated into their everyday lives and those of their acquaintances and peers.

Age differentials

The potential for negative predispositions to be overcome if people see that there is a reason to make an effort to use the Internet is illustrated by the most striking WIP and OxIS findings supportive of the concept of a digital choice: the differentials in take up of Internet use between different age groups. This shows that younger people are considerably more likely to be users than older people. Internet use by age differences are dramatic in every nation in the WIP dataset, with use by sixteen-to-twenty-four-year-olds consistently higher than use by fifty-five-to-sixty-four-year-olds (see Figure 3.5).

Furthermore, the OxIS data show the persistence of a profound gap in use between younger and older age groups, with little change between 1995 and

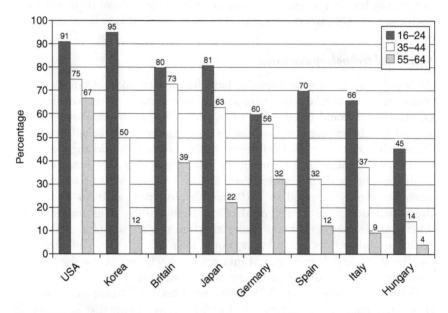

Figure 3.5 Cross-national Internet use by age, *c.*2003 (source: World Internet Project (www.oii.ox.ac.uk/research/?view=wip)).

2003 in the proportion of sixteen-to-twenty-four-year-old and fifty-five-to-sixty-four-year-old respondents that have been going online. This evidence supports the digital choice concept, particularly since multivariate controls for socioeconomic status do not account for these age differences in take up.

The complementary value of the digital choice perspective

The concept of a user-controlled digital choice is resisted by many analysts, who argue that choices are limited and structured by socioeconomic circumstances. However, income and other key social and economic status variables do not in themselves explain all choices, such as those reflected in the large age differentials identified above. In addition, 7 per cent of non-users in the OxIS survey decided not to go online despite having access to the technology within their households, where they also had potential support in exploiting that access. Cost could be among the reasons for this digital choice not to use the Internet because narrowband households would face additional costs for more users, which could be reflected in the finding that 14 per cent of those who were online did not use email although many free email programmes were available. This highlights the contingent and conditional nature of Internet use. People choose to use only those parts of the Internet they perceive are of value to their own lives.

This is not to argue that digital choice provides a better explanation than other viewpoints for all non-use. The evidence from OxIS showing that the majority of people who have never used the Internet do not ask someone else to use it on their behalf, with over half not knowing someone they could ask to go online for them, indicates that many non-users are socially and technically distanced from the Internet. This reinforces the need to combine notions of digital choice with an understanding of digital divides. They are complementary rather than alternative explanations for Internet use and non-use.

Sociability: an example of the impact of digital choices

Sociability has been one of the expected areas of Internet impact that has pitted Utopian against dystopian perspectives. Early ideas of the effect of the Internet upon social life often included gloomy predictions that growing use of the Internet would cause people to become less sociable and neglect offline relationships, considered more genuine and profound, in favour of online relationships, which were seen as potentially based on insubstantial role-play (Kraut *et al.*, 2002). Other theories maintain that the Internet facilitates sociability by helping to maintain existing social relationships or favouring the creation of new ones (Mesch and Talmud, forthcoming). Evidence on the impact of the Internet on social relationships is mixed, with some studies showing that time spent online detracts from time spent on face-to-face relationships (Nie and Erbring, 2000; Nie *et al.*, 2002), and other studies suggesting the Internet plays a more complementary role with face-to-face patterns of communication (Katz and Rice, 2002).

Cross-national evidence from the WIP surveys supports the view that the Internet has not disrupted existing social relations, with people overwhelmingly thinking that going online had not changed the amount of time they spent with family and friends. Of those that did think there had been a change, more thought time spent with family and friends had increased rather than decreased as a result of going online.

OxIS data also show that there is very little evidence that Internet users employ other kinds of media to communicate with friends and family less than do non-users.[5] OxIS findings also indicate that experienced users employ the Internet more to communicate with friends and family than do inexperienced users, but do not use other media less, resulting in more overall communication among experienced users than either novice users or non-users (Rice *et al.*, 2004). In addition, Internet users spend more hours a week meeting with friends and family than do non-users (56 per cent vs 47 per cent).

Given the importance of social communication to mental well-being, it is interesting to note that Internet users in the OxIS sample are more likely than current Internet non-users (70 per cent vs 57 per cent) to say they have someone they can 'confide in when depressed'. Users also show slighter greater levels of life satisfaction (83 per cent vs 76 per cent).

Sceptics may wonder what offline activity is being sacrificed to the time spent online. However, Internet users in WIP studies generally watch less television than non-users, which does not give grounds for alarm about the decline of social capital. The impression given in its early days that Internet use causes a reduction in social capital may have been a by-product of the kind of people who went online early.

The stereotypical early users, such as those with personal computers in their homes, were younger men and boys who tended to be fascinated by the technology and relatively less socially oriented, contributing to the idea that the technology was isolating and a replacement for human connections. As Internet use has diffused to include the majority of people, so Internet users have become more like the general population. Users seem to have generally employed the Internet to support their social relations, maintaining and enhancing offline relationships and building new ones in ways that can have a transformative impact on reconfiguring access within society.

Thus, far from undermining social connectedness, the findings reported here suggest that the digital choices made by Internet users are directed at complementing and supplementing users' existing social networks. It illustrates how outcomes of Internet use are shaped by the values articulated through these choices, rather than through any straightforward, deterministic path dictated by an in-built bias in the technology. Digital choices not only change the ways in which people keep in touch and communicate with one another, but also enable people to reconfigure their social networks, such as by making friends with those they meet online.

Conclusion

This chapter has highlighted two key themes identified in WIP surveys from twelve countries and in-depth OxIS data in Britain, which reflect a surprising degree of consistency between countries. One is the finding of how digital choices made about the use and non-use of the Internet can reconfigure access to people, information, services and technologies (Dutton, 1999, 2004). In helping to do this, the technology offers individuals and nations new opportunities to maintain and enhance their relative communicative power, making access to and effective use of the Internet a major social and policy issue.

The second theme is the significance of 'digital divides' as a continuing element that reinforces existing social inequalities and stratifications. This complements the identification of digital choice as an important shaper of outcomes, such as those relating to sociability or the degree to which older people tend to avoid the Internet. Moreover, OxIS data enable a deeper analysis of peoples' reasons for their choices about activities like going online and dropping offline, providing evidence of the significance of both digital divides and digital choice.

The notion of digital choice, supported by the evidence reported here, has important policy implications. Many countries have sought to attack the problem of digital divides primarily in terms of ensuring that people have the necessary physical access and technical ability to use the Internet, and by supporting the development of appropriate information infrastructures, for example through investment in extending broadband availability and Internet access in public libraries and schools. Our findings support these as important but not sufficient strategies.

Access to infrastructure is not equivalent to its take up. As shown above, many who have meaningful access to the Internet decide not to use it. Policy-makers therefore need to focus on influencing digital choices as well as closing digital divides. This requires focused activity in understanding and addressing the difficult and major challenges involved in encouraging resistant groups to choose whether or not to go online, on the basis of a more informed foundation of experience. Such efforts need to take account of the Internet as an experience technology and prioritise finding out what actually motivates people to use the Internet, particularly the hardest-to-reach groups who are least attracted by the Internet's possibilities, such as the elderly. Policies can then focus on demonstrating to such groups how the Internet could enhance their lives, which will require developing more opportunities for the kinds of people who are currently non-users to gain experience with the Internet and Web.

Acknowledgements

This work is based on the OII's Oxford Internet Surveys (OxIS) www.oii.ox.ac.uk/research/project.cfm?id=8, and the Institute's participation in the World Internet Project, www.worldinternetproject.net.

Notes

1 See www.worldinternetproject.net for more on the WIP.
2 A number of questions common to all member countries allow for cross-national comparison of findings. Each country also asks questions that are unique to their own survey, allowing for flexibility and responsiveness to the issues that are in the forefront in their national contexts.
3 England, Wales and Scotland only. See www.oii.ox.ac.uk/research/?rq=oxis/index for more on OxIS, including its latest 2005 survey.
4 Only 2 per cent of past users said that they stopped using the Internet because it was too difficult to use.
5 For example, OxIS shows that 65 per cent of current Internet users telephone friends and/or family who live close by, but not within walking distance, at least once a week, compared to 68 per cent of non-users. In addition, 84 per cent of current Internet users often or sometimes telephone friends and/or family who live in another country or city, compared to 84 per cent of non-users.

References

Bromley, C. (2004) Can Britain close the digital divide? In Park, A., Curtice, J., Thomson, K., Bromley, C. and Philips, M. (eds) *British Social Attitudes: The 21st Report*, London, Sage.

Castells, M. (1996) *The Rise of a Network Society: The Information Age*, Oxford, Blackwell Company.

Castells, M. (2001) The digital divide in a global perspective. In Castells, M (ed.) *The Internet Galaxy*, Oxford, Oxford University Press, pp. 247–274.

Chen, W. and Wellman, B. (2003) Charting and bridging digital divides: comparing socioeconomic, gender, life stage and rural–urban Internet access and use in eight countries. AMD Global Consumers Advisory Board (ESAB), October.

Comstock, G., Chaffee, S., Katzman, N., McCombs, M. and Roberts, D. (1978) *Television and Human Behavior*, New York, Columbia University Press.

Dutton, W.H. (1999) *Society on the Line: Information Politics in the Digital Age*, Oxford, Oxford University Press.

Dutton, W.H. (2004) Reconfiguring access. In Dutton, W.H., Kahin, B., O'Callaghan, R. and Wyckoff, A.W. (eds) *Transforming Enterprise*, Cambridge, MA, MIT Press.

Dutton, W.H. and Shepherd, A. (2005) Confidence and risk on the Internet. In Mansell, R. and Collins, B.S. (eds) *Trust and Crime in Information Societies*, Cheltenham, UK, Edward Elgar.

Dutton, W., Blumler, J.G. and Kraemer, K.L. (eds) (1987) *Wired Cities: Shaping the Future of Communications*, New York, G.K. Hall, Macmillan.

Dutton, W.H., Kahin, B., O'Callaghan, R. and Wyckoff, A.W. (eds) (2004) *Transforming Enterprise*, Cambridge, MA, MIT Press.

Hargittai, E. (2002) Second level digital divide: differences in people's online skills. *First Monday*, 7(4).

Katz, J.E. and Rice, R.E. (2002) *Social Consequences of Internet Use*, Cambridge, MA, MIT Press.

Kraut, R., Kiesler, S., Boneva, B., Cummings, J., Hegelson, V. and Crawford, A. (2002) Internet paradox revisited. *Journal of Social Issues*, 58(1), 49–74.

Liff, S. and Shepherd, A. (2004) An evolving gender digital divide. *OII Issue Brief No. 2*, Oxford, Oxford Internet Institute, University of Oxford.

Mesch, G.S. and Talmud, I. (forthcoming) Similarity and the quality of online and offline social relationships among adolescents in Israel. *Journal of Research in Adolescence*.

Mesthene, E.G. (1997) The role of technology in society. In Teich, A. (ed.) *Technology and the Future*, New York, St Martin's Press.

Nie, N.H. and Erbring, L. (2000) Internet and society: a preliminary report. Stanford, CA: Stanford Institute for the Quantitative Study of Society.

Nie, N.H., Hillygus, D.S. and Erbring, L. (2002) Internet use, interpersonal relations, and sociability. In Wellman, B. and Haythornthwaite, C. (eds) *The Internet in Everyday Life*, Oxford, Blackwell Publishing.

Norris, P. (2001) *Digital Divide*, Cambridge, Cambridge University Press.

Rice, R., Shepherd, A., Katz, J.E. and Dutton, W.H. (2004) Social interaction and the Internet: comparative results from the US and Britain. Paper presented at the International Conference of the Association of Internet Researchers, Brighton, University of Sussex, 19–22 September.

Rose, R. (2004) Governance and the Internet. In Yusuf, S., Altaf, M.A. and Nabeshima, K. (eds) *Global Change and East Asian Policy Initiatives*, New York, World Bank Group.

Sackman, H. and Nie, N. (eds) (1970) *The Information Utility and Social Choice*, Montvale, NJ, AFIPS Press.

Simon, H. (1955) A behavioural model of rational choice. *The Quarterly Journal of Economics*, LXIX (February), 99–118.

Wilhelm, A.G. (2004) *Digital Nation: Toward an Inclusive Information Society*, London and Cambridge, MA, MIT Press.

4   The social impact of broadband Internet in the home

Ben Anderson and Yoel Raban

The broadband 'revolution'

At the time of writing there is an almost ceaseless stream of news flashes and marketing messages trumpeting the future social and economic (not to ignore profitable) opportunities of broadband Internet access in the home. This has not gone unnoticed in policy circles since the early 1990s (Bangemann, 1994; DTI, 1994). More recently, and as a natural progression from the Bangemann report, the eEurope 2005 Action plan[1] states:

> broadband enabled communication, in combination with convergence, will bring social as well as economic benefits. It will contribute to e-inclusion, cohesion and cultural diversity. It offers the potential to improve and simplify the life of all Europeans and to change the way people interact, not just at work, but also with friends, family, community, and institutions.
>
> (CEC, 2002: 8)

But is this happening, and what evidence do we have of the difference that broadband makes to the domestic user? This chapter uses data from the e-Living survey to assess at least some of these issues empirically.

The processes of choosing a broadband connection, the characteristics of those who do so and the possible effects this has have all been the focus of a number of academic studies, as well as many private and public market research surveys such as the Flash Eurobarometers funded by the European Commission (Gallup Europe, 2002).

Many of these studies concentrate on modelling and forecasting demand based on hypothetical price and charging schemes or potential applications, and are of less interest here (see, for example, Madden and Simpson, 1997; Ida and Kuroda, 2004; Savage and Waldman, 2005).

Others have used survey data to study the characteristics of early adopters of broadband. For the USA in 2000, Kridel and colleagues (2002) found that broadband adopters tended to be younger and have higher income and education levels. For Korea, Lee *et al.* (2003) note that the mobilisation of demand through IT literacy activities particularly targeting housewives, the elderly, military personnel and farmers may have had a significant effect in driving up demand and thus uptake. They also suggest that Asian cultures are more likely to use the Internet for inter-personal communication than non-Asian cultures, and that the increased affordances for this aspect of usage may also have contributed to increased demand for broadband although, as we shall see, this may also be true of non-Asian cultures. For New Zealand, Paynter and Chung (2003) showed that early broadband adopters were more likely to be male, to be those with higher computer skills and who used the Internet more per day. Interestingly, educational status, age and income made no difference. Finally, for the UK, Robertson and colleagues (2004) found that educational attainment, disposable income and the presence of children were all indicators of Internet adoption and had a marginally stronger effect for broadband as opposed to narrowband.

A few studies have focused on patterns of usage. For example, Hoag (1998) used a single cross-sectional survey of cable modem and narrowband users in the USA to establish that there were few socio-demographic differences between the two groups (confirmed by Anderson *et al.*, 2003), but that broadband users tended to make more use of FTP and the Web than narrowband users and also to spend more time online. She also showed that they made more use of a wider range of applications and were more satisfied with their Internet experience.

Using Pew Internet data for the USA, Horrigan and Rainie (2002) showed that broadband users spent more time online, did more things and did them more often than narrowband users. As with some of the other studies, they also suggested that home broadband users were 'typical early technology adopters', being disproportionately well educated, wealthy and male.

However, as we will elaborate below, such studies of *difference* tell us nothing at all about broadband-related *changes.* Indeed recent authors have noted that few academic publications focus on the impact of broadband on social and personal issues in contrast to the developmental and macro-economic issues (Firth and Mellor, 2005). Firth and Mellor note that the results of even these economic analyses tend to provide more rhetoric than empirical analysis and they call for a diverse analysis of the outcomes of broadband Internet access.

By following individuals over time, the e-Living project has produced one of the few datasets that can distinguish the effects of moving to broadband from the effects of heavy Internet users becoming broadband users. We will provide an illustrative example of this key distinction below.

Using wave one (2001) and wave two (2002) of the e-Living longitudinal household panel survey, we initially provide descriptive data on the uptake of household broadband Internet access in the six countries (UK, Italy, Germany, Norway, Bulgaria and Israel). Then, rather than repeat previous cross-sectional analyses of uptake, we use the unique longitudinal nature of the e-Living data to develop models of the 'impact' of switching to broadband between wave one (2001) and wave two (2002) on time spent using the Internet, social leisure, TV watching and e-commerce. We focus on these issues because they are germane to a number of academic, policy and commercial pre-occupations:

- Does broadband Internet access lead to more time being spent online? Or is it that people can do more in the same amount of time that is available to them?
- Might broadband Internet access lead to less social engagement in a dystopian future as some might suggest (Nie and Hillygus, 2002)?
- Might the usage of broadband, whether for content or for new forms of leisure, lead to a reduction in TV viewing and an attendant switch in potential advertising revenues?
- To what extent does broadband enable more (or more valuable) e-commerce transactions by households?

The chapter concludes with a summary of the results and a brief discussion of their implications.

Definitions

What do we mean by 'broadband'? According to the ITU (2003) 'Broadband is commonly used to describe recent Internet connections that are significantly faster than today's dial-up technologies, but it is not a specific speed or service.' Recommendation I.113 of the ITU Standardization Sector defines broadband as a transmission capacity that is faster than primary rate ISDN, at 1.5 or 2.0 Mbit/s. Elsewhere, broadband is considered to correspond to transmission speeds equal to or greater than 256 kbit/s, and some operators even label basic rate ISDN (at 144 kbit/s) as a 'type of broadband'. In this chapter, while not defining broadband specifically, 256 kbit/s is generally taken as the minimum speed and so we use the following definitions:

- Analogue = narrowband Internet access (does not include ISDN).
- Broadband = cable modem/ADSL.

Penetration of broadband Internet access in households

To provide context to the analysis that follows, Table 4.1 compares the results of e-Living wave two with Eurobarometer (EB) 135 (2002) and ITU (2003) data to show levels of broadband Internet uptake in households in 2002. In most cases, the differences between the surveys are in the order of $+/-4$ per cent, which is to be expected. However, the e-Living results for Germany estimate fewer Internet households in general and fewer ISDN/broadband in particular than does the EB 135. Comparison with the ITU source, which also contains mostly 2002 data, suggests that whilst the

Table 4.1 Broadband uptake in selected European countries in 2002

	Per cent with Internet access	Per cent of Internet households with analogue modems only	Per cent of Internet households with at least ISDN	Per cent of Internet households with broadband[8]
UK (Flash EB 135)	50.0	85.0	4.0	12.0
UK (ITU BoB)	–	–	–	10.5
UK (e-Living wave two)	47.0	87.0	3.2	9.7
Italy (Flash EB 135)	36.0	79.0	10.0	9.0
Italy (ITU BoB)	–	–	–	14.7
Italy (e-Living wave two)	31.1	77.3	8.2	13.0
Germany (Flash EB 135)	48.0	56.0	47.0	34.0
Germany (ITU BoB)	–	–	–	21.6
Germany (e-Living wave two)	41.5	49.8	39.8	8.7
Norway (ITU BoB)	–	–	–	7.2
Norway (e-Living wave two)	57.3	30.0	55.5	15.0
Bulgaria (e-Living wave two)	4.6	90.9	1.5	7.6
Israel (ITU BoB)	–	–	–	14.1
Israel (e-Living wave two)	43.5	71.2	6.1	22.5

Notes
Comparison of results from e-Living wave two and Flash Eurobarometer 135 both collected November 2002 (weighted for non-response) and the ITU's Birth of Broadband 2002 data, rows may sum to more than 100 per cent as multiple answers allowed.
The ITU figures are taken from the Annexe table on page 21 of the report's executive summary and it should be noted that there are apparent arithmetical errors within the ITU Report's table. We have provided the corrected figures here. The ITU figures represent broadband subscribers as a percentage of Internet subscribers (not Internet households) and so may be larger than both the e-Living and EB 'household level' figures.

e-Living figures for Germany may have been an underestimate, the EB figures were certainly an overestimate.

However, the e-Living results suggest that, in 2002, in the e-Living countries, broadband Internet access was most prevalent in Israel and Norway, with Italy and the UK roughly equal. Bulgaria may appear to have had a broadband penetration rate within Internet households similar to that of the other countries, but this in fact represents five households! Of course this is a view of history. By 2005, these figures have changed substantially so that, for example, in the UK, more than 55 per cent of Internet households had broadband access (Dutton *et al.*, 2005).

Routes to broadband

Even though they describe the recent past, the two waves of e-Living data provide a unique resource to analyse the routes that households are taking to broadband and, indeed, their routes out again.

Table 4.2 pools data for all six countries and suggests that about 0.7 per cent of those who had no personal computer (PC) or Internet access in 2001 had become broadband users in 2002, 3.6 per cent of those with a PC but no Internet had moved to broadband, whilst 11 per cent had a PC and narrowband Internet access before switching. On the other hand, 87 per cent of those who had no PC or Internet were still in the same state and 54 per cent of those with a PC but no Internet had also not 'progressed' to Internet access of any kind. Intriguingly, some 14 per cent $(1.6 + 2.8 + 10.8)$ of those who had some form of broadband (ISDN or above) in 2001 had reverted to narrowband, or some even to no Internet access by 2002. Clearly whilst there is adoption going on, there is also dis-adoption and considerable stasis (non-adoption).

Table 4.2 Routes to broadband (e-Living wave one and two, weighted for non-response)

Internet access 2002	Internet access 2001			
	No PC, no Internet (%)	*PC but no Internet (%)*	*PSTN*	*Broadband[1]*
No PC, no Internet	87.30	11.10	2.40	1.60
PC, no Internet	6.00	53.70	4.20	2.80
PSTN	5.40	24.50	73.50	10.80
ISDN	0.60	6.40	7.40	66.30
Broadband	0.70	3.60	11.00	15.80
Something else	–	0.70	0.70	1.10

Note
1 Defined as 'at least cable modem or ADSL' – may also include other such as WIFI, ethernet etc.

The difference broadband makes

There is considerable interest in the potential effects of broadband, not only on Internet use or e-commerce but also on other activities such as TV viewing and social and leisure activities. However there is little or no evidence for these 'effects' from anything other than cross-sectional surveys which cannot, other than by error-prone respondent recall, account for the historical behaviour patterns of those who are broadband adopters. As a result the apparent changes in behaviour that are attributed to broadband adoption may in fact be due to differences between broadband and narrowband users in terms of socioeconomic status or Internet usage levels. This confusion is apparently endemic in the ICT market research community at this time (e.g. Nielsen/NetRatings, 2003; Kerner, 2004) and also, more surprisingly, in some quasi-academic literature (see, for example, Horrigan and Rainie, 2002). As an example, Nielsen/NetRating's May 2003 press release on broadband implied that the difference in online time between narrow and broadband users measured in a cross-sectional survey was 'caused' by the switch to broadband.

Difference vs change

To continue with this example, we might hypothesise that moving to broadband would increase the minutes spent online due to the probable switch to flat-rate pricing. On the other hand, we might hypothesise that people would spend less time as the speed should enable them to complete their tasks more quickly. Or indeed there may be no difference in time spent online since there may be only a fixed portion of time available to individuals in any given day for Internet use. Let us first consider the case of a cross-sectional survey.

Figure 4.1 shows the typical results of a cross-sectional survey and, by comparing the means, we can see that, in the UK, Norway and Israel, broadband users do indeed spend more time online than narrowband users. However, we cannot conclude from this chart alone that broadband is causing this difference; it is just as likely to be caused by the socio-demographic profiles of early broadband users.

Figure 4.2 addresses this problem by comparing the mean minutes spent online by narrowband users who did not move to broadband (wave one or two: PSTN 2001 and 2002) with those who did (wave one or two: PSTN → BB (before/after)). Now we can see that those who moved to broadband were already heavier users of the Internet before they switched; indeed this may have been one reason for them to do so. We can also see that it is only in the UK that moving to broadband from narrowband is associated with heavier Internet use in terms of minutes per week online.

Of course, this is still a relatively simple picture. We do not know the influence of Internet experience, age, gender or education, all of which may be mediators of Internet use, as may changes in life stage or lifestyle such as

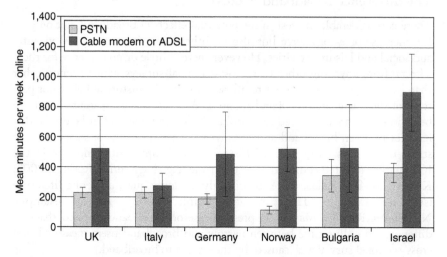

Figure 4.1 Mean minutes online per week for narrowband and broadband users (e-Living wave two, 2002, weighted for non-response).

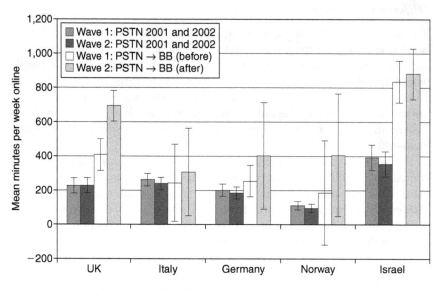

Figure 4.2 Mean minutes online per week for narrowband and broadband users as well as for broadband adopters (e-Living waves one and two, 2002, weighted for non-response).

getting (or losing) a job, becoming a parent or retiring. To overcome this problem, we need to use longitudinal regression models to predict current behaviour on the basis of historical behaviour and changes between waves one and two such as adopting broadband or losing a job. The remainder of the chapter does precisely this.

Table 4.3 shows the specification of these models. In the case of Internet and TV time, it is worth noting that, in order to ensure an approximation to the normal distribution of the dependent variable, we have used the square root of Internet time. In each case we have pooled all Internet users at waves one and two in all six countries in order to achieve a reasonable sample size, but have included dummy variables for the countries as controls to negate inter-country differences.

In the remainder of the chapter we present summaries of models we have developed to test the effects of adopting broadband on Internet time, TV watching time, social leisure activities and online spending which, taken together, represent a range of potential 'impacts' of broadband that are of interest in policy and commercial contexts. Two of these models (Internet time and e-commerce) produced evidence of effects and are discussed first, whilst the other two produced no evidence of effects.

Internet time model

In this case we want to know if moving from narrow to broadband is associated with an increase or decrease in time spent online, whilst controlling for previous Internet usage and other transitions.

For the Internet time model we used the time spent online at wave one to predict the time spent online at wave two; a range of socio-demographic variables, a number of transition variables, such as retiring or losing a job, and dummy variables for each country. We also included a dummy variable for switching to broadband, the respondent's wave-one Internet experience, a set of Internet behaviour change variables and a measure of change in TV watching.

Figure 4.3 shows the results of running this model. As we can see, the strongest predictor of current Internet time by a considerable margin was the amount of time spent online last year. This is hardly surprising – people's habits do not change that quickly. Switching to broadband was the next strongest predictor followed by changes in two ICT behaviours – the frequency of emailing family and friends and the number of different online activities. These last two suggest that there is at least a mutually reinforcing relationship between email and other activities and time spent online as we might expect. Thus the more email people send and the more online activities they do, the more time they spend online. In the context of the *information* society, it is interesting to note that the effect for email (*communication*) was marginally stronger than the number of other online activities.

We can also see that retirement and losing a job made no difference, and nor did gaining a job.

Table 4.3 Longitudinal model specifications

Dependent variables

Wave two weekly Internet minutes	Wave two weekly TV minutes	Wave two online spending (euros) in last three months	Wave two out of home leisure	Details out of home leisure
Y	Y	Y	Y	Country dummies (UK, Italy, Germany, Norway, Bulgaria, Israel)
Y		Y		W 1: minutes per week using Internet
		Y		W 1: minutes per week using TV
		Y		W 1: online spend in last 3 months
			Y	W 2: out of home leisure
Y	Y	Y	Y	W 1: gender (1 = female)
Y	Y	Y	Y	W 1–W 2: was single, now married
Y	Y	Y	Y	W 1–W 2: was single, now living as a couple
Y	Y	Y	Y	W 1–W 2: got job
Y	Y	Y	Y	W 1–W 2: retired
Y	Y	Y	Y	W 1–W 2: became unemployed
Y	Y	Y	Y	W 1–W 2: couple has split

W 2–W 1: change in hours worked, non workers = 0	Y	Y	Y
W 1: Education level – GCSE or equivalent	Y	Y	Y
W 1: Education level – A level or equivalent	Y	Y	Y
W 1: Education level – Degree or equivalent	Y	Y	Y
W 1: aged 16–24	Y	Y	Y
W 1: aged 25–34	Y	Y	Y
W 1: aged 35–44	Y	Y	Y
W 1: aged 45–54	Y	Y	Y
W 1: aged 55–64	Y	Y	Y
W 1: aged 65–74	Y	Y	Y
W 1: aged 75–84	Y	Y	Y
W 1: aged 85+	Y	Y	Y
Broadband switch dummy: (1 = went from PSTN to BB W 1–W 2; 0 = stayed with PSTN)	Y	Y	Y
W 1: Internet experience (years)	Y	Y	
W 2–W 1: change in frequency of email sent to family and friends	Y	Y	
W 2–W 1: change in number of different online activities done in last 3 months (sum of list of 10)	Y	Y	Y
W 2–W 1: change in minutes per day using TV	Y	Y	
W 2–W 1: change in minutes per week using Internet	Y	Y	Y

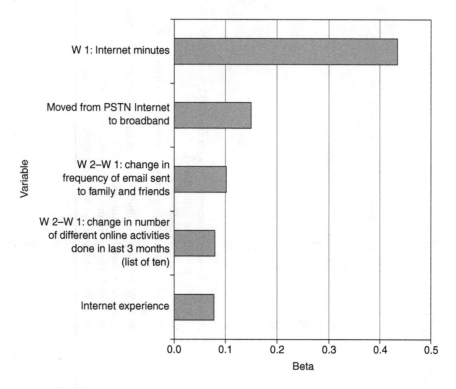

Figure 4.3 Internet time model results (substantive variables with $p < 0.05$ shown, values = beta (standardised coefficients), adjusted $R^2 = 0.352$, controls not shown).

E-commerce model

In this case we wanted to know if moving from narrow to broadband was associated with an increase or decrease in overall online spending. This model was again broadly similar to the previous two but includes the wave one and two spend variables and leaves out the ICT behaviour variables relating to email as we had no a priori reason to suppose that this will be linked to online spending. However we included Internet experience at wave one as it is known to correlate with online spending, as well as the level of Internet use at wave one (minutes online) and the change in time spent online between waves one and two.

The results of this model were rather similar to those for online time, except that now no effect was found for those who moved from narrow to broadband. Instead, the amount of online spend in the previous year together with time online and Internet experience were excellent predictors of current online spend. Undertaking more activities online and spending more time online was linked to spending more.

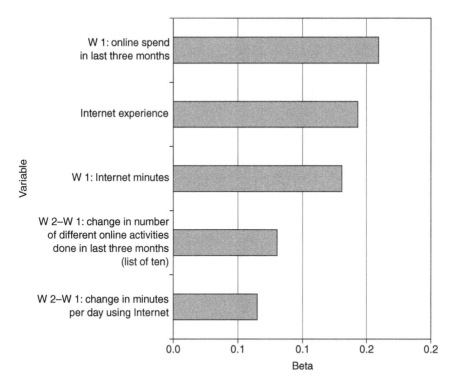

Figure 4.4 E-commerce model results (substantive variables with $p < 0.05$ shown, values = beta (standardised coefficients), adjusted $R^2 = 0.200$).

TV time model

In this model we wanted to know if moving from narrow to broadband was associated with an increase or decrease in time spent watching TV whilst controlling for previous TV usage.

The specification for this model was almost identical to the previous one, with the only difference being the use of TV watching time in wave two as estimated by the respondents as the dependent variable. We also kept the longitudinal ICT usage variables to see if changes in online activity had any effect on TV time.

Although the model explained 33 per cent of the variance in the wave-two TV watching time (not shown), the only two variables that proved statistically significant were the amount of time spent watching TV at wave one, getting a job (negative) and the years of Internet experience (negative). No changes in Internet access mode or online behaviour had any significant effect on time spent watching TV.

Social leisure model

In this model we wanted to know if moving from narrow to broadband was associated with an increase or decrease in out-of-home social activity.[2] This model was similar to the previous three but, instead of the online spend variable, we used an index of social leisure constructed from the following question items describing the frequency of:

1   Playing sport, keep fit or go walking.
2   Going to the cinema, a concert, theatre or watch live sport.
3   Have a meal in a restaurant or cafe, or go for a drink to a bar.
4   Attending activity groups such as evening classes.
5   Meeting with friends.

These items were measured on a scale of 0–7 with 0 meaning 'never' and 7 meaning 'most days'. The index used was simply the sum of these scores for each item so the more frequently an individual took part in these activities, the higher their score.

Although the model explained 44 per cent of the variance (again, not shown), the only variables that showed any statistically significant effects on the wave-two leisure score were the active leisure score for wave one and age (all age groups had significantly lower scores than the sixteen-to-eighteen-year-olds). Getting broadband Internet was not significant and nor was increasing time spent or activities undertaken online.

We repeated this analysis for each component part of the social leisure index and the patterns were identical in that switching from narrowband to broadband Internet made no difference to these scores.

Conclusions

The penetration of broadband Internet was still at an early stage in 2001 and 2002. Israel ranked with the UK, Germany and Norway in terms of households with PCs, but the UK had proportionately more narrowband (analogue modem) Internet households than any other country. ISDN dominated in Norway and, to some extent, in Germany. Some households had multiple modes of access, the most frequent in the UK being analogue modem and cable modem/ADSL and ISDN with analogue modem/cable in Germany and Norway. This reinforces a finding from earlier research, which suggested that new cable modem and ADSL users were retaining their analogue modem access in case of broadband service failure (Anderson *et al.*, 2003).

The four models that we have presented in this chapter have used unique longitudinal data to examine the effect of moving to broadband on four 'representative' activities of interest primarily to the ICT industry but also to policy-makers – Internet time, TV time, amount of money spent online and out-of-home social leisure activities. As we noted in the introduction to this chapter, a range of authors from market research consultancies to academics have commented on the impact of broadband on these aspects of life. It turns out that such 'impacts' are hard to substantiate when we have 'before' and 'after' data on the same individuals and can control for a range of other simultaneous life changes.

The greatest effect on time spent online is not moving to broadband, although this was significant, but the previous behaviour of an individual. We also noted the strong positive effect on time online of the frequency of emailing friends and relatives, thus confirming Kraut *et al.*'s similar finding for the USA (2000) and highlighting that it is not only Asian Internet users who are driven to a great extent by social communication. This should remind us that those looking for 'killer applications' may need to investigate 'social' rather than 'consumption' software more fully.

Given previous findings that have used longitudinal data to show that increased Internet time had a negative effect on television use (Gershuny, 2003), the results we see here suggest that, whilst this may be so, the result does not hold for switching from narrowband to broadband Internet at home. Indeed our results demonstrate the resilience of time spent watching TV to a range of life transitions.

We have no evidence that switching to broadband will have any effect on the amount of money individuals spend online. As with time online, we can instead see a steady progression of online spend driven largely by experience, not only in terms of years spent online, but in terms of breadth of Internet use. We can also see an overriding effect for successful previous e-commerce – since the driving factor for spend this year is the amount spent last year.

We also have no evidence that switching to broadband will have any effect on social leisure activities, even though more time may be spent online in contrast to the concerns of those such as Kraut *et al.* (1998) and Nie and Hillygus (2002).

Overall, the process of experienced or heavy Internet users moving to broadband largely explains the effects we see. Broadband users were, at this time at least, an unrepresentative group of Internet users. In the future, and possibly quite soon in some countries, less-experienced Internet users, as well as new users, will move to broadband. In this case we may see more of a broadband effect, although the constraints of everyday life suggest that it is only a small group of people in any cohort who exhibit significant behavioural change. There is simply not that much slack in most people's lives for major shifts in behaviour in the short term.

Finally we must also express some concerns about the potential distribution of any social benefits of broadband. We have seen that in the case of the Internet time and online spend models, it is those who have the most experience and greatest breadth of use who are doing and spending more. If this pattern continues, then broadband access will not change the structural problems already found in narrowband – those who have the knowledge and experience gain the most benefit, whilst those who lack the skills, knowledge and perhaps self-confidence are left further behind (Selwyn, 2005). This is not an issue that will be solved by technology, or by policies that focus on penetration and access, as opposed to utility, value and social outcomes.

Acknowledgements

This research was partially funded by the European Commission funded Framework 5 project e-Living (IST-2000-25409).

Notes

1 europa.eu.int/information_society/eeurope/2005/index_en.htm.
2 Unfortunately within this dataset we have no measures of intra-household social activity with which to test the hypothesis that heavier Internet usage may lead to less intra-household communication.

Bibliography

Anderson, B., Gale, C., Jones, M.L.R. and McWilliam, A. (2003) Domesticating broadband – what really matters to consumers. In Turnbull, J. and Garrett, S. (eds) *Broadband Applications and the Digital Home*, London, IEE.

Bangemann, M. (ed.) (1994) *Europe and the Global Information Society: Recommendations to the European Council*, Brussels, HLEG INFO-SOC.

CEC (2002) *eEurope 2005: an Information Society For All – an Action Plan*, Brussels, Belgium, Commission of the European Communities.

DTI (1994) *Creating the Superhighways of the Future: Developing Broadband Communications in the UK*, London, HMSO.

Dutton, W., Di Gennaro, C. and Hargrave, A.M. (2005) The Internet in Britain. *The Oxford Internet Survey (OxIS) May 2005*, Oxford, Oxford Internet Institute.

Firth, L. and Mellor, D. (2005) Broadband: benefits and problems. *Telecommunications Policy*, 29, 223–236.

Gallup Europe (2002) *Flash Eurobarometer 135: Internet and the Public at Large – Results and Comments*. Online, available at: ec.europa.eu/public_opinion/flash/fl13s_en.pdf.

Gershuny, J. (2003) Web use and net nerds: a neo-functionalist analysis of the impact of information technology in the home. *Social Forces*, 82, 141–168.

Horrigan, J.B. and Rainie, L. (2002) *The Broadband Difference: How Online American's Behavior Changes with High-speed Internet Connections at Home*, Washington, DC, Pew Internet and American Life Project.

Ida, T. and Kuroda, T. (2004) Discrete choice analysis of demand for broadband in Japan. *Interfaces for Advanced Economic Analysis Discussion Papers*, Kyoto, Kyoto University.

ITU (2003) Birth of broadband. *International Telecommunication Union Internet Report*, Geneva, ITU.

Kerner, S. (2004) *More Broadband Usage Means More Online Spending*, ClickZ Network.

Kraut, R., Lundmark, V., Patterson, M., Kiesler, S., Mukopadhyay, T. and Scherlis, W. (1998) Internet paradox: a social technology that reduces social involvement and psychological well-being? *American Psychologist*, 53, 1017–1031.

Kraut, R., Mukhopadhyay, T., Szczypula, J., Kiesler, S. and Scherlis, B. (2000) Information and communication: alternative uses of the Internet in households. *Information Systems Research*, 10, 287–303.

Kridel, D., Rappoport, P. and Taylor, L. (2002) The demand for high-speed access to the Internet. *Topics in Regulatory Economics and Policy*, 39, 11–22.

Lee, H., O'Keefe, R.M. and Yun, K. (2003) The growth of broadband and electronic commerce in South Korea: contributing factors. *The Information Society*, 19, 81–93.

Madden, G. and Simpson, M. (1997) Residential broadband subscription demand: an econometric analysis of Australian choice experiment data. *Applied Economics*, 29, 1073–1078.

Nie, N.H. and Hillygus, D.S. (2002) The impact of internet use on sociability: time-diary findings. *IT & Society*, 1, 1–20.

Nielsen/NetRatings (2003) *Broadband Revolutionizing Europe's Internet Behaviour*, London, Nielsen/NetRatings.

Paynter, J. and Chung, W. (2003) Factors influencing broadband uptake in New Zealand. *Innovation: Management, Policy & Practice*, 5, 170–188.

Robertson, A., Soopramanien, D. and Fildes, S. (2004) Understanding residential Internet service adoption patterns in the UK. *Telektronikk*, 4, 84–94.

Savage, S.J. and Waldman, D. (2005) Broadband Internet access, awareness, and use: analysis of United States household data. *Telecommunications Policy*, 29, 615–633.

Selwyn, N. (2005) Whose internet is it anyway? Exploring adults' (non)use of the internet in everyday life. *European Journal of Communication*, 20, 5–26.

5 The mysterious east

Pluses and minuses in the e-Europe equation

Maria Bakardjieva

Introduction

In the two consecutive waves of the e-Living study that splashed on the shores of a still largely uncharted e-Bulgaria in the autumn of 2001 and 2002, respectively, respondents were asked to what extent they agreed with the statement: 'The Internet is a mystery to me.' In 2001, 72 per cent agreed with this. A year later, the mystery was not anywhere close to being dispelled for 68 per cent of respondents.

Mystery shrouds the process of penetration of new information technologies in societies like Bulgaria. What is going on behind the small numbers and the subtle fluctuations in them over time? Samples sizes around 1,500 that would normally be representative of the Bulgarian population in measuring any widespread attribute fail to capture the parameters of Internet use due to the negligible number of actual users. What, then, are the specific developments unfolding in Bulgaria or any other similar low-penetration country? Can the presence and use of information technologies, and the Internet in particular, be expected to grow steadily and eventually catch up with the rest of e-Europe? Or are there insurmountable obstacles to be faced? Is there any course of political or industrial action that can lead to faster equalisation between the candidate countries and the current members of the European Union in this particular sphere? This chapter will engage these questions by putting together survey-generated numbers and observations collected in the course of a qualitative study of the Internet in Bulgaria carried out in 2003–2004.[1]

Mapping e-Bulgaria

A large-scale survey conducted by the Bulgarian National Statistical Institute[2] in 2004 provides the latest picture of IT penetration in Bulgarian society. The survey is representative of the Bulgarian population between sixteen and seventy-four years of age. It finds personal computers in close to 15 per cent of the Bulgarian households and Internet connections in 10 per cent of them. Most often, households access the Internet via a modem, followed by broadband connections of different kinds, such as cable, ADSL and LAN. Only a small fraction of households connects through satellite or mobile phone. Mobile phones, for their part, are present in 46 per cent of the households. As to the actual utilisation of these technologies, the survey registers that 23 per cent of the studied population have used a computer in the preceding three months, while during that period the Internet has been accessed by 16 per cent of the people between sixteen and seventy-four years of age. Note that the latter number is significantly higher than the share of users registered by the earlier e-Living study (2001 – 7 per cent; 2002 – 6 per cent), and reasonably close to the share of those Bulgarians who in 2002 strongly rejected the claim that the Internet was a mystery to them. Yet, significantly, 82 per cent of the population had not been online in the past year, or ever (see Figure 5.1).

The National Statistical Institute report points out that education is an important factor influencing the frequency of Internet use, as is age. The percentage of university graduates who use the Internet on a daily basis is higher than in the other categories (3.8 per cent), although those with high-school education do not fall far behind (3.0 per cent). Age may be an intervening factor, in that young people who have not yet completed a university degree form an active user group (see Figure 5.2).

The significant presence of youth among the daily users in the high-school education category is reinforced by the fact that its representatives most often access the Internet from an 'other' public place, which in the Bulgarian context in all likelihood means an Internet club. Home-based Internet use is still quite rare. Only 3.3 per cent of university graduates, 2.8 per cent of those with completed high-school education and 0.5 per cent of people with elementary education say that they use the Internet from home (see Figure 5.3).

With respect to the purposes for which the Internet is used by the Bulgarian population, the choices given to respondents by the National Statistical Institute's study remain confined within a set of unfortunately ambiguous categories that conceal as much as they reveal (see Figure 5.4).

The all-embracing category of 'searching for information or online services' eclipses numerous possibilities that pertain to different spheres of

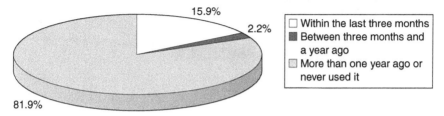

15.9%

2.2%

□ Within the last three months
■ Between three months and
  a year ago
□ More than one year ago or
  never used it

81.9%

Figure 5.1 Internet usage by the population as of 31 March 2004 (source: National Statistical Institute, 'Survey on Information and Communication Technologies Usage in Households', 2005, www.nsi.bg).

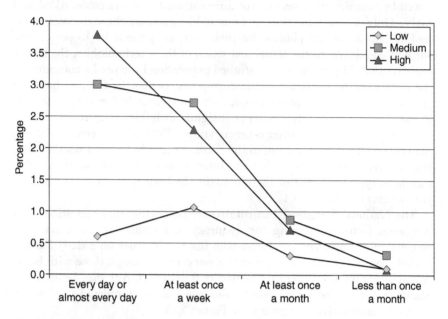

Figure 5.2 Frequency of Internet use of the population by educational level (source: National Statistical Institute, 'Survey on Information and Communication Technologies Usage in Households', 2005, www.nsi.bg).

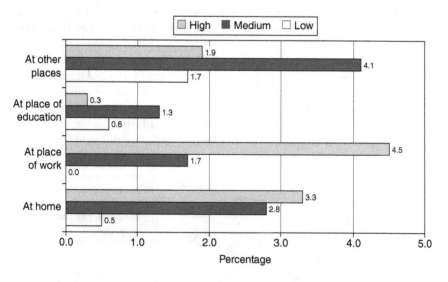

Figure 5.3 Internet access by location and educational level (source: National Statistical Institute, 'Survey on Information and Communication Technologies Usage in Households', 2005, www.nsi.bg).

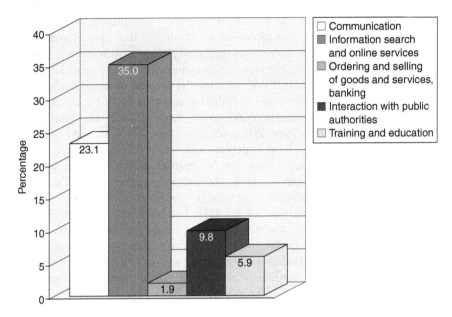

Figure 5.4 Internet activities by purpose of usage (source: National Statistical Institute, 'Survey on Information and Communication Technologies Usage in Households', 2005, www.nsi.bg).

activity, motivations and interests. 'Interactions with public institutions' and 'education and learning' could find different interpretations among different respondents and thus contribute to the skewing of the overall picture. Would, for example, somebody's search for information for the purposes of an educational course fall under 'education and learning' or 'searching for information'? How much real interaction with a public institution does it take to differentiate that category from 'searching for information'? If anything becomes clear from this section of the study, it is that the 'ordering and selling of goods and services and banking' is very rarely the purpose for which Bulgarians use the Internet (mentioned by 2 per cent of Internet users). Sadly, after thousands of users have been asked why they go online, the actual motivations for doing this and the usefulness of the Internet for Bulgarians remain a mystery.

Looking beyond the number of users, the Bulgarian context is characterised by the transitional state of the telecommunications infrastructure, which inherited from the socialist state a respectable penetration rate, but a low technical quality of the telecommunications network. At 26 per cent, the level of digitalisation of this network is amongst the lowest in Europe. The main player in the telecommunication market, the Bulgarian Telecommunications Company (BTC), held an actual monopoly in the past as it owned the main telecommunications backbone as well as the 'last mile' connectivity infrastructure in the country. This monopoly has been challenged, but not radically transformed, during the years following the turn to a market economy. The privatisation of the BTC has been a contested process which advanced slowly and hesitantly due to numerous political squabbles and conflicting interests. In the meantime, new providers have gradually entered the market and spurred the growth of data-transfer networks. According to the 2004 e-Bulgaria report published by Applied Research and Communication Fund (ARC Fund, 2004), the number of optical lines connecting large Bulgarian cities has grown steadily over the past few years, along with the international connectedness of the national telecommunications system. These are, by themselves, favourable conditions for further Internet penetration. However, computer ownership and access to the Internet remain unaffordable to a large portion of the Bulgarian population. The monopoly position of the BTC has resulted in high telephone rates, which continue to obstruct the advancement of the Internet. Thus local phone costs constitute 80 per cent of the cost of dial-up Internet access. Consequently, in 'purchasing power parity equivalent' dial-up costs are higher in Bulgaria than the European Union maximum costs.[3] The prices of LAN access average around 12 Euro a month, and those of cable around 30 Euro a month, at a time when the average household income in the country has been about 242 Euro per month.[4] Thus, while these access modes remain relatively expensive for the average Bulgarian, they represent an attractive alternative to dial-up.

Internet use in Bulgaria typically starts at the workplace. About 40 per cent of businesses have been connected to the Internet in 2004 and an estimated 11–14 per cent of employees have had access to the network (ARC Fund, 2004).[5] Workplace use policies are mostly liberal, which allows employees not only to explore the Net at will, but also to do it for numerous personal purposes. Skills are picked up informally with the help of colleagues in the course of the working day, and it is at the workplace that people discover the usefulness of the network in many areas of professional and personal interest, as well as for interpersonal communication. A lot of chat activity, some observers believe, also takes place at work, in the absence of screening or monitoring.

Connecting from home: costs and benefits

While the opportunity to use the Internet at work arises as a result of business processes and management decisions, the step of becoming a domestic (home-based) Internet user requires personal motivation, which, as the data suggest, is rare. This arouses even more curiosity as to who these people are and what drives their choices. To answer this question, I turn to the analysis of fifty qualitative individual interviews with Bulgarians who use the Internet at home carried out in 2004. Respondents were recruited through the personal networks of the author and a Bulgarian research assistant. We recruited people whom we knew to be home users, trying to diversify along gender, age, occupation and education as far as possible. Far from being representative of the Bulgarian population, our group of respondents can be seen as reflecting the features of the current domestic Internet users in the country – people of working age, between twenty and forty years old, professionals with university education, both males and females. An examination of respondents' stated household incomes shows that most of them had almost twice the average household income for the country. According to data from the Bulgarian National Statistical Institute, the average household income in Bulgaria for the month preceding the study, July 2004, was 473 Bulgarian Leva.[6] Most of the fifty people interviewed, with only a few exceptions, stated household incomes higher than 800 Bulgarian Leva. Another attribute distinguishing the people in our respondent group was utilisation of a computer at work. All these features are in line with the Internet-user profile sketched by the e-Living study. While no more than 11 per cent of the wave-one sample identified university as the type of educational institution they had last attended, just over 50 per cent of all Internet users had been to university. Viewed from a different perspective, the same dataset reveals that, among those respondents whose last-attended educational institution was university, 32 per cent had used the Internet, while only 6 per cent of those with high-school education and 0.3 per cent of those with primary or elementary school education had done so. Similarly, 47 per cent of the people who said they used a computer at work also used the Internet, versus only 7 per cent of those who did not operate a computer at work.

My investigation of home-based Internet use in Canada in the late 1990s (Bakardjieva, 2005) demonstrated that the computerisation of the workplace had been the driving force behind much of the overflow of Internet use into the home. It is very likely that a similar development has taken place in Europe. The influence of this factor is even more decisive in the Bulgarian context, where the level of computer literacy in the general population is low and the cost of networking is quite high to the average person. Without a clear understanding, and some practical experience of the benefits of Internet use, few people would make the decision to experiment with a home subscription. Even when these benefits are understood in principle, the initial investment in computer equipment, software and subscription is so high relative to the average income that it is hardly reasonable for a person who hasn't already accumulated some of this personal 'e-capital' by way of work to jump into the networked world. Further, justification of such an expense is more easily found if the prospective user expects to realise economic gain with the help of his or her computer and network connection. Not surprisingly, most of the users interviewed in the qualitative study employed their Internet connections to do extra work, and directly or indirectly, for earning some extra income.

In a very rough and sweeping way, Internet penetration in Western societies, where it first found a home, can be seen as passing through three stages: the hobbyist, the economic/professional and the mass/mundane stage. Most EU member states, despite the differences in user numbers and connection speed, find themselves at the mass/mundane stage where the Internet is conceptually and financially accessible to the average person and has truly become a part of everyday life with a large presence in the home. The Internet in Bulgaria, in contrast, is still at the economic/professional stage, where motivations related to professional development and increased income lead the way to adoption and use, particularly within the home setting.

Thus, the home-based Internet user in Bulgaria is typically a professional person with some level of post-secondary education.[7] The aspiration to be a 'world-class' professional noted by Miller and Slater (2000) in their study of Internet use in Trinidad represents a powerful driver of Internet adoption in Bulgaria as well. Accessing professional information online holds a prominent place in the accounts of the Internet users interviewed. This ability is seen as a factor increasing competitiveness, along with self-confidence and satisfaction. The 'catching-up' mentality with respect to the so-called 'developed world' is a marked characteristic of Bulgarian culture which finds expression at the level of personal choices and decisions as well. In the case of professional people, it is manifested in the need for constant reassurance that one is up-to-date with the information in one's professional area as well as the need to measure up one's skills with the world standards. For some categories of professions, such as programmers, designers and those in business, the open channel to the online stock of information and field of action sometimes translates into concrete profit through contract work and business deals. Some of our respondents had jobs that dealt with Web design or site maintenance, so in a sense, as one respondent put it, the Internet was giving them both 'bread and circuses'.

There are also the users for whom 'the circuses', or the entertaining, and social functionalities of the Internet are central, but these are usually family members of professionals who have brought the connection to their homes, or the rare members of the new Bulgarian 'leisure class' who can pursue their curiosities and the hype of the day without concern for the cost and time involved. A minimal Internet access realised through an old computer and a dial-up pay-per-use card can be found in the homes of people whose main motivation is to email family and friends belonging to the substantive lot of Bulgarian migrants that left the country in the past fifteen years.

Most of the home-based Internet users interviewed employed several languages in their online pursuits. This is logical to expect in light of the fact that professional goals lead home-based subscription. Quality professional information from the spheres of science, technology, media, business and non-profit/non-government activity is abundant in English, French and a few other languages, while it is hard to find in Bulgarian. Thus the mastery of a language different from Bulgarian increases the gains from the home Internet connection and justifies its existence. At the same time, some of the respondents who only used sources in Bulgarian mentioned the usefulness of legal, governmental and financial information for their work. This can be taken as a hint that the faster development of Bulgarian-language resources useful to particular professional categories, and in business activities, should be a priority for content providers at all levels. Commercial content providers at this stage concentrate their efforts on entertainment and news and, in the best case, on e-commerce functionalities. A more focused attention to the creation of information resources to be used by distinct occupational groups may speed up adoption and help individuals to overcome the existing language-based barriers and inequalities. In a long-term perspective, however, a wider adoption of the Internet could be anticipated, with the gradual rise in foreign-language competence among the population, especially the younger generations. An interesting detail that came out of the interviews was the fact that many respondents mentioned Russian as a language they used on the Internet. With resources in Russian growing at a fast rate and the proximity between the two languages, it would be interesting to watch whether a certain revival of the old cultural bond would occur in the new media context.

Examining the minuses of e-Europe Plus, it is therefore important to emphasise that, compared to the EU member states, the Bulgarian Internet lacks content. Due to the relatively low-spread knowledge of Western languages, the mass of the Bulgarian population can make little use of the vast resources available online. Another question, of course, is that of the relevance of such resources to the lay user. Arguably, the pervasive interest in global popular culture can constitute a motivation for logging on for those who have basic knowledge of English, French, German or Spanish, but this has to be weighed against the prices of computer equipment, software, subscription and an average monthly household income of approximately 242 Euros. With that said, an active and committed Internet service- and content-provider community is growing in Bulgaria.[8] It manifests a spirited effort to construct what is widely referred to as 'the Bulgarian Internet Space'. The Bulgarian Internet space, as envisioned in the discourse of this community, is a space of business, government, culture and civic dialogue that expands with every new site and online initiative that uses the Bulgarian language and reflects Bulgarian experiences, issues and concerns. Tuning into this discourse, one is struck by the obvious and yet somehow elusive realisation that the global, interconnected and all-embracing Internet is the terrain of multiple nation-scapes[9] which make it attractive and meaningful to particular people in particular points of the globe. Or, to paraphrase Miller and Slater (2000: 1), the Internet is not a monolithic or placeless 'cyberspace'; rather it is numerous screens of content, meaningful and useful to diverse people in diverse real-world locations. Hence, there is everything to be gained by an ethnographic approach that construes content as a cultural artefact produced by local forces with local interests and desires in mind; by investigating how Internet content is being produced and consumed in different languages, amidst different cultural settings. The next section will elaborate on the connection between Internet adoption and content supply as it is played out in the Bulgarian situation.

Internet ruses

A recent Bulgarian phenomenon, that started out around 2001, is the proliferation of Internet provision in cities through LANs. According to the ARC Fund's 2004 e-Bulgaria report, there are around 200–300 LAN-based Internet service providers in larger Bulgarian cities that offer around 64 kbps international and 256 kbps national capacity.[10] These providers enter in contractual agreements regarding their mutual transfer of traffic and, through such cooperation, increase the speed of local access. The common approach taken by such companies is to establish a base in a particular neighbourhood, to connect to the services of a bigger wholesale Internet provider, and from there, to spin their own local networks by drawing cable between buildings, sometimes underground, but often simply dangling it through the air. The local base in many cases is a neighbourhood Internet club where computer games and Internet access are offered on a pay-per-minute basis.[11] The business of such companies has typically started with the club and later moved on to establish the LAN service. Internet clubs of this type are capital-modest enterprises which survive on sheer ingenuity, diversity of services and careful tracking and cultivating of demand. Public discourse around these clubs is ambiguous. They are touted as abject joints of drug peddling by some and as laudable hubs of computer education and meaningful pursuits for the youth by others. Many Internet clubs, especially at the early stage of their existence, relied on pirated software and entertainment content such as films, music, etc. to attract clients. Furthermore, they provided devices such as CD burners for users to copy and take away content from the Internet.

After a number of police raids on Internet clubs, this kind of shady activity has been carried over to the so-called 'free servers', affectionately called 'the frees' by young Bulgarian computer and Internet fans. The free servers allow subscribers of the particular LAN maintaining the server, as well as those coming from other LAN providers, to tap into an ample stock of pirated software, films and music. Visitors from outside LANs are charged on the basis of traffic and in this way a lively competition in increasing the attractiveness of their content arises between different providers. Free servers are more difficult to monitor and police than Internet clubs. Their owners have come up with evasive arguments and tactics when confronted with the accusation of copyright infringement.[12] Illegal content, the argument goes, is uploaded on the server by users themselves (at no charge). The LAN operator does not censor and should not be held responsible for the copyright violations that individual users choose to commit on its facilities. As soon as the company operating the service is notified by law-enforcing organisations that illegal content resides on its server, it immediately does the right thing, i.e. takes it down. The law-enforcing system in Bulgaria is notoriously slow and inefficient, and lacks understanding and experience in policing digital technology. This makes the shelf life of the pirated software – films, music, games, etc. – that users upload on such free servers long enough for others to benefit and for the popularity of the LAN providing the service to grow unabated. Thus, users and Internet entrepreneurs have become accomplices in a game of sorts that prolongs the practice.[13]

There is a widespread attitude in Bulgarian culture holding that the Western intellectual property and copyright laws do not apply to 'us' who make much less money and cannot afford to pay the prices of intellectual products. A typical expression of this view is contained in the following quotation found in a Bulgarian online forum:

> If they shut down the frees and P2P networks, HOW the hell can people buy original soft[ware], music, go to the movies to see the new films, or even rent DVDs and videocassettes in a country where the average salary is 100 EU? One question: How are we going to work on the computers, if we need to buy original software? The stupid Windows alone costs almost two times the average salary, that is, you have to starve for two months in order to buy yourself an operating system.... The games are also half a salary.... Let the companies that want everything to be legal make all these much cheaper. People in the US go to the movies 3–4 times a week because with their salaries and prices, they can afford to do that. In practice, in Bulgaria the prices are like those in the US, but the salaries are like in Bulgaria. So they can't [make me believe] the nonsense that the frees will be shut down. They will shut down themselves when there is no more interest in them, that is, when people have enough money to buy legal software.
>
> (April, 2003)

Several of the experts interviewed in the course of this study also insisted that 'people in Bulgaria cannot afford to buy legal software'. Was that to mean, then, that the people of this nation would have to stay away from computer and Internet technology until such time that their disposable income comes into line with Western standards? Nobody seemed prepared to suggest this alternative. Thus piracy has emerged as a reasonable solution to the dilemma and the mass of Bulgarian computer and Internet users go for it without much, or in fact any, moral remorse. An expert estimated that about 80 per cent of the Internet traffic in Bulgaria is generated by the 'free servers' and pointed out that this hurts legitimate content providers who lose out in the traffic competition.

Another subversive practice, undertaken mostly by younger people, from high school students to young professionals with some basic knowledge of computers and networks, represents a kind of 'poaching' by users on the terrain of ISPs themselves. This is the widespread sharing of Internet subscription among neighbours by simply drawing cables along apartment building corridors or across the open spaces between these buildings (wireless local networks are still rare in Bulgaria due to the older equipment used). Some users would even run an improvised, out-of-the-bedroom, micro-business operation where they would offer neighbours the opportunity to join their 'sub-network' for a fee. In other cases, the format is a simple sharing of the network connection officially obtained by one user and splitting up the fee charged by the commercial ISP among several co-users.

How are we to interpret these popular practices that undoubtedly beget new Internet users in Bulgaria like nothing else? If we are to resort to the discourse portraying Eastern Europe as the Mecca of piracy and calling for urgent measures to stop the plague, we would have missed a significant side of the social process through which the Internet makes its way into this country. These practices, I argue, provide the routes along which Internet adoption advances, despite economic and infrastructural difficulties. 'Sly as a fox and twice as quick, there are countless ways of making-do', writes de Certeau (1984: 29) in his analysis of popular tactics and the ways of using a system that ordinary people devise in the face of the disciplining and controlling strategies of the powerful. De Certeau's concept of 'ruses' captures nicely the kind of actions described in this section. Tactical ruses, in de Certeau's terminology, are 'clever tricks of the "weak" within the order established by the "strong", an art of putting one over on the adversary on his own turf, hunter's tricks, manoeuvrable, polymorph mobilities, jubilant, poetic, and warlike discoveries' (1984: 40). There are, certainly, no clear demarcation lines between weak and strong as well as between adversaries in the situation I am trying to analyse here. I am cautious not to poeticise these practices out of proportion either, as there are definitely illegitimate elements at play in them, which may erect obstacles before a more 'normal' course of Internet adoption. However, it should be recognised that they represent a form of creative manoeuvring undertaken by entrepreneurs and users facing deterring economic conditions and an absence of decisive administrative steps towards creating a favourable environment for the penetration of the Internet. These actors refuse to be captives of economic circumstances and lack of political will. They try to take their fortune into their own hands and, interestingly, choose solutions involving attempts at a 'potlatch economy', a notion borrowed by de Certeau from Mauss to signify 'an interplay of voluntary allowances that counts on reciprocity and organizes a social network articulated by "the obligation to give"' (1984: 27). In this case, the obligation to give is applied to things that actually are not users' own (software, music, films), but the principle remains valid. The sharing of connections, for its part, can be seen as cooperative utilisation of a scarce resource, a commendable form of action, even if unacceptable to commercial providers.

Should the goal of pubic policy be to sanction and eradicate these Internet ruses, or should it take them as examples of how a wider popularity of a new medium could be achieved where straight market mechanisms would not work? The Net has to have sufficient relevance for users in order for them to make the investment of time and money necessary for joining. Films, music and games are a common denominator lure that, when offered for free, generates excitement in the general population. But there are surely legitimate ways to create a stock of meaningful information and entertainment services that would be similarly attractive. A number of such possibilities have been tentatively marked by different actors. The online versions of daily and weekly newspapers represent a productive route for expanding the 'Bulgarian Internet space' in directions that can capture the interest of more potential users. Better tools for searching and organising the Bulgarian content that is already online would make the Internet more practically useful to citizens in the course of pursuing interests and needs stemming from everyday-life situations and activities. The experience of the free servers demonstrates that the supply of meaningful content could be the key to encouraging more people to join the still-feeble e-Bulgaria. Content should be understood as a multidimensional entity. E-government by itself will not be sufficient to tip the scale of the public interest. Educational, entertainment, professional and practical-reference types of content should be perceived as parts of an inseparable system and should be built in a balanced way. The elaboration of a strategy for stimulating the creation of Bulgarian content in all areas, and the dedication of relevant funding to that goal, should be put on the agenda of public policy, if the building of e-Bulgaria is to be pursued seriously by the current or successor administrations.

Talking about content in this sense, I do not mean only information put online for the public to consume, but importantly also content that would lead to increased public participation in the Bulgarian Internet space. The forums hosted by newspapers are an indicator of the potential of such formats to attract a devoted audience willing to contribute opinions. A recent initiative entitled 'Our Memories: I Lived Socialism' undertaken by an NGO, the New Culture Foundation, became an interesting experiment in enacting 'the new ways of talking' (Diana Ivanova, director, pers. comm.) made possible by the Internet. The small organising committee, comprising two journalists, a writer and a psychiatrist, created a site where citizens were invited to share their personal memories of the times of 'socialism'. The proclaimed credo of the group was that all stories, no matter what their political and ideological underpinnings, had the right to be heard, i.e. published on the site, and that a tolerant discussion around the inevitable conflicts and contradictions would have a healing effect on Bulgarians. Sharing memories was seen as a way to come to terms with the personal and collective past of Bulgarians and to facilitate a confident transition into the future. The site has become widely known through promotion in the mass media and has indeed accumulated numerous personal stories of fascinating diversity, reflection and debate. This marked a productive collaboration between 'old' and 'new' media.

Various other forms of collaboration between Internet forums and traditional media have emerged in the practice of some newspapers as well. The daily *Sega*,[14] for example, regularly invites prominent personalities to respond to questions (and challenges) coming from members of the online forum in real time. The content of these exchanges is subsequently edited and published on the pages of the newspaper (both the paper and online editions). Needless to say, such interflow between online conversation and the widely distributed and read 'regular' pages of the newspaper raises the profile of the forum participants and makes their voices heard within larger circles of readership. In a further innovative move, journalists in charge of different newspaper columns or thematic areas have entered into online, and sometimes also face-to-face, dialogue with the members of the forums pertaining to their columns. This relationship inevitably influences the direction of journalists' thinking and planning, gives them new ideas and makes them vividly aware of the reactions of their readers. A more dialogic journalism could potentially take shape in this changed communicative situation, although it would be premature to proclaim it at this early stage before the practice has been reflexively conceptualised and cultivated by editors and journalists.

Conclusions

Developments like those recounted in the above two anecdotes are examples of steps that could lead to increasing the civic value of being an Internet user in Bulgaria. If the network is to become a field actively employed for participatory civic debate that is reflected in the media and picked up by audible public discourses, its attraction to a wider variety of people would be enhanced just as much, and even more, than by the possibility of commercial applications. E-commerce will take years to become a feature of Bulgarian everyday life due to the specific circumstances characterising this country's banking system, credit and retail practices, and shopping habits. E-government, by itself, can represent only a limited enticement for users to join the Internet. Free entertainment, which has proved its effectiveness as such an enticement, can be expected to dwindle as copyright legislation is more systematically enforced. Taken together, this means that, under the current conditions, Internet penetration will be slow and restricted to certain social groups such as professionals, business people, young people speaking foreign languages, family members of migrants and a few others.

Another possible course of development, which does not figure on the Bulgarian agenda at this point in time, could be inspired by the ideas of the Open Source and Open Culture movements. During his visit to Bulgaria in May 2005, in relation to the newly initiated Open Culture Project,[15] Lawrence Lessig[16] argued in a newspaper interview that the next big growth spur of the global computer market can only come through the use of Open Source software. The users who will be purchasing the next billion computers will reside in China, India and other developing countries, and will not be able to afford an operation system costing $100. The whole package should not exceed $100 in order to be accessible to the people in such countries, Lessig insisted.[17] Bulgarians are obvious candidates for a $100 dollar computer package until such time that their earning power catches up with their brethren in Old Europe. Needless to say, the $100 should be inclusive of the modem. For this reason, a policy of wider adoption, application and support of Open Source software may be a promising choice for Bulgarian businesses and public organisations. With respect to content, works of Bulgarian culture may have a better chance to become the substance of an appealing Bulgarian Internet space, if they are to be distributed under Creative Commons[18] licences rather than remaining confined within old media and old copyright legislation. In theory, Europe Plus countries like Bulgaria could turn into productive laboratories for testing out such industrial and legal innovations and in this way leave their own, original mark on Internet development globally.

Acknowledgements

This research was supported by a fellowship from the Oxford Internet Institute. The author also wishes to acknowledge the invaluable assistance provided by the Bulgarian e-Living team and the editors of this book.

Notes

1 The qualitative study involved interviews with experts from the spheres of technology, policy and the budding Bulgarian Internet industry, ethnographic observations, as well as in-depth interviews with fifty home-based Internet users with diverse demographic characteristics.
2 The survey collected data from 4,414 households and 10,150 individuals between sixteen and seventy-four years. It was designed in accordance with the requirements of Eurostat. Its methodology was harmonised with the directives of the European Union and the European Parliament (National Statistical Institute, 2005a).
3 The comparison is for off-peak hours (see ARC Fund, 2004, E-Bulgaria Report).
4 This is the average household income for July 2004, calculated by the National Statistical Institute (2004).
5 The number of Internet-connected businesses quoted in a study by the National Statistical Institute (2005b) is 62 per cent, possibly because of differences in the methodology.
6 Equal to EU 242 (see National Statistical Institute, 2004).
7 According to the results published in the *SIBIS Pocket Book* 2002/03 (SIBIS Project and European Communities, 2003), Bulgaria is among the European countries most severely divided with respect to access and use of the Internet along educational lines (2003: 156).
8 *Firsts in the Bulgarian Internet* (Belogusheva and Toms, 1993, in Bulgarian) details the chronology of the emergence and growth of this community between 1990 and 2002.
9 The allusion to Appadurai's (1996) 'global flows' is intentional.

10 ARC Fund, 2004, E-Bulgaria Report 2004.
11 Not counting these privately owned and operated Internet clubs, in 2003, Bulgaria had 0.01 Public Internet Access Points (PIAPs) per 1,000 inhabitants, as noted in the e-Europe Final Progress Report (European Ministerial Conference, 2004).
12 See Aleksiev, S., 2003: 2.
13 In April 2005, due to fear of Bulgaria being included in the Special 301 Report by the US Trade Representative listing countries with intellectual property rights protection problems, the National Service for Combating Organised Crime held several meetings with 'free server' providers and organisations of copyright holders. The objective was to elaborate a regime of efficient intellectual property protection on the Internet. A number of raids on LAN companies and limitations on the operations of the free servers followed. In response, the users of these servers began actively discussing and regrouping with a view to switching to P2P and 'torrent' technologies.
14 See www.segabg.com/.
15 See open-culture.net/.
16 Lawrance Lessig is a Stanford law professor, chair of the Creative Commons project and author of *Free Culture* (2004) among others.
17 *Capital*, Issue 21, May 2005.
18 See creativecommons.org/.

Bibliography

Aleksiev, S. (2003) Bulgaria piracy heaven. Online, available at: www.svetlozar.com/research/analyses/2003,06,19,,001.html (accessed October, 2004).

Appadurai, A. (1996) *Modernity at Large: Cultural Dimensions of Globalization*, Minneapolis, University of Minnesota Press.

ARC Fund (2004) E-Bulgaria Report. Online, available at: www.arc.online.bg/artShow.php?id=4235 (accessed 25 August, 2005).

Bakardjieva, M. (2005) *Internet Society: the Internet in Everyday Life*, London, Thousand Oaks, New Delhi, Sage.

Belogusheva, R. and Toms, J. (2003) *Firsts in the Bulgarian Internet*, Sofia, IK Siela (in Bulgarian).

De Certeau, M. (1984) *The Practice of Everyday Life*, Berkeley, LA, London, University of California Press.

European Ministerial Conference (2004). e-Europe final progress report. Online, available at: www.emcis2004.hu/dokk/binary/30/17/3/eEurope__Final_Progress_Report.pdf (accessed 21 October, 2005).

Lessig, L. (2004) *Free Culture*, New York, Penguin Press.

Miller, D. and Slater, D. (2000) *The Internet: an Ethnographic Approach*, Oxford, New York, Berg.

National Statistical Institute (2004) Households income, expenditure and consumption. Online, available at: www.nsi.bg/BudgetHome_e/BudgetHome_e.htm (accessed 21 October, 2005).

National Statistical Institute (2005a) Survey on information and communication technologies usage in households. Online, available at: www.nsi.bg/ (accessed 21 October, 2005).

National Statistical Institute (2005b) Survey on information and communication technologies usage in enterprises and e-commerce. Online, available at: www.nsi.bg/ (accessed 21 October, 2005).

Ognyanova, K. (2005) Don't shut the Internet, but sue the criminals! Interview with L. Lessig. *Capital*, 21 (in Bulgarian).

SIBIS Project and European Communities (2003). *SIBIS Pocket Book 2002/03 Measuring the Information Society in the EU, the EU Accession Countries, Switzerland and the US*, Bonn: Empirica GmbH.

6 Gender and ICTs

Tal Soffer and Yoel Raban

Introduction

In this chapter we look at the same issues addressed in Chapter 2 by Raban but with a different purpose, to examine gender differences in ICT usage. The aim of this chapter is to describe the differences between men and women regarding ownership, usage and diffusion of ICTs. Is there a gender-related digital divide (gender gap in ICTs) and, if so, what are its causes? The gender gap is a major issue that has been addressed by researchers in the past. The studies related to the gender gap in ICTs started as emerging technologies penetrated rapidly into our lives. This reality changed traditional patterns of daily life and introduced new ways of work and leisure (Mackenzie and Wajcman, 1999).

Our approach to analysing gender gaps is straightforward. We use OLS regressions for men and women to explain the differences in Internet use and Internet usage time. By comparing the impacts of demographics, income, work status and other variables on Internet use and usage time, we can determine the sources of the gender gaps.

Possible determinants of the gender gap

There are several different theories regarding the causes of the gender gap in general, and in ICTs in particular. One theory simply claims that girls inherently have a different approach towards technology compared to boys (Turkle, 1995), though education must be a part of this. Indeed, many studies indicate that education level is one of the major factors that influence ICT access and usage in general. The literature on gender emphasises the importance of this variable and shows a gap between men and women in their education level in general, and in technology education in particular. The technological gap between the genders starts even in the kindergarten, where educators tend to 'push' boys into computers and technical games and girls into playing social games. This reflects directly on future decisions regarding education, occupation and even way of life (Dryburgh, 2000). In the teenage period, girls' self-confidence in technical subjects is lower than that of boys and they tend to avoid maths, science and computer studies (Miller *et al.*, 1996). A different approach emphasises the lack of an imitator model for girls. Usually young women do not see many women in key positions in the fields of science and technology, who could be a model for imitation or a 'mentor' for them (Faulkner, 2001; Lee, 2002). The 'patriarchy' approach claims instead that technologies are usually designed and dominated by men and are also poorly related to women's needs and interests (e.g. Cockburn and Ormrod, 1993).

In this chapter, we analyse the determinants of the gender gap with respect to Internet use and usage time. We focus on demographics (work, marriage, education, age, income) and on attitudes towards computers and the Internet as its main determinants. Perhaps the most important, however, is gender differences in the extent and nature of work. The literature regarding women's participation in the labour force emphasises the gap between men and women in general, and in work status, wage, occupations distribution and career choice in particular (Ahuja, 2002; SIGIS, 2002). Although this trend has changed in recent years and more women are joining the labour force, there still remains a wide gap between the genders. Examining the differences between men and women in work status in the e-Living sample, which forms the basis of the analysis presented below, we find a considerable gap of 17 per cent in labour force participation. The participation rate for men was around 60 per cent or just over in most countries (except in Bulgaria), while women's participation rates range from 33 per cent in Italy to 55 per cent in Norway. In some countries, the gender gap is fairly narrow, at around 9 per cent – 10 per cent in Israel and Bulgaria, around 15 per cent in Norway, but above 20 per cent in Italy, the UK and Germany. Only in Scandinavian countries is women's participation in the labour force as high as amongst American women. Finally, although this work participation gap seems quite persistent for all age groups, in some countries (Germany and Norway) it declines with age.

Women work less and therefore have more time to use domestic ICTs, but they also earn less, and so have fewer resources with which to buy them. The time issue, though, is more complex. Although men work more than women, women's work 'is never done', and this is especially so for women in employment. Women and men allocate their time during the day differently. In the second wave of the e-Living study (2002), we collected diary data that included various activities carried out by respondents during a twenty-four-hour period. Looking at these data, we find that, on average, men and women spend the same time (around six hours a day) on both paid and unpaid work activities. However, the most significant activity for women is unpaid work (including shopping, house maintenance, childcare), which lasts around four hours during the day. For men, the major activity is paid work that lasts on average around four hours a day, while unpaid work lasts about two hours.

ICTs ownership and use

In this section, we study the differences between the genders regarding personal use of computers, Internet and mobile phones in the six countries studied in e-Living. Table 6.1 shows that in all countries (except for Bulgaria) ICT usage by women is lower than that of men.

The mobile phone is the most popular ICT. One of the reasons for this is that it is easy to operate and provides immediate opportunities for communication with others with no limit on time and space. The ownership of mobile phones for both men and women is high compared to computer and Internet use. However, there is still a gap between men and women. The average ownership rate is 70 per cent for women compared to 83 per cent for men. Looking at the gender gap in mobile phone ownership across countries, Italy, Germany and Norway have the highest gap with 17 per cent, followed by the UK (9 per cent), Bulgaria (8 per cent) and Israel (7 per cent).

The survey shows that in all countries there is a gap between men and women in PC use. In Italy, Germany and Norway the gap is 17–18 per cent. In the UK it is 11 per cent. Bulgaria and Israel have the lowest gap – 1 per cent and 3 per cent respectively. Similar results were published in recent studies (DTI, 1999; SIGIS, 2002a).

As for Internet use, studies show that users are most likely to be men (SIGIS, 2002b). Overall, men have higher usage rates than women. However, surveys show that there has been a strong growth in the use of the Internet among girls, reducing the gender gap in the adolescents' age group (Berg *et al.*, 2002). In our study we still see a gender gap in all countries surveyed concerning Internet use, averaging around 12 per cent. The highest gap is in Norway (21 per cent) and the lowest is in Bulgaria (2 per cent).

Table 6.1 ICTs use by gender (%)

	UK		Italy		Germany		Norway		Bulgaria		Israel	
	M	F	M	F	M	F	M	F	M	F	M	F
Have mobile	80	71*	88	71*	78	61*	89	72*	21	13*	82	75*
Use computer	68	57*	60	42*	71	53*	83	66*	18	19	62	59*
Use Internet	60	53*	52	33*	60	43*	78	57*	13	11	54	46*

Notes
M = male, F = female, * – difference significant at $p < 0.05$.

Internet diffusion and usage intensity

In recent years there has been a strong growth in access and use of ICTs like home computers, the Internet and mobile phones (SIGIS, 200b2). More women are joining the 'ICT Club', using mobile phones, computers and the Internet. Some reports claim that the gender gap in ICT usage has narrowed in recent years. In this chapter we examine this issue and try to see if there is a gender digital divide in Internet use. In order to answer this question, we carried out a diffusion analysis of Internet adoption by gender. The diffusion is based on respondents' experience with the Internet, which was converted into the year of Internet adoption. Figure 6.1 shows Internet use diffusion in the pooled sample.

We can see that the rate of Internet adoption has grown for both genders between the years 1991 and 2001, but also that the rate of women's adoption is lower than that of men. The adoption's rate of the Internet for women in the year 2001 was around 40 per cent, while the men's rate was around 55 per cent. However, the annual addition of male Internet users is lower than that for women in the years 2001 and 2002. It seems that, although women are considered late adopters, they have succeeded in narrowing the gap during recent years to less than 20 per cent, on average, by 2001. But, as Internet adoption has been slowing for both men and women, a certain gap is likely to remain.

The examination of usage patterns was carried out in response to studies published on this issue which claim that it is not enough to seek to explain why people decide to adopt a particular technology. Great importance should be attributed to examining the nature of use, as adoption in itself

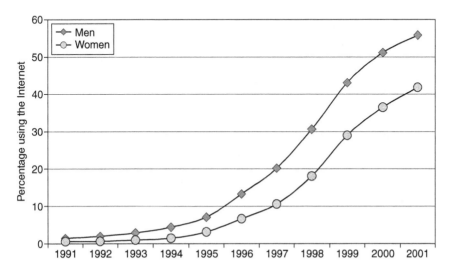

Figure 6.1 Internet use diffusion curve by gender.

does not fully measure the actual use of technology. As mentioned in Raban's chapter, Internet penetration in most European countries is quite high. It is therefore becoming more important to study Internet usage patterns. Boneva *et al.* (2001) confirm in their study the declining trend of the gender gap. They claim that the gender gap in Internet use has been narrowing, but different gender usage patterns and application preferences nevertheless persist. Other studies in this area indicate that women's interest in and usage of computers and the Internet is very different from that of men. For example, women tend to search the Web mostly for health information and educational purposes, while men are more likely to seek news and entertainment online (Boneva and Kraut, 2003). Moreover, there are gender variations in terms of intensity of usage, where women tend to spend less time using computers as well as the Internet at home compared to men (SIGIS, 2002b).

Research on diffusion of innovations mostly uses time as a measure for intensity of use of a new technology. The more people who are willing to spend time using the new technology, the more it will be considered as a success for the adoption process. As mentioned before, there is a gender gap regarding ICT access. This gap appears in Internet usage intensity as well. In general, women tend to use the Internet for less time than men in all the surveyed countries. The usage intensity gap is around ten minutes per day, which is about 30 per cent of the daily usage of men. Another factor that measures intensity is the depth of Internet use, measured by the numbers of activities people engage in on the Internet. Women are involved in less online activities than men. The average number for women's online activities is three, compared to 3.5 for men. Except for Italy, the depth of Internet use for men is significantly higher than that of women in all countries.

Explaining the gender gap

The gaps are not always large, but why do they exist at all? We first analyse the differences in Internet use by using logistic regression on the pooled sample by gender. We assume that Internet use is basically determined by demographics, such as marital status, education and age, but also by work status and income. We do not include current attitudes towards the Internet as one of the explanatory variables, since they may have changed since the decision took place. The e-Living data were obtained during 2001 and 2002, and for most individuals the decision to start using the Internet took place before that period.

Table 6.2 describes the results of a logistic regression where Internet use is the dependent variable. In order to concentrate on gender gap issues, we decided to use the pooled sample of all six countries. We can see that work status has a positive and significant impact on Internet use of both men and women. The workplace is indeed a conducive environment for

Table 6.2 Logistic regression coefficients of Internet use by gender and country (odds ratio)

	Men	*Women*
Age	0.93***	0.94***
Work status (0, 1)	1.30**	1.85***
Marital status (0, 1)	0.85	0.70***
High-school education (0, 1)	2.44***	2.21***
Higher education (0, 1)	7.87***	6.27***
Low-income group (0, 1)	0.42***	0.27***
High-income group (0, 1)	2.70***	2.29***
Time (2002 = 1)	1.27**	1.27**
UK	50.21***	39.53***
Italy	23.34***	13.20***
Germany	46.83***	23.23***
Norway	70.55***	32.44***
Israel	13.75***	6.87***
R^2	0.42	0.38
N	4,609	5,601

Notes
$* < 0.05$, $** < 0.01$, $*** < 0.001$.

Internet use. It seems that the impact is larger for women than for men, so transition to the workforce can benefit women more than men in terms of Internet use.

There is a distinct gender difference with regard to the impact of marital status. Being married has no significant impact on men's Internet use, but it does for women. Married women are less likely to use the Internet than unmarried women. There could be several explanations for this. We think that one important reason could be the difference in allocation of time between men and women. Men spend more time on paid work and may allocate some time at home for Internet use. Women, especially married women, spend more time on domestic chores, which eats into free domestic time, thus leaving them not only perhaps with less time at home for the Internet, but more specifically with less time to experiment with this, and to become familiar with its intricacies.

Other important determinants of Internet use are education and income. Both have a significant impact for men as well as for women, but again we can see a certain gender difference. The impact of education on Internet use is higher for men, and so is the impact of income.

The next table shows the results of a linear regression describing Internet intensity (daily time spent on the Internet) as a function of computer attitudes and other explanatory variables. We assume that attitudes towards the Internet, along with depth of Internet use as well as time spent watching television, are all exogenous to Internet usage time. Attitudes towards

Table 6.3 Standardised coefficients for men and women of OLS regression with
Internet usage time (log form) as dependent variable

	Men	Women
Positive attitude index	0.18***	0.22***
Number of online activities	0.18***	0.21***
TV watching time per day	0.14***	0.15***
Age	−0.07**	−0.02
Work status (0, 1)	−0.06**	−0.06**
Marital status (0, 1)	−0.08**	−0.09***
Emails sent per day	0.17***	0.17***
ISDN or faster (0, 1)	0.13***	0.05*
Time (2002 = 1)	−0.05**	−0.06**
UK	−0.14	−0.19*
Italy	−0.05	−0.11
Germany	−0.18*	−0.18*
Norway	−0.33***	−0.38***
Israel	0.05	0.04
R^2	0.29	0.34
N	2,144	1,866

Notes
* <0.05, ** <0.01, *** <0.001.

computers and the Internet are formed gradually, and depend mostly on past
experience. In this sense, present usage intensity may affect future rather
than current attitudes. The depth of Internet use is also formed gradually
over time and depends mostly on past experience. Usage satisfaction gained
from past experience tends to reinforce the current depth of use. TV-
watching time is influenced by past habits and not by the current intensity
of Internet use. Here, again, viewing habits are formed over an extended
period of time and cannot be changed instantly.

Attitudes towards computers and the Internet are measured by the level
of agreement to several questions, such as 'the Internet is a mystery to me'.
The index is computed by adding positive measures and subtracting negative ones. This impact is higher for women compared to men. In general, the
data show that attitudes towards computers and the Internet are higher for
men than for women (an average value of 2.6 for men compared to 2.3 for
women). It could be argued that since men's attitudes are high already, an
increase in women's attitudes will cause a greater impact on usage intensity.
A similar argument may be used with regard to depth of use. Men are
already heavier Internet users, in term of the number of activities performed
by them (3.3 activities compared with 2.8). In this case, increasing the
depth of women's use will have a greater impact on usage time.

Looking at other determinants, we see that the impact of TV-watching
time, work status, marital status and email activity are almost identical for

men and women. The impact of age is small and significant for men, but it is not significant for women. Having a broadband Internet connection (including an ISDN or faster connection) is associated with a more significant increase in usage time for men compared to women. Since men are heavier users, in terms of usage time and depth of use, they utilise the faster connection more than women.

But what is the main impression we gain from these analyses? While for both men and women the characteristics of intensive users of the Internet are different from those of *mere* users, and although there are some differences in the gender patterns of both (highlighted above), the gender profiles of both usage and usage intensity are remarkably similar. Whatever induces a man to use the Internet a lot might also induce a woman to do so. In the case of use itself, the only differences that stand out are country differences. Whatever it is that gives rise to such variation in the gender gap by country, which we have already demonstrated in Table 6.1, specific individual-level factors do not seem to make much additional difference to the gender distribution of Internet usage. This implies an institutional-level basis for the difference, rather than a psychological or social–psychological explanation.

Conclusions

Are there policy issues that derive from the above discussion? We feel that there are, but these derive from policy in other areas such as employment or the family rather than directly from the field of ICT development.

There are still some persisting gender gaps in ICT use and usage intensity in most countries. When we look more closely at Internet use, we see gender gaps ranging from as low as 2 per cent (Bulgaria) to 21 per cent (Norway). We show that the gender gaps may be explained by certain gaps in the determinants of Internet use. One of the strongest gender gap determinants is workforce participation. The work environment today brings people closer to computers and the Internet. As women's work participation rises, it is possible that the ICT gap will continue to close, but policy is a major factor influencing work participation in the first place. Education is similarly often given as a key factor for ICT use. Our analysis shows that, although education is an important predictor of Internet use, the education gap between men and women is already rather low, so this may not be an area where policy could have a strong impact. As expected, income is also an important determinant of Internet use. Even if men and women in couples share their income, income is a policy issue in the case of single people or lone parents.

As for Internet usage intensity, we find a gender gap in all countries. A part of this usage intensity gap may be related to allocation of time to daily activities. Women generally need more time for domestic activities than men, so that if they also work they have less free time for Internet usage. But besides that, our analysis shows that women's attitudes towards computers and the Internet are in general more negative than men's. Attitudes sometimes change rather slowly, so efforts in this area should start early in life, during primary education. In the USA and some European countries, efforts have been made to increase women's knowledge and interest in computer science and technology studies. Preliminary results can perhaps be seen in the growing numbers of women in science and technology fields in recent years (Margolis and Fisher, 2002; European Commission, 2004). Such efforts should be continued with more vigour in the future.

Acknowledgements

We would like to acknowledge Mr Amram Turgman for his devoted statistical assistance.

Bibliography

Ahuja, M.K. (2002) Women in the information technology profession: a literature review, synthesis and research agenda. *European Journal of Information Systems*, 11, 20–34.

Boneva, B. and Kraut, R. (2003) Email, gender and personal relationships. In Wellman, B. and Haythornewaite, C. (eds) *The Internet in Everyday Life*, Malden, MA, Blackwell Publishers, pp. 372–403.

Boneva, B., Kraut, R. and Frohlich, D. (2001) Using e-mail for personal relationships: the difference gender makes. *American Behavioral Scientist*, 45(3), 530–549.

Berg, V., Gansmo, H.J., Hestflatt, K., Lie, M., Nordli, H. and Sørensen, K.H. (2002) *Gender and ICT in Norway: an Overview of Norwegian Research and Some Relevant Statistical Information*, Online, available at: www.rcss.ac.uk/sigis/public/download/SIGIS_D02_Part5.pdf.

Cockburn, C. and Ormrod, S. (1993) *Gender and Technology in the Making*, London, Sage.

Dryburgh, H. (2000) Under representation of girls and women in computer science: classification of 1990s research. *Educational Computer Research*, 23(2), 181–202.

DTI (1999) *Women and Information and Communication Technologies: a Literature Review*. Online, available at: www.rcss.ed.ac.uk/sigis/public/backgrounddoc5/women.

European Commission (2004) *She Figures 2003: Women and Science Statistics and Indicators*, Luxembourg. Online, available at: ec.europa.eu/research/science-society/pdf/she_figures_2003.pdf.

Faulkner, W. (2001) The technology question in feminism: a view from feminist technology studies. *Women's Studies International Forum*, 24, 79–95.

Lee, J.D. (2002) More than ability: gender and personal relationships influence science and technology involvement. *Sociology of Education*, 75, 349–373.

MacKenzie, D. and Wajcman, J. (1999) Introductory essay: the social shaping of technology. In MacKenzie, D. and Wajcman, J. (eds) *The Social Shaping of Technology*, Milton Keynes, Open University Press, pp. 3–28.

Margolis, J. and Fisher, A. (2002) *Unlocking the Clubhouse: Women in Computing*, Cambridge, MA, MIT Press.

Miller, L., Chaika, M. and Groppe, L. (1996) Girls: preferences in software design: insights from a focus group. *Interpersonal Computing and Technology: an Electronic Journal for the 21st Century*, 11(2), 27–36.

SIGIS (2002a) *Love, Duty and the S-Curve: an Overview of Some Current Literature on Gender and ICT*. D02 part 1. Online, available at: www.rcss.ed.ac.uk/sigis/public/D02_Part1_pdf

SIGIS (2002b) *Information Society, the Internet and Gender: a Summary of Pan-European Statistical Data*. D02, part 2. Online, available at: www.rcss.ed.ac.uk/sigis/public/download/SIGIS_D02_Part2.pdf

Turkle, S. (1995) *Life on the Screen: Identity in the Age of the Internet*, New York, Simon & Shuster.

7 ICT use and the elderly

Cohort, lifestage or just irrelevant?

Deborah DiDuca, Caroline Partridge and Jeroen Heres

The European policy context

Europe has an ageing population. By 1995, seventy million people over the age of sixty were living in the Union, almost 20 per cent of the total population. By 2020, this figure will rise to 25 per cent and the number of people over eighty-years-old will more than double (Seniorwatch, 2002). There will therefore be more older people in absolute as well as relative terms, there will be considerably more older 'old' people, there will be fewer family (informal) carers, and there will be a smaller workforce if current employment and retirement practices persist. We cannot ignore these facts, but we also cannot ignore the associated media attention which tends, rather predictably, to focus on the negative aspects of this demographic trend.

The broad aim of the 2005 eEurope action plan was very much in lin with taking into account the needs of the ageing population, for example:

> To make the European Union the most competitive and dynamic knowledge-based economy with improved employment and social cohesion by 2010.

Yet nowhere was the ageing population mentioned as an integral part of an explicit aim. This is not to say that the European Commission did not recognise the trends for this population segment but, rather, that the Commission did not emphasise this population segment when considering the provision of new technologies as a driver for social inclusion.

However, the ageing population was, together with increasing international competition, the main concern leading to the Lisbon agenda formulated by the EC in 2000. After a recent review on the achievements made during the past five years, the EC decided to focus efforts on two main areas: productivity and employment; and the need for urgent action is confirmed by the report from the High Level group chaired by Wim Kok last November (HLEG, 2004). According to the group's report,

The Lisbon strategy is even more urgent today as the growth gap with North America and Asia has widened, while Europe must meet the combined challenges of low population growth and ageing. Time is running out and there can be no room for complacency.

(2004: 6)

While the ageing society is part of the problem, it is also considered as part of the solution:

pursuing active employment policies which help people in work and provide incentives for them to remain there, developing active ageing policies to discourage people from leaving the workforce too early...

(CEC, 2005)

The concept of life-long learning should also increase employability and enable people to stay employed and productive longer. However, it is important that this is seen not just in economic terms, but also in terms of the effects that extended learning and increased workforce participation would have on the quality of life of the older population. It is also important to be wary of the emphasis on productivity and workforce participation, in terms of ensuring that inclusive policy development takes into account the 'old old', that is, people in their seventies and above, who may not wish, nor be able to, rejoin the workforce. As the new European Commissioner for Information Society and Media, Viviane Reding (2005), has stated:

I will make sure that we create an information society for all, including the older generations, people with disabilities and people who are simply not familiar with new technologies.

The private-sector context

Along with the implicit assumptions made by the EC regarding older people, there is also the related phenomenon of 'design bias' – which is currently rife in large IT corporations (e.g. Moore, 2002; Bodoff, 2003). The tendency is to look to youth when designing new products and services, because they are seen as 'lead users' and as such are seen as being more prepared to support, purchase and even help to develop 'innovative' or 'disruptive' services. Innovation is seen very much as a province of the young, therefore many designers will tend towards designing for this age group, hoping to disrupt other companies, and equally to prevent their own company from being disrupted. It must also be remembered that: 'Companies like to be seen as young, innovative, sexy. This means that aging is not something they like to be identified with' (Bodoff, 2003).

In both research and design circles, working with young people is generally more appealing than working with the older population – it has the appearance of being more exciting, more cutting-edge and, in design terms, the youth are perceived as more concerned with aesthetics than older people. To combat this, several bodies, however, including The Helen Hamlyn Research Centre at the Royal College of Art in London have set up R&D initiatives to promote inclusive design methods, i.e. design methods that produce generic products and services that are useful, usable and pleasurable for everyone.

There are also biases inherent in current IT advertising. For example, a survey of 45,000 over-fifties by marketing agency Millennium (Malkani, 2004) showed that 86 per cent felt ignored by the marketing industry, and 70 per cent felt patronised by current advertising campaigns. A recent UK survey of 'baby-boomers' by Demos (2004a), however, showed a common appreciation of a certain kind of humour in advertising; that of the 'parent' figures being more 'childish' than their offspring, as reflected in current adverts in 2005 for Vauxhall cars, amongst others. But we cannot assume from this that all older people would appreciate this humour, as Demos stated: 'the idea of a "grey market" is itself an incoherent category, referring as it does to everyone from 40 to 100. Marketers would never dream of segmenting the youth market with such sloppiness' (2004: 44).

The Baby Boomers (those born between 1945 and 1965) mentioned above are themselves beginning to explode some of the myths about ageing. In the UK, the oldest of these reach retirement age in 2005, and there has been much speculation about their role as retirees and how it will differ from previous generations. These are the people for whom new campaigns are currently being designed, that reflect their supposed affluence, individualism, youthfulness and general refusal to accept the status quo (Demos, 2004a). Again, the emphasis is on the Baby Boomers rather than the 'old old', and again, this could lead to a new type of exclusion.

Common assumptions about older people

The basic assumptions about older people and technology, which exist both in the public and private sectors, therefore appear to be as follows:

- older people are more technophobic;
- older people are less concerned with aesthetic issues;
- older people are less likely to innovate;
- older people are less likely to purchase innovative products and services;
- older people find it more difficult to learn new IT-related skills;
- older people are less interested in technology;
- older people aren't excluded from IT;
- it doesn't matter how you advertise to older people.

It is possible that these assumptions, if not properly investigated, could lead to erroneous policy and design decisions, which could actually be harmful to Europe's ageing population. Therefore we need to understand the older population with regard to their multiple and varied attitudes towards technology, and also whether there are changes to policy, education, advertising and design that we can make that will facilitate positive changes to those attitudes, which in turn may increase productivity and workforce participation amongst those in the older population/s who are able to carry on working, and may also increase the quality of life for those who are not.

Empirical analysis

Several of the issues raised above can be clarified by examining the e-Living data. For example, we can analyse older people's attitudes to, and usages of, technology and compare this with other groups. In addition, we can use the panel nature of the data to examine transitions of key significance to this age group, such as retirement, with respect to indicators of quality of life. In the following sections we make a number of comparisons, in order to help to clarify the roles that ICT can play in the lives of the older population.

Attitudes to ICTs

In order to analyse the effect of age and ICT experiences on attitudes to ICTs, we developed two regression models for each of eight attitudinal statements. These statements were:

- 'The Internet is a mystery to me' – asked of all.
- 'I am interested in new technologies' – asked of all.
- 'Computers are intimidating to use' – asked of all but with some non-response/don't know responses.
- 'Computers can be fun' – asked of all but with some non-response/don't know responses.
- 'Everyone depends on computers too much nowadays' – asked of all but with some non-response/don't know responses.
- 'Computers will make life much easier if you have one' – asked of all but with some non-response/don't know responses.
- The Internet is fun' – asked of all Internet users (home or work).
- 'The Internet is very useful to me' – asked of all Internet users (home or work).

In all cases respondents were asked to respond on a scale of 1 (strongly disagree) to 5 (strongly agree).

In each case the first, simple model analysed only the effects of being in older age groups compared to being in the youngest (sixteen-to-twenty-four). The second included variables measuring years of Internet experience (0–n) and sum of PC skills (see Brynin, this volume) as measures of ICT experience.

As we can see from Table 7.1, in all cases older people and especially the sixty-five-plus groups have significantly more negative attitudes to ICTs

Table 7.1 Effects of age and ICT experience on attitudes to ICTs (e-Living wave one, weighted for non-response, dummies for countries included but not shown)

	The Internet is a mystery to me	The Internet is a mystery to me	I am interested in new technologies	I am interested in new technologies	Computers are intimidating to use	Computers are intimidating to use	Computers can be fun	Computers can be fun
Age (16–24)								
25–34	0.151**	−0.017	−0.024	0.073	0.054	−0.054	−0.164***	−0.120***
35–44	0.352***	0.03	−0.075	0.100*	0.201***	0.009	−0.186***	−0.110***
45–54	0.604***	0.132*	−0.240***	0.019	0.387***	0.106*	−0.400***	−0.291***
55–64	0.970***	0.243***	−0.544***	−0.150**	0.619***	0.183***	−0.508***	−0.341***
65–74	1.321***	0.330***	−0.822***	−0.290***	0.850***	0.250***	−0.602***	−0.369***
75+	1.542***	0.354***	−1.026***	−0.390***	1.145***	0.420***	−0.876***	−0.596***
Years of Internet use	–	−0.111***	–	0.029***	–	−0.048***	–	0.007
Sum of PC skills	–	−0.262***	–	0.158***	–	−0.163***	–	0.070***
Adjusted R^2	0.163	0.353	0.138	0.207	0.109	0.201	0.0921	0.113
N	10,022	10,022	10,098	10,098	9,543	9,543	9,489	9,489

	Everyone depends on computers too much nowadays	Everyone depends on computers too much nowadays	Computers will make life much easier if you have one	Computers will make life much easier if you have one	The Internet is fun	The Internet is fun	The Internet is very useful to me	The Internet is very useful to me
Age (16–24)								
25–34	−0.035	−0.077	−0.141**	−0.081	−0.157***	−0.137***	−0.170**	−0.111*
35–44	0.02	−0.066	−0.085	0.027	−0.229***	−0.187***	−0.253***	−0.121*
45–54	0.089	−0.039	−0.213***	−0.051	−0.449***	−0.388***	−0.455***	−0.264***
55–64	0.123*	−0.077	−0.351***	−0.094	−0.627***	−0.526***	−0.609***	−0.305***
65–74	0.137*	−0.146*	−0.518***	−0.162**	−0.504***	−0.370***	−0.823***	−0.418***
75+	0.269***	−0.078	−0.654***	−0.219*	−0.623***	−0.434***	−0.992***	−0.440**
Years of Internet use	–	−0.066***	–	0.047***	–	0.023**	–	0.076***
Sum of PC skills	–	−0.048***	–	0.084***	–	0.067***	–	0.200***
Adjusted R^2	0.0221	0.0499	0.0336	0.0716	0.062	0.0809	0.347	0.444
N	9,690	9,690	9,505	9,505	6,024	6,024	6,238	6,238

than the sixteen-to-twenty-four age group. However, when we take account of ICT experiences, the scale of these effects is considerably reduced. In further analysis, selecting just those who were PC users (not shown), the age effects completely disappeared in nearly all cases when ICT usage was controlled.

These results can be interpreted as reflecting an age-related negative attitude towards technology which is fundamentally altered by experience of ICTs. Thus age is not necessarily the determinant of using or owning a computer (Cooper and Victory, 2002; Greenspan, 2003), but may instead be an indicator of a combination of factors that happen to correlate with older people, to do with culture (life experiences), education, wealth and, perhaps most importantly, previous experience of technology.

When we examine the typical characteristics of all the adopter types (i.e. innovators, early adopters, early majority, late majority, laggards: Rogers, 1995), we can see that, in most cases, the characteristics of the 'late majority' and the 'laggards' happen to coincide with typical characteristics of today's elderly population. The most important implication for future uptake of technology is that if the typical characteristics of 'the elderly' change over time, so might their adoption patterns. For example, a recent report examining the demographics of Internet users found that 'Seniors [who use the Internet] are more likely than their offline peers to be married, highly educated and enjoying relatively high retirement incomes' (Pastore, 2001).

Other research (Zimmer and Chappell, 1999) has found that older adults who do *not* conform to typical laggard characteristics are often willing and eager to embrace new technologies:

> Older adults of today have lived through a radical transformation of their technological environment.... Homes are now equipped with video cassette recorders (VCRs), microwave ovens, satellite televisions, home alarm sensors, home computers and a barrage of communication devices, all unknown to today's cohort of older adults while they were growing up.
>
> (1999: 222)

Time spent online

The amount of time that people spent online can be examined using, amongst other sources, data from the e-Living project. An example of one of the dimensions examined was how many hours participants with Internet access spent online per day. Figure 7.1 illustrates the findings.

The most interesting finding is that, although the 'youth' demographic tends to spend the most time online, this is not the case in all countries, as the data for Israel shows. Whilst the data for those aged seventy-five and over needs to be viewed with caution due to small *n*, those aged sixty-five-plus spend *at least as much* time online than do some of the younger cohorts

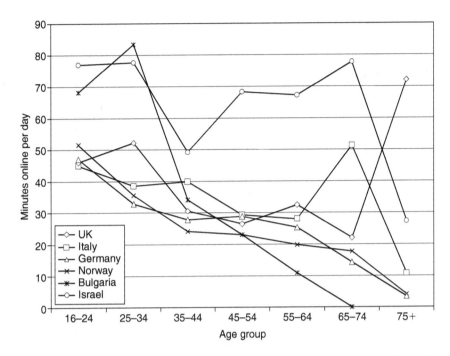

Figure 7.1 Internet home daily use by Internet users in each age group for each country (e-Living wave one (2001), weighted for non-response).

in some countries (UK, Italy, Israel), presumably because they have more leisure time at their disposal. This effectively illustrates the point that once older adults have adopted a technology, they use it as much as any other cohort, and may use it more, due to having more time available.

Social communication online

We also compared the frequency of communicating with friends and family by email across all age groups of Internet users, and no significant differences were found in the UK or Israel. Some were found in the other participating countries, as follows:

- Italy – Under-thirty-fives used email more than forty-five-to-sixty-four-year-olds.
- Germany – sixteen-to-twenty-four-year-olds used email more than thirty-five-to-fifty-four-year-olds; sixty-five-to-seventy-four-year-olds used email less than the under-thirty-fives.
- Norway – fifty-five-to-sixty-four-year-olds used email less than all the younger age groups.

Again, these differences are in the direction indicated by the list of common assumptions at the beginning of this chapter, but again, this could be due to other, more robust factors related to age.

Depth of Internet use

'Depth' (richness) of Internet use is also worth examining, as it helps to address the assumptions that older people are technophobic, less interested in technology, and less likely to innovate. This was examined by totalling the number of online activities per individual. This total was then compared across age groups, and the only significant difference found (in numbers of online activities) was between the sixteen-to-twenty-four-year-olds and sixty-five-to-seventy-four-year-olds (for the whole (weighted) sample). As it was hypothesised that the nature of online activity would change with age, the separate activities were also compared across ages. Some activities, such as online library services and medical services, increased slightly with age, whereas others, such as online job seeking and banking, decreased slightly. However, the overall number of online activities showed little variation. Interestingly, one of the activities that increased slightly with age was classified simply as 'other' – perhaps indicating an even greater range of online activity for the older population.

The total number of online activities was correlated with the responses to the attitude questions for the total (weighted) sample, controlling for age (as a continuous variable). Significant ($p < 0.01$) negative correlations were found between the total number of online activities and negatively phrased attitude questions; that is, the less the number of online activities, the more negatively technology was viewed by the respondents. This was with the exception of the item 'everyone depends on computers too much nowadays', which was only significant at the $p < 0.05$ level. Significant ($p < 0.01$) positive correlations were also found between the total number of online activities and the positively phrased attitude questions; that is, the more the number of online activities, the more positively technology was viewed by the respondents.

Responses to the attitude questions were also correlated with frequency of communicating with friends and family by email and frequency of using the Internet at home (controlling for age as a continuous variable) amongst those with an Internet-connected PC. Again, positive attitudes correlated highly ($p < 0.01$) with high frequencies of email and Internet use, and negative attitudes correlated highly with low frequencies of email and Internet use, with the exception of the item 'Everyone depends on computers too much nowadays', which showed no relationships with measures of frequency of use. Therefore we can state that there is a definite association between people's experience of, and attitudes towards, computers and the Internet.

The e-Living data also illustrates that PC ownership and Internet access increase both with income and with education level, both of which have been found to be related to age.

We can therefore state with some certainty that although people's attitudes to technology appear to become more negative with age, this is in fact due to several different factors, including access (which is strongly related to income and education level, both of which have been shown to vary with age), experience and depth and frequency of usage.

The next subsection will examine the retirement transitions in the e-Living data, to try to clarify the effect that retirement has on a number of dimensions of quality of life.

Retirement transitions

The e-Living dataset gives us an opportunity to examine some of the short-term effects of retirement on aspects of people's quality of life. More causal explanations are possible than would be the case with cross-sectional data, and this section analyses the effects of retirement on access to and usage of ICTs, as well as aspects of quality of life.

Eighty-nine people who were in paid work at wave one described themselves as retired in wave two. It must also be noted that, during the same period, forty-five people who described themselves as retired at wave one described themselves as being in paid work at wave two. Clearly retirement is not a one-way process.

In order to examine the effects of retiring, we developed a number of models similar to those presented in Table 7.1, but which instead uses the lagged endogenous approach (Finkel, 1995) to predict wave two values of quality of life, wealth and income from wave one values, whilst including a contrast variable for those who retired from paid work between waves (coded one) compared to those who did not (coded zero). This enables us to analyse the effects of retirement. Given the small number of retirees, it is not possible to run these models separately for each country, although we do, as above, include a dummy for each country as control variables.

As we can see, retirement significantly affected (positively) only satisfaction with free time. However, it is worth noting the effect on overall quality of life (positive), income (negative) and Internet minutes (strongly positive) which, although not statistically significant, may be indicative of the likely effects with a larger sample size, as is the effect on number of online activities. The latter may, of course, be suggestive of decreased Internet usages for work purposes after retirement.

Interestingly adopting the mobile telephone during the timeframe in which retirement occurred had a positive effect on both satisfaction with free time and on satisfaction with the local environment. Adoption of the Internet, on the other hand, had no such effects.

Table 7.2 Effects of retirement on a range of quality of life aspects and time spent online (all aged over 45, weighted for non-response, constant and country included but not shown)

	W 2: overall life satisfaction	W 2: satisfaction with free time	W 2: satisfaction with local environment	W 2: satisfaction with communications with family and friends	W 2: household income	W 2: minutes online per week	W 2: number recent online activities
W 1: overall life satisfaction	0.370***	–	–	–	–	–	–
W 1–2: retired	0.163	0.849***	0.117	0.005	–0.336	75.237	–0.258
W 1–2: adopt mobile telephone	–0.017	0.213*	0.161*	–0.047	–	–	–
W 1–2: adopt Internet	0.094	–0.032	0.106	0.068	–	–	–
W 1: satisfaction with free time	–	0.393***	–	–	–	–	–
W 1: satisfaction with local environment	–	–	0.404***	–	–	–	–
W 1: satisfaction with communications with family and friends	–	–	–	0.221***	–	–	–
W 1: household income	–	–	–	–	0.514***	–	–
W 1: Internet minutes per week	–	–	–	–	–	0.498***	–
W 1: number recent online activities	–	–	–	–	–	–	0.501***
Adjusted R^2	0.389	0.248	0.396	0.188	0.394	0.277	0.231
N	1,267	1,276	1,268	1,276	849	379	395

In conclusion

Evidence so far

Referring back to the list of assumptions at the beginning of this chapter, we appear to have shown, at first glance, the prevalence of negative attitudes towards technologies amongst the older population. However, our analyses have also shown that this negativity appears, on the whole, due to lack of experience of the relevant technologies. It must also be noted that agreement with the phrase 'The Internet is a mystery to me' does not in itself entail a reluctance to learn about the Internet – it could just as likely be an indication of lack of opportunity to learn about the Internet.

We have little evidence either way for the assumption that older people are less likely to innovate, although the relative lack of age differences in depth of Internet use is an indication that this assumption could also be erroneous. It is also worth noting that older people were the first to use their answer phones to screen phone calls rather than just to answer calls when they were not available (Haddon, 2003). This 'creative misuse' is one form of user innovation.

We have some evidence that older people are less interested in technology, but that this can be altered through training and/or other forms of experience, and that older people are in fact excluded from IT, albeit in fairly subtle ways, through common design, research and advertising practice, as well as for socioeconomic reasons. These include a general design bias in favour of the young an IT education bias in favour of the young and an assumption that older people are less interested in technology simply because they are older.

Encouraging depth-of-use

There are several possible ways in which computers, the Internet (particularly broadband) and mobile technologies could become embedded in the lives of the older populations of Europe, and also encourage them to 'innovate'.

Through civic participation services

The EC eEurope Action Plan 2005 focuses on the interactivity of online public services, stating that it is vital that users are able to interact with and input to the services being offered. Much 'social capital' research (e.g. Putnam, 2000) has emphasised the reluctance of the youth to participate in community or society activities, pointing to the generation of seniors as being the ones who initiate community actions, belong to more formal groups and communities, and vote more regularly, and this is also true of the e-Living sample (see Ling, this volume). It surely makes sense, then, to target the older population when developing online civic participation services, as these will initially be the people most likely to respond and interact. The motivation to be a part of their local community, apparently much stronger in the older populations who have greater free time, will encourage the older populace to embrace the technologies that enable this participation.

Through education

The rising popularity of online life-long learning services, particularly in the United States and increasingly in Europe, indicates older peoples' enthusiasm for education. The commercial success of bodies such as the University of the Third Age demonstrate the need for leisure-learning facilities amongst the older population, whilst the early redundancies encouraged by many large corporations throughout the 1990s have fostered many work returnees, often requiring 'reskilling' in order to facilitate continued workforce participation. Sadly, the research and design emphasis in educational technology has been very much geared towards the young, as demonstrated by the sheer number of UK government initiatives for IT in schools, colleges and universities.

Through health services

The majority of 'health services' using IT are already being designed with 'the elderly' in mind. However, there is now an increasing emphasis by many leading companies (e.g. Guynes Design, Intel, General Electric) on retaining independence later in life through the use of sophisticated, unobtrusive health monitoring devices, both wired into the home and worn by the individual. Little research has so far been done on the acceptance of these devices; however, there are suggestions that aesthetics are perhaps more important to the older population than commonly assumed, i.e. people won't wear ugly, grey boxes, no matter how useful they are. Therefore, although the design of health services for the older population is further advanced than design of any other service types for this age group, there is still a need for aesthetic concepts to be better incorporated into this design process. Designs of health products and services are also increasingly following the principles of 'inclusive design'; that is, designs that are usable, useful and pleasurable for all, regardless of age and/or 'disability'.

Through leisure

Despite people working until later in their lives, those that do work tend to have increased leisure time due to less family commitments and more flexible working hours. Retired people also have more leisure time than those in employment, therefore the use of technology to enrich leisure time would be welcome.

The e-Living data has shown that participation in several leisure activities decreases slightly with age; however others increase, including reading, at least up to age sixty-five.

This increase in reading with age up to around sixty-five also demonstrates the potential here; much printed matter is relatively inaccessible to those members of the older population with failing eyesight, and broadband services could again address this problem given the relevant design agendas.

The older population at present has, at least until retirement age, more 'spending power' in terms of disposable income and free time, particularly after the youngest of their offspring has left home. It would therefore seem sensible to concentrate on entertainment and leisure services for the older population.

Through communication services

Isolation can be a particularly acute problem for the elderly, as their children leave home, their spouses die, and getting out becomes more difficult due to physical infirmity or disability. According to Demos (2004b), other risk factors for isolation in old age are also increasing, including rates of childlessness and divorce, single-person households and widely distributed social networks. They estimate an increase of 33 per cent in socially isolated older people in the UK by 2021.

Those in their fifties, now, however, have a more extended family to keep in touch with than younger people (either that, or a stronger desire to keep in touch with extended family) – this communication can be greatly aided by the use of Internet technologies. It has been observed that these age groups will use the communication technologies they grew up with. However, research into Internet use has shown that the main use by the older population is to communicate with friends and family, therefore designing communication services tailored to the older population would seem to be one way to tackle the increase in social isolation noted above.

Further research

Longitudinal research is needed that focuses on the Baby Boomers. This research could capture their retirement transitions over the next twenty years or so, and would answer many of the current questions about this generation, the most important one being; will they adopt the attitudes and behaviour of the current seniors in our society, or will they approach retirement in different ways?

More qualitative research is also urgently needed with the older population, to assess the reasons behind their comparative lack of engagement with IT, in order to ensure that they are included to a greater extent in the future of eEurope. This inclusion is also vital for Europe's long-term economic prosperity. Therefore we need to ascertain the factors that could encourage this inclusion, through the use and appropriation of new technologies, both by the over-fifties and the 'old old'.

Acknowledgements

Thanks to Ben Anderson for help with the analysis!

This work was partially funded by the European Commission funded Framework 5 project e-Living (IST-2000-25409) and the Framework 6 funded project SOCQUIT (IST-2002-507753).

References

Barclays Small Business Report (2003) *Quarterly Report on Small Business Statistics, January 2003*. Online, available at: www.bankofengland.co.uk/qrsbjan03.pdf (accessed September 2004).

Bodoff, R. (2003) *Progress and Possibilities – State of Technology and Aging Services*. Center for Aging Services Technologies white paper. Online, available at: www.agingtech.org/history.aspx (accessed 4 May, 2004).

CEC (2005) Working together for growth and jobs: a new start for the Lisbon Strategy. *Communication to the Spring European Council*. Brussels, Commission of the European Communities.

Christensen, C.M. (1998) *The Innovator's Dilemma*, New York, Harper Business Press.

Cooper, K.B. and Victory, N.J. (2002) A nation online. *US Department of Commerce, Economics and Statistics Administration*. Online, available at: www.esa.doc.gov/Word/anationonline2.doc.

Demos (2004a) *Eternal Youths*. Online, available at: www.demos.co.uk/catalogue/eternalyouthsbook/ (accessed September 2004).

Demos (2004b) *Home Alone*. Online, available at: www.demos.co.uk/catalogue/homealonebook/ (accessed September 2004).

European Commission (2002) *Increasing Labour Force Participation*. Online, available at: www.ceps.be/files/TF/communicationstockholm.pdf.

Finkel, S. (1995) *Causal Analysis with Panel Data*. Thousand Oaks, CA, London, Sage.

Greenspan, R. (2003) Surfing with seniors and boomers. *ClickZ Stats & Demographics*. Online, available at: www.clickz.com/stats/big_picture/demographics/article.php/5901_1573621.

Haddon, L. (2003) What is innovatory use? A thinkpiece. In Haddon, L., Mante-Meijer, E., Sapio, B., Kommenon, K.-H., Fortunati, L. and Kant, A. (eds) *The Good, the Bad and the Irrelevant: the User and the Future of Information and Communication Technologies*. Conference Proceedings, 1–3 September, Helsinki.

HLEG (2004) *Facing the Challenge: the Lisbon Strategy for Growth and Employment*. Report from the High Level Group chaired by Wim Kok. Brussels, European Commission, High-Level, Expert Group.

Malkani, G. (2004) Affluent over-50s accuse advertising industry of ignoring the 'grey pound'. *Financial Times*, 26 April.

Moore, C. (2002) The new heart of your brand: transforming your business through customer experience. *Design Management Journal*, Winter, 39–48.

MORI (2002) *e-MORI Technology Tracker*, August.

Pastore, M. (2001) Online seniors enthusiastic about Internet use. *ClickZ Stats & Demographics*. Online, available at: www.clickz.com/stats/big_picture/demographics/article.php/5901_881201.

Pearson, I. and DiDuca, D. (2005) Spiritual revival towards 2010 – traditional religion or nouveau-hippies?. *The Journal of Communications Network*, 4(1).

Putnam, R. (2000) *Bowling Alone: the Collapse and Revival of American Community*, New York, Simon & Schuster.

Reding, V. (2005) Innovation, creativity and inclusion. Interview in *EURESCOM Message*, 1.

Rogers, E.M. (1995) *Diffusion of Innovations* (4th edn), New York, The Free Press.

Seniorwatch (2002) *Older People and Information Society Technology: a Comparative Analysis of the Current Situation in the EU and of Future Trends*. Online, available at: www.seniorwatch.de (accessed March 2005).

Zimmer, Z. and Chappell, N.L. (1999) Receptivity to new technology among older adults. *Disability and Rehabilitation*, 21(5/6), 222–230.

8 UK Children Go Online

A child-centred approach to the experience of using the Internet

Sonia Livingstone and Magdalena Bober

Children go online – a new research agenda

Many households, especially those with children, now have domestic Internet access, and 98 per cent of UK nine-to-nineteen-year-olds have used the Internet, mainly at home (75 per cent) and/or at school (92 per cent) (Livingstone and Bober, 2004). As we move beyond the present climate of speculation and hyperbole, sound empirical evidence and a sceptical mindset is much needed. In response, a growing body of academic research is examining the social shaping and social consequences of new information and communication technologies, particularly the Internet, in relation to work, leisure, politics, culture and the family (Lievrouw and Livingstone, 2002).

Considerable attention, and anxiety, is focused on children and young people. They are seen as 'the digital generation', being in the vanguard of new skills and opportunities, yet also vulnerable and potentially at risk (Livingstone, 2003). Children and young people are generally enthusiastic and creative adopters of the Internet – for communication, entertainment and education. Parents hope that home access will improve their children's educational prospects, although many are unsure how to guide their children towards valuable sites, and they are concerned about online dangers. In school, pupils increasingly rely on online educational resources, and the Internet is becoming a key mediator of informal learning, linking home and school. Meanwhile, commercial interests increasingly centre on the development of online contents and services that target the youth market, together with some public-sector initiatives directed at children and young people.

Our research project, *UK Children Go Online* (www.children-go-online.net), has explored the nature and meaning of children's Internet use, combining qualitative work with a national survey of Internet-related attitudes and practices among 1,511 nine-to-nineteen-year-olds and their parents across the UK (Livingstone and Bober, 2004, 2005). The project asks how the Internet may be transforming, and may itself be shaped by, family life, peer networks and informal learning processes. Taking a 'child-centred' focus, the project regards children as active and interpretative agents who appropriate and shape the meanings and consequences of the 'new' through a series of well-established social and semiotic practices. It seeks to contextualise the Internet within an account of the changing conditions of childhood, acknowledging also the ways in which children themselves play a role – through their imaginative responses, their creative play, their micro-practices of daily life – in establishing the emerging uses and significance of the Internet (James *et al.*, 1998; Seiter, 1999; Buckingham, 2002).

In this chapter we present qualitative research findings, drawing on a series of fourteen focus-group discussions with children and young people aged nine-to-nineteen, conducted during summer 2003 (Livingstone and Bober, 2003). Given the often-polarised approaches to children's Internet use – focused on either the opportunities or the risks that may arise – our aim is to encompass both, so as to develop an integrated view that balances the positives and the negatives.

Opportunities for learning and literacy

Parents commonly say that supporting their children's education is their main reason for investing in a home computer and Internet access. Yet in pointing to the 'uncertain pedagogy of the home computer', Buckingham (2002) identifies some unresolved questions regarding the benefits of domestic Internet use. What skills are children learning through computer use? Is the Internet better than books and encyclopaedias? Are young people developing new styles of learning? In stark contrast to other expensive domestic goods, the computer and Internet are associated with an image of the child as expert. Although many households contain a computer-literate parent, children are likely to consider their parents less knowledgeable when it comes to using the Internet.

> My dad hasn't even got a clue. Can't even work the mouse . . . so I have to go on the Internet for him.
>
> (Nina, 17, from Manchester)

Possessing a type of expertise valued by adults has significant consequences (Facer *et al.*, 2001; Ribak, 2001). Children gain status through the public valuing of their ability to access information resources in a way which is, perhaps, unprecedented. Papert (1996) points out that, for children, computers are about mastery; the Internet may offer an experience of mastery not otherwise forthcoming in their lives. More concretely, they gain responsibility, and therefore some power, in the home through taking on new tasks – researching family holidays, finding information, even helping with the accounts. Thus children are reversing the hierarchical teacher–pupil relationship. In so far as children act as pioneers of technological developments, they may retain their advantage. On the other hand, for the 'expert' child to ask for advice or help is to relinquish some social status, possibly inhibiting such requests.

Is this expertise broader than a set of specific technical skills? Is it rather, as it was for print media, a matter of literacy, a whole way of thinking and knowing (Livingstone *et al.*, 2005)? This emerged as a theme when we asked children *how* they had gained their Internet skills and why some people lacked them. Many young people stress the importance of learning by trial and error instead of reading a manual or being taught formally how to use the Internet – a process of 'learning through play' or 'learning by doing'.

> I think it's better to do like trial and error because you can like learn from the mistakes from it, and you can find new places and stuff, for different sorts of things.
>
> (Kim, 15, from Essex)

For most young people, the key contrast to the Internet is with books – a 'boring' world of libraries and indexes, authoritative sources, endless lines of print and too few images. Using the Internet as an information resource is far more fun and far more rewarding – producing images as well as text, interesting and quirky facts, as little or as much detail as needed, and all without going to the library. These views are particularly common among children and younger teens.

> Encyclopaedias are hard to use really. . . . Because there's so many, and you don't actually know which one of them to use. And how to get what you really want, except if you have a very long time.
>
> (Prince, 16, from London)

Interestingly, some older teenagers return to books. They are 'more serious about their school work' as they get older.

> You don't always find what you're looking for. And when you get to college you're more serious about your work, so you choose the books. . . . Helps you out more in the long run than just going on the Internet and getting the first thing you find.
>
> (Mitch, 17, from Essex)

Both these discussions, however, acknowledge the difficulties of the Internet as an information source, pointing up the limits of young people's expertise online.

Despite their distinctive expertise, young people admit to aspects of Internet use that they find problematic. They cannot always find what they are looking for, although they know of different searching strategies. They are overwhelmed by the amount of information and find it difficult to obtain or select what they need.

I'll sometimes type in something, and I'll get pages of, you know ... for that search, and it's just, I can never find what I'm looking for. Unless you are willing to spend an hour going through each page. It's ridiculous.

(Hazel, 17, from Essex)

Even more important than the efficiency of their searching is their evaluation of the information obtained. Myths about the Internet are commonplace, especially among the younger respondents, and in general an awareness of the motives behind websites and a critical attitude towards their trustworthiness is only now developing. Most tend to trust the information found online – particularly if it is professionally presented and if it neatly fits their requirements. Others have a more critical attitude, realising that the source of information is often unknown and cannot be checked.

It's like you don't know who's doing what, whose website it is, who wants what, who wants you to learn what. So you don't know who's put what information there, but ... it's reliable – but you don't know who's put it, who wants you to gain what from that information.

(Faruq, 15, London)

The question of media – or Internet – literacy, encompassing not just how to find but also how to evaluate sites, is surely crucial if children are to benefit from the educational and informational opportunities provided by the Internet. It seems that, although they are enthusiastically developing a range of skills for Internet use, becoming increasingly sophisticated as they get older, children's so-called expertise is, none-the-less, limited in important ways. This is partly a matter of training, partly the responsibility of teachers and parents, but also a matter of interface design (Machill *et al.*, 2003; Livingstone *et al.*, 2005), for the difficulties of searching should not always be laid at the door of the user. Lastly, much depends on the quality of online experiences. Feeling encouraged and confident to explore the Internet freely is crucial to getting the most out of it.

Pleasures of communication and connection

Adults may wish children to go online for educational reasons. Children's own motivation primarily centres on the new opportunities for communication. What changes are underway in social networks as online communication becomes commonplace? The most striking change is the way young people are embracing 'constant connection' – they are, and wish to be, 'always on', continuously in touch with their friends.

Even if you've just seen them at school like, it'll be like you're texting them or talking to them on the phone or on MSN.

(Kim, 15, Essex)

The content of these conversations may seem mundane or trivial to adult observers, being focused on day-to-day topics, gossip and talk for the sake of talk. But the point is less the content than the contact, the keeping in touch, being in the loop, all of which takes a considerable effort to sustain.

Online communication is rarely an escape from or an alternative to real life. The popular opposition between online and offline, or virtual and real, communication is inappropriate. Young people are not divided into sociable kids who meet face-to-face and isolated loners who chat to strangers online. Rather, young people use both online and offline communication to sustain their social networks, moving freely among different communication forms (Ling, 2004). The more they meet offline, the more they also meet online, or so it would seem. Hence, for all but the already-isolated – for whom the explanation lies elsewhere – the Internet appears to foster rather than under-mine existing social contacts (Slater, 2002), connecting children more fully into their local networks.

'Local' is the key term here because, as the integration of online and offline communication implies, contacts are generally local rather than distant (or 'virtual'), with friends rather than strangers. Access to new com-munication technologies need not result in a larger or geographically wider social circle. Particularly, we see little evidence for the 'global village' hyped in earlier discussions of the Internet. However, the Internet does permit some broadening of everyday networks, strengthening already-existing rela-tionships which are otherwise hard to maintain – friends from abroad, distant relatives, staying in touch with people who have moved.

> I think mobile phones and the Internet are a good way of keeping in contact with friends. For example, I have friends in other countries who use MSN. I can send them an email every day rather than phoning them up and running up a huge phone bill, or sending them a text message. And it's just a good way of keeping in contact with people.
>
> (Lorie, 17, from Essex)

Some young people told us that they have built up large friendship networks on the Internet and report large numbers of contacts on their MSN 'buddy list', mostly friends from school or 'friends of friends'.

The question of making new friends online is the subject of some debate among young people themselves. Most say they were not interested in talking to people they did not know on the Internet, preferring to communicate with friends as they feel they can relate better to them.

> If you're talking to someone on the Internet who's a friend, you actually talk to them saying stuff, but feelings and everything are real, and the stuff you're saying means stuff, but if you're talking to someone you haven't met, how do you know if what they're telling you is the truth? You don't really mean some things you say, like, it is a bit fake.
>
> (Mark, 17, from Essex)

Children who have chatted to strangers online describe it as 'weird', referring to unknown online contacts as 'dodgy'. They say they 'don't see the
point in meeting up with someone they don't know'. Teens tend to prefer
instant messaging to chat rooms because 'you know who you're talking to' –
a phrase used over and over in the focus groups. They are clearly aware of
adverts and media reports warning children of online dangers.

When interviewing teens in 2001 (Livingstone and Bovill, 2001), it was
common practice among them to agree, before the end of the school day, to
meet later in a certain chat room at a certain time. Notwithstanding the
public perception of chat rooms as a place designed for meeting strangers,
teens treated chat rooms as places for their personal network to meet up. This
illustrates the process of social shaping (Mackenzie and Wajcman, 1999), with
users creatively reshaping the chat room into something more suited to their
needs, for here the demand for a communicative form led to the subsequent
development of the technology – instant messaging. Today, teens meet using
instant messaging, leaving chat rooms to the playful games of younger teens.

This activity of adapting the communicative form to one's communicative
needs and interests points up a broader theme in the focus groups, namely the
complexity of the choices underlying young people's uses of media. While
public discourse tends to judge online communication against an ideal of
face-to-face communication, young people themselves embrace a wider range
of options – face-to-face, writing, email, instant message, chat rooms, telephone, SMS. In other words, rather than accepting the supposed superiority
of face-to-face communication, young people evaluate the suitability of different options for different communicative needs according to a range of criteria,
such as urgency and complexity of a message, mobility, cost or privacy.

> Text message – if you want to speak to them immediately. 'Cause email,
> they've got to be on the Internet, they've got to see it. For emergencies.
> And for convenience.
>
> (Stuart, 17, Manchester)

> Emailing, I just do it like if it's not a long bit to say and not a short bit
> to say . . . But text messaging I just ask questions – it's just short ques-
> tions. And phoning, I just have a long conversation with people, about
> nothing really.
>
> (Beatrice, 13, from Essex)

The mobile phone enables children and young people to be in contact with
their friends from anywhere (Ling, 2004); by comparison, the fixed location
of the desktop computer is an important constraint.

> I think using mobile or text is a bit easier because you can do it while,
> like while you're in the middle of the supermarket, and then you can
> arrange to meet someone.
>
> (Joe, 13, Derbyshire)

Children are very conscious of the financial cost when choosing which communication technology to use. Often having to pay their mobile phone bill themselves, they prefer to use the mobile for sending text messages than for calls. And they prefer instant messaging to texting because it is 'like sending a text to someone but with no money' (Jim, 14, from Essex).

More personal issues are also at stake when choosing how to communicate with friends. Talking in a private online space enabled friends to be more open with each other, an important factor in girls' friendships. Face-to-face communication, in this context, is too visible and, thus, subject to peer pressure.

> When you're like talking to them face-to-face, you're like – you've got other people around you, and they can't tell you what they really think. So like instant messaging, you can.
>
> (Beatrice, 13, from Essex)

Some children, boys particularly, prefer online communication for private conversations as a face-saving device. Here too, face-to-face conversation, far from being ideal, can be risky and difficult for teenagers.

> I once dumped my old girlfriend by email.... Well, it was cowardly really. I couldn't say it face-to-face.
>
> (Cameron, 13, from Derbyshire)

Older teenagers, on the other hand, prefer to hold private conversations face-to-face, which they think is more secure than online communication. They are concerned about the possibility of someone 'spying' on online conversations. The confidence with which some of them talk about private and personal conversations suggests they have moved on from the problems of embarrassment and peer pressure which preoccupy younger teens – now they are more concerned that their privacy is secure.

> If you wanted to have a private conversation, then I'm sure you'd talk to them face-to-face rather than using the Internet, because if you know they can be listened to, or someone else can see what you're doing, then I wouldn't have thought that you'd want that to happen. So you'd therefore talk to them, meet up and talk to them face-to-face.
>
> (Hazel, 17, from Essex)

In sum, children and young people relish this new and complex communication environment. They make subtle and deliberate choices according to multiple criteria, some of which concern the medium and some of which concern the age or personality of the child. We still know too little about the implications of online peer networks for identity. Suffice it to say that through their enthusiastic experimentation, young people are again pioneers in constructing the emerging perceptions and conventions surrounding different forms of communication.

Risks of content and contact

Use of the Internet poses particular threats to children and young people. Consistent with the three categories of online threat identified by Childnet International (Williams, 2001), the research literature thus far has concentrated on exposure to sexual and pornographic content, on the incidence of exploitative and dangerous contacts, and on issues of privacy, advertising and commercialism. The focus groups did not address advertising, branding or online commercialism other than in relation to young people's readiness to trust, rather than critically evaluate, online information. This section will concentrate on pornographic content and unsafe contact.

Attempts to map the availability of online pornography find much that could upset or embarrass children (Feilitzen and Carlsson, 2000). Whether pornographic websites are experienced as problematic by young people and their families is less clear (Sutter, 2000). Thus far, it seems that not all risks taken result in worrying incidents, and not all worrying incidents result in actual or lasting harm. But there are also sufficient reasons for concern.

Young people commonly claim to have come across pornography online, usually accidentally. They see it as part of the media environment more generally, it also being available through videos, magazines and newspapers. Here gender plays more of a role. While some respondents regard it as unwelcome, especially the younger teenage and mid-teen girls, others, especially teenage boys, express curiosity about sexual matters and are not opposed to seeing it.

> It's just what teenagers do, I mean, it's only hormones. Some people deal with it, some people don't. Some people I know they go on it because – some people just have fun.... I just find it's a good experience!
>
> (Amir, 15, from London)

Consequently, they do not think online pornography should be restricted. Young people do, however, agree that it is more available online than offline.

> I don't think there is realistically any way it can be censored completely. So I think, yeah, you just have to try and avoid it as best as possible.
>
> (Scott, 17, from Essex)

> The Internet is just like life as I see it, but just easier. So if these 13 or 14 year olds want to find stuff, they're going to find it in real life or on the Internet.
>
> (Lorie, 17, from Essex)

For some young people, especially girls, the greater exposure to pornography online than offline is problematic. This is particularly because it is not restricted to leisure contexts, but also intrudes into educational uses.

> Yeah, these boys, they just go onto the Internet, they download it, they put it on as screensaver. . . . It's just disgusting.
>
> (Tanya, 15, from London)

Other respondents appear more indifferent towards pornography.

> I think there's way too much hype about it. Because I use the Internet loads. And you so, so, so rarely come across something that maybe like a pop-up for a porn site. But that's hardly . . . Once you're into your teenage years, you've got used to the idea that people have sex. It's not really that scary any more.
>
> (Milly, 15, from Essex)

However, although teens may consider that they can protect themselves, all agree that younger children should be protected, for example by setting up Internet filtering software.

> It doesn't really bother me. I know it's there, and you can just move on to something else you find. . . . It doesn't really matter when you're our age. But I mean, for little kids . . . maybe the parents should set it up. But when you're like seventeen or about – it doesn't really matter. Just ignore it, just move on.
>
> (John, 17, from Essex)

Notwithstanding considerable public concern over questions of content, most attention has centred on the growing incidence of unwanted or inappropriate sexual contact made to teenagers by adult strangers. Fortunately, many young people are now getting the message. We have seen that chat rooms are losing popularity in favour of instant messaging. In part, this reflects the success of media awareness campaigns warning children of the risks.

> There's obviously the scare of paedophiles and people like that on chat rooms. . . . It's on the news, and there are ad campaigns against it. It's just a kind of thing that you realise there's probably someone on it who is a paedophile or like a child sex-abuser or someone, and you don't really want to kind of meet one of them or speak to one of them.
>
> (Alan, 13, from Essex)

> Because adults can like turn their voices into younger children, and like they can ask for pictures and stuff and ask to meet you. If you give away your name and address, they could . . .
>
> (Ellen, 10, from Hertfordshire)

While increased safety awareness is a positive outcome of media publicity, this is associated with considerable parental anxiety. For some, a further outcome is a simple ban on the use of chat rooms, email or specific content.

You're not allowed to give your last name to any website.

(Holly, 10, from Hertfordshire)

At home I'm not allowed to go on chat rooms.

(Ellen, 10, from Hertfordshire)

For young children, restrictive responses are perhaps appropriate, although children's understanding of these responses reveal a confusing mix of reality and myth.

My mum doesn't let me go on chat rooms.... They find out your address and come and rob you and things. That's why I don't go on it.

(Adrian, 10, from Hertfordshire)

I would say that chat rooms would be dangerous because, like Cameron said before, you don't know who you're talking to. And then if you give your address then they can come and kidnap you or something. And take you away. It's just I think it's on the news. I remember someone's got into a chat room and gone off to Paris.

(Joe, 13, from Derbyshire)

While younger children have been impressed by media stories, older teenagers seek to assess the risks by comparing them with other risks encountered in real life. Interviews with parents confirm that fears of danger to young people on the street are more salient than online threats (Livingstone, 2002). Given that young people are highly constrained in their freedom offline, to increase constraints online is unfortunate.

On the Internet you feel physically safer because you know no-one can beat you up on the Internet and do any physical harm. When you live round my way ... it gets a bit rough sometimes, you know, you don't want to go out on the streets that much.

(Steve, 17, from Manchester)

The Internet you can control what's going on, but when you're outside, you can't.

(Prince, 16, from London)

Perhaps the perception of the 'comparative safety' of the Internet leads some teens to take greater risks than is advisable. In the focus group discussions, we identified several hints as to why safe practices might be ignored on occasion (O'Connell, 2002).

First, even among those aware of the risks, young people may gain social status by meeting people on the Internet.

> I've got about five buddies on my thing but you can't really say, oh, this is a young girl, she's got brown hair, blue eyes, 'cause she could be an old – she could be a he and it's an old man but I suppose it's quite nice to just say, oh, I've met someone on the Internet.
>
> (Rosie, 13, from Derbyshire)

Second, when young people encounter dubious aspects of the Internet, they may avoid talking to their parents about this as this, in turn, risks losing them their Internet access.

> Talking to them about Internet is bad for you and stuff. They might try and think about taking the Internet off your computer, which isn't good for us.
>
> (Amir, 15, from London)

Third, when young people get involved in an interesting conversation, they simply forget about the risks.

> When you're actually on the chat rooms, you don't think of what's happened to this person, if someone's chatting to you, you're having an interesting conversation.
>
> (Amir, 15, from London)

Fourth, young people may think they are safe in chat rooms because they see themselves as sensible.

> I also think that people have got common sense. If you hear on the news because someone got lost because they went to a chat room and chatting to people, I think they'll use their common sense to know they shouln't do this. . . . And I also think it's the situation some people are in, to just go in chat rooms and stuff – maybe the family's not settled and things like that.
>
> (Prince, 16, from London)

As in other safety or public information campaigns, it seems that it is easier to get the message across than it is to ensure safe practices under all circumstances. In addition to seeking to maintain high levels of safety awareness, public campaigns could become better targeted to counter the specific conditions that lead some children to take risks online. At the same time, also in response to the risks, parents are developing rules for managing their children's Internet use, rules that children sometimes evade and sometimes comply with (Livingstone, 2006; Livingstone and Bober, 2006).

What difference does the Internet make?

Interestingly, among the majority with access, the Internet is regarded with some ambivalence. We asked children about the importance of the Internet for them, and how they would feel if it ceased to exist. Despite their huge enthusiasm for the Internet, its importance to them remains relative – both relative to other media and other leisure activities. Many children prefer other activities (such as playing sports, meeting friends or going outside) or other media (such as television or games consoles), seeing the Internet as something for use 'on rainy days' (Livingstone, 2002).

The importance of the Internet depends on a child's age, among other factors. Whereas younger children have grown up with it, older teenagers remember the times before the Internet existed and, perhaps, have a different approach to this technology.

> My younger cousins, they're all under the age of eleven – and they're now coming into an age where the Internet is all they've ever known. Where we, really, when we were young, we were still doing all the [outdoor] activities, and the Internet wasn't really around. So we've got balance. But maybe in five or ten years' time that will change.
>
> (Lorie, 17, from Essex)

When asked what they would do if the Internet disappeared tomorrow, some initial responses were of horror. However, after a little reflection, the major message concerned the convenience of the Internet. In other words, while children and young people recognise its usefulness, especially for schoolwork, and say they would miss Internet access, they are confident that eventually they would find alternative ways to do the same things; others find that losing other technologies, such as satellite television or the mobile phone, would be more 'devastating'.

> It would make life harder because you'd have to go out and hunt for the information at different libraries and things and wait for them to get the books in, and something that would take half an hour or an hour, would take two to three weeks.
>
> (Steve, 17, from Manchester)

> I do use it a lot but it's kind of like – if you lost the Internet I wouldn't be as bothered as if we'd lost Sky digital. I would be bothered. I wouldn't be as bothered because like if we didn't have Sky, I'd be distraught. Yeah, but if we lost the Internet I'd probably be like, oh no, oh no. I'd be upset for like a couple of days. . . . I'd just live on text messaging. Yeah. Because you can get chat rooms on your phone, so I don't see what's wrong with that.
>
> (Rosie, 13, from Derbyshire)

Some older teenagers are more critical towards the Internet, saying that they would not miss the Internet as it does not necessarily improve learning, and the information is also available from alternative sources.

> If we didn't have the Internet, we'd get everything we have on the Internet somewhere else. And I don't think the Internet is the solution to anything. And especially not education because there are too many distractions. Um, and I just think the Internet can be an easy way of doing things, but it won't actually change anything like education.
>
> (Marie, 16, from Essex)

Clearly the Internet is not so much taken for granted that young people cannot contemplate life without it, although this may be changing. Although the Internet is highly convenient for schoolwork, it is gaining its most insistent role in everyday life through its impact on communication habits. Indeed, staying in touch with their peer group becomes increasingly important as they grow older, form their identities and gain independence from their parents. In short, the crucial issue concerns the peer group norms. If the Internet disappeared tomorrow, young people are confident they would adjust. But given that the Internet is widely but not universally available, for those few who lack access, the shift to an online peer culture may well exclude them socially as well as add barriers to their educational performance.

Conclusions

This chapter has shown that, in relation to parents and teachers, children are gaining valued social status by their 'expertise' in using the Internet, a status that gives them confidence to learn from the technology though also, perhaps, inserting a barrier that undermines adult support for their Internet use. Less is known about what they learn from the Internet, although there are signs that a more informal and creative – although often uncritical – mode of learning characterises their engagement with the Internet, posing some challenges for media (or Internet) literacy education. Children are especially enjoying the new opportunities for communication opened up by the Internet. Despite adult anxieties that this communication paves the way for inappropriate contact with strangers, most online talk is with local friends, exploiting the distance the Internet puts between communicative partners, so that young people can achieve intimacy while avoiding embarrassment or losing face. Lastly, as part of growing Internet literacy, the chapter charts young people's struggles to grasp the risky or unwelcome aspects of online contact and content, revealing some subtle and thoughtful, if not always informed, responses to these new challenges.

As young people go online, integrating the online and offline, there are clearly implications for their lives that extend far beyond leisure, the traditional focus of media research. When television arrived, the home was conceived as a sanctuary, apart from the demands of work and community. Today the Internet is finding its place in a very different kind of home, defined through its connections with, rather than separation from, work, school, community, even the global community. Within this, family members live increasingly individualised lifestyles, and here too the Internet facilitates, blurring boundaries between home and work, public and private, education and entertainment, citizen and consumer. The child sitting and staring at the computer screen, far from being off in a world of their own, is connected with many others, familiar and new, and this brings dangers as well as opportunities.

However, the historical lesson of previously-new media is one of diversification rather than displacement, with repositioning and specialisation of older media (Bolter and Grusin, 1999). Little evidence here or elsewhere supports claims for the child as dramatically affected by the supposed harms (or benefits) of changing media, inviting research to locate the young Internet user within intersecting social contexts (home, family, peers, school, community, nation). Our findings also make us wary of overstating the creativity and innovativeness of children's responses to, or shaping of, the Internet, notwithstanding our child-centred approach. Still, the present findings concern the first generation of young people to access the Internet en masse, and further developments in the communications environment and, accompanying this, in the contexts of childhood and family life, will continue to pose many questions for the future.

Acknowledgements

This research was funded by an Economic and Social Research Council grant (RES-335-25-0008) as part of the 'e-Society' Programme, with co-funding from AOL, BSC, Childnet-International, Citizens Online, ITC and Ofcom.

Bibliography

Bolter, J.D. and Grusin, R. (1999) *Remediation: Understanding New Media*, Cambridge, MA, MIT Press.

Buckingham, D. (2002) The electronic generation? Children and new media. In Lievrouw, L. and Livingstone, S. (eds) *The Handbook of New Media*, London, Sage.

Facer, K., Sutherland, R., Furlong, J. and Furlong, R. (2001) What's the point of using computers? The development of young people's computer expertise in the home. *New Media & Society*, 3(2), 199–219.

Feilitzen, C., von and Carlsson, U. (eds) (2000) *Children in the New Media Landscape: Games, Pornography, Perceptions*, Gothenburg, Sweden, Nordicom.

James, A., Jenks, C. and Prout, A. (1998) *Theorizing Childhood*, Cambridge, Cambridge University Press.

Lievrouw, L. and Livingstone, S. (eds) (2002) *Handbook of New Media: Social Shaping and Social Consequences*, London, Sage.

Ling, R. (2004) *The Mobile Connection: the Cell Phone's Impact on Society*, San Francisco, Elsevier.

Livingstone, S. (2002) *Young People and New Media*, London, Sage.

Livingstone, S. (2003) Children's use of the Internet: reflections on the emerging research agenda. *New Media & Society*, 5(2), 147–166.

Livingstone, S. (2006) Children's privacy online. In Kraut, R., Brynin, M. and Kiesler, S. (eds) *Domesticating Information Technologies*, Oxford, Oxford University Press, pp. 145–167.

Livingstone, S. and Bober, M. (2003) *UK Children Go Online: Listening to Young People's Experiences*, London, London School of Economics and Political Science. Online, available at: www.children-go-online.net.

Livingstone, S. and Bober, M. (2004) *UK Children Go Online: Surveying the Experiences of Young People and their Parents*, London, London School of Economics and Political Science. Online, available at: www.children-go-online.net.

Livingstone, S. and Bober, M. (2005) *UK Children Go Online: Final Report of Key Project Findings*, London, London School of Economics and Political Science. Online, available at: www.children-go-online.net.

Livingstone, S. and Bober, M. (2006) Regulating the internet at home: contrasting the perspectives of children and parents. In Buckingham, D. and Willett, R. (eds) *Digital Generations*, Mahwah, NJ, Erlbaum, pp. 93–113.

Livingstone, S. and Bovill, M. (2001) *Families and the Internet: an Observational Study of Children and Young People's Internet Use*, London, London School of Economics.

Livingstone, S., van Couvering, E.J. and Thumim, E. (2005) *Adult Media Literacy: a Review of the Literature*, London, Ofcom.

Machill, M., Neuberger, C. and Schindler, F. (2003) Transparency on the net: functions and deficiencies of Internet search engines. *The Journal of Policy, Regulation and Strategy for Telecommunications*, 5(1), 52–74.

Mackenzie, D. and Wajcman, J. (eds) (1999) *The Social Shaping of Technology* (2nd edn), Buckingham, Open University Press.

O'Connell, R. (2002) *Young People's Use of Chat Rooms: Implications for Policy Strategies and Programs of Education*, Cyberspace Research Unit, University of Central Lancashire.

Papert, S. (1996) *The Connected Family: Bridging the Digital Generation Gap*, Atlanta, GA, Longstreet Press.

Ribak, R. (2001) 'Like immigrants': negotiating power in the face of the home computer. *New Media & Society*, 3(2), 220–238.

Seiter, E. (1999) *Television and New Media Audiences*, New York, Oxford University Press.

Slater, D. (2002) Social relationships and identity online and offline. In Lievrouw, L. and Livingstone, S. (eds) *The Handbook of New Media*, London: Sage, pp. 534–547.

Sutter, G. (2000) 'Nothing new under the sun': old fears and new media. *International Journal of Law and Information*, 8(3), 338–378.

Williams, N. (2001) *Are We Failing Our Children?*, London, Childnet International Publications.

9 Web-use and Net-nerds

The impact of information technology in the home

Jonathan Gershuny

Norman Nie's Net-nerds

What follows was stimulated by Nie and Erbring (2000), who concluded on the basis of cross-sectional evidence that Internet use reduces social contact. I contend that their finding is methodologically flawed because longitudinal panel survey materials are necessary to draw any such implication; I argue for a 'neo-functionalist' theoretical perspective within which the impact of such new technologies may more helpfully be considered; and I illustrate these propositions through the analysis of a UK panel study of time-diarists.

Technologies as chains of provision for services

What follows relates particularly to the currently contested issue of the 'time displacement' results of the Internet.[1] It concerns the role of technical change in delivering 'final services' – those ultimate consumption experiences which are the real purpose and end point of all economic activity.

There are many alternative chains or sequences of activity that might lead in principle to the same or a similar final service. A woman might plant and harvest her own wheat, mill it herself, bake, slice the bread, butter her own sandwich and eat it. Or she might enter a café, eat a sandwich and pay for it. There are fundamental differences in the sensations she might experience as a result of these two chains of activity. But it would also surely be perverse to deny that there are also some important similarities, a degree of functional equivalence. Rather similar sorts of wants are satisfied by quite different sequences of various sorts of paid and unpaid work and consumption – by, in the broadest sense of the word, different technologies.

Thus, in the 1950s, people progressively reduced time at the cinema, but bought televisions and produced a similar final entertainment service themselves at home – a change in the balance between different modes of provision for passive entertainment. This change in the 'modal split' has clear reflections both in employment and time-use data. Using this approach, and combining the conventional National Accounts statistics with time-budget studies, it is possible to produce comprehensive accounts of societies' time use, broken down by paid and unpaid work and consumption time, across a complete set of 'final service functions' (Gershuny, 2000: Table 8.1, 224–225).

This is a neo-functionalist approach, where the functions are wants for particular sorts of final consumption experiences. The functions – the particular set of wants that are satisfied by the economic system – are not determined by any inevitable forces, whether biological or economic. They are merely the outcomes of historical processes, contingent, culturally diverse, and varying widely over time and between countries. But, while they are socially constructed (Berger and Luckman, 1967: 70–85), they are nevertheless real, and innovations in modes of provision for them drive economic change. And with economic change, comes change in patterns of time use.

It is in this sense that the authors cited by DiMaggio *et al.* (2001) refer to 'time displacement'. There is a functional equivalence of time spent watching television and time spent at the cinema. Historical and cross-national comparative time-use studies of the diffusion of television use across the developed world suggest that time spent watching television 'displaced' time at the cinema (e.g. Szalai, 1972). DiMaggio *et al.* pose the question of whether the Internet has similar effects in relation to television, as well as other leisure activities, citing studies for and against such time-displacement effects.

In fact, once we set out this neo-functionalist perspective explicitly, it becomes clear that there are a number of different ways that the diffusion of new technologies may affect time-use patterns. For example:

- Technical change may increase the productivity of paid work in production of 'basic' commodities, in turn freeing time to be transferred to chains of provision for more sophisticated or luxury wants.
- Increased productivity may be accommodated through more intensive consumption without ever-rising unemployment (Linder, 1970).
- Unpaid work time may be substituted for paid service work through 'self-servicing', using domestic washing machines for laundry services, driving private cars instead of purchasing transport services, and so on (Gershuny, 1978, 1984).
- And new technologies lead to 'displacement' of consumption time – the TV vs cinema example.

It is likely that home-based computing technologies, with associated telecommunications infrastructure developments, will have a similar scale of impact to the mid-twentieth-century self-servicing innovations. New consumer information systems, systems for purchase and delivery of goods and services, new systems for provision of advice and training, have already emerged as Net-based commodities, and there are opportunities for much more of this sort of change. These imply a number of different possibilities: the 'time displacement' case – with Internet time, considered as a leisure or final consumption activity, displacing, for example, social contact or television – is, in fact, just one among a considerably wider group of such phenomena.

Let us consider just two further cases, of more complex chains of consequences, which are perhaps more generally representative of the effects of a multi-purpose consumer technology (or it may be more appropriate to consider it as a 'technological infrastructure') such as the Internet.

The final service function may be subject to inelastic demand, in the sense that its end could be achieved more efficiently in time as a result of the technological change, and the resulting time savings could then be devoted to satisfying other wants. This corresponds to the historical case of the declining social time devoted to food production. For example, home Internet time may take on a new role in an existing chain of intermediate production activities such as shopping. Home shopping using the Internet could lead to a substantial reduction in time spent shopping away from home (and related travel) by consumers, while in turn: generating new paid employment both directly in software and telecommunications industries, and indirectly in construction and home-delivery services; and freeing time that consumers could use to satisfy wants for other forms of consumption, which might not directly involve the Internet at all (and might well generate yet more new paid employment).

On the other hand, the final service function may be subject to elastic demand: the technology might improve the efficiency and effectiveness (i.e. either the volume or the quality of result) of time devoted to the satisfaction of a particular class of want, to such a degree that consumers want more of it. To use the old language of production for the chain of provision as a whole, in such a case, growth in output of the service function is greater than productivity growth and leads to more consumption time; this is the historical case of the effect of domestic radio and television technologies on time spent in passive home-leisure consumption.

Questionnaires, diaries and time-use estimates

It has been demonstrated repeatedly (e.g. Hoffman, 1981; Niemi, 1983; Robinson and Godbey, 1997) that questionnaire-based estimates of work time are unreliable; while most employed people are aware of their contractual hours of work, their actual hours of work very frequently differ from these. In fact, except in exceptional circumstances (e.g. employees clocking on and off, or the self-employed billing clients for work actually done), there is no reason for anyone to know the answer to this sort of question, any more than one might know the weekly time devoted to watching television or washing dishes. A diary-based methodology, which involves the establishment of a random sample of records of sequences of recent activities (ideally in the respondents' own words), together with estimates of the clock time of the start of each activity, seems altogether more reasonable.

The data

What follows is based on the Home-on-Line (HoL) time-diary panel study (Lacohee and Anderson, 2001) based at ISER, University of Essex. The HoL study had an initial random probability sample of 1,000 UK households, with an over-sample to provide 50 per cent of the achieved household sample with home computer access (the UK average was 32 per cent at the time of the first wave in 1999: Taylor *et al.*, 2000). All adult (sixteen or over) members of households were interviewed. Two further annual waves in the early spring of 2000 and 2001 were undertaken. Wave one consisted of computer-aided personal (CAPI) interviews, while waves two and three involved an initial telephone (CATI) interview. Each wave consisted of a multistage investigation, consisting of an initial household interview with a randomly selected household informant, followed by individual interviews with all adult household members. A seven-day self-completion time-use diary was left behind for all adults, together with children over ten (using a slightly simplified design, results of which are not discussed further here), with a request to complete this at least once per day, and then mail back at the end of the designated week. Rules for inclusion in the subsequent waves follow those of the British Household Panel Survey; broadly, all members of wave-one respondent households, plus all current co-residents, are interviewed in subsequent waves. There have been previous diary-panel studies (Harvey and Elliott, 1983; Juster, 1985; Kraut *et al.*, 1998 discuss the specific issue of the impact of the Internet on sociability). The present study is, however, the first nationally representative panel study using a seven-day diary suitable for exploring changes in time use at the individual level.

The main analysis in what follows is of two-wave transitions (wave one → wave two pooled with wave two → wave three, together with wave one → three transitions for those absent in wave two). (Longitudinal weights to compensate for differential non-response and attrition have been calculated, but are not used here, on the grounds that they are inappropriate to the regression analyses.)

IT in the home: a very *small* revolution

Our substantive starting point must be the diffusion of home computing. The British Household Panel Survey suggests that, in 2000, around 50 per cent of the UK population was in households possessing home computers. But the distribution of access was socially skewed. Approximately two-thirds of those in households above the mean income have access, but fewer than one-quarter of those in below-mean-income households, and there were negligible levels of ownership in households below the official half-median income poverty line. This constitutes a substantial 'digital divide'.

To get a proper perspective on the nature of the putative IT revolution, we need to see how home computers are actually used in the home. Relatively little time is devoted to home computing overall – hardly two hours per week for working-age men, around one hour per week for working-age women. There is also a very strong social-class gradient in the amount of time used for this purpose: men in higher professional and managerial occupations spend four hours per week in computer-related activities, similarly placed women, three hours per week. Those in manual occupations spend hardly one hour per week in these activities. Plainly, if there are *any* observable effects of the Internet, these are going to be small ones.

Cross-sectional differences between users and non-users

Consider first the straightforward comparisons of time data for Web-users and non-users. The brief summary of the results is that there is little sign of the Nie *et al.* finding in the UK time-diary data. Similar non-results have been reported both from US questionnaire evidence (Wellman *et al.*, 2001), and from time-diary materials (Kestnbaum *et al.*, 2002).

Table 9.1 illustrates in the most straightforward of ways the most basic of the objections to the simple comparison of Web users and non-users: users and non-users differ also with respect to other variables. Web-users have substantially more paid and less unpaid work, for example. Some of this is explained by gender (for instance, the work/unpaid work differences only apply to men). However, some of the associations persist once we control for gender – for example, time spent watching TV. Indeed, the Nie and Erbring finding that television watching time is much lower among Web-users appears to be supported. But is this really because of Web-use, or because Web-users do more paid work? Some findings also reflect interactions between gender and Web-use. The two time-use categories most closely connected with the Net-Nerd hypothesis – 'going out' and 'visits' – show something of this sort: relatively small differences for men, but really quite substantial differences between female users and non-users, with the former apparently 'going out' a lot more, but visiting friends' houses a lot less – which might in turn suggest that female users and non-users are in some sense 'different sorts of women'.

This is clearly not the right way to go about the analysis. Three distinct problems are emerging:

1 There may be other 'third variables', measured in the survey, but not yet included in the analysis, causally prior to both Net use and social activity, which confound our view of the connection between them.

2 Some of these 'third variables' (e.g. employment status) have very strong connections with particular categories of time use (paid work) so the effect of the variable might be either direct (i.e. employed people are the sort who do less visiting) or a result of time-use crowding (employed people have less free time for visiting).

Table 9.1 Web users and non-users: time in various activities (pooled data 1999–2001) (minutes per day)

	All			Men		Women	
		Non-user	User	Non-user	User	Non-user	User
Paid work, FT education, assoc. travel	227	220	255**	258	294*	192	200
Unpaid work, shops etc., assoc. travel	209	215	185***	167	151	251	232
Sleep, personal care, meals at home	620	624	603***	611	587**	634	626
Social life, 'going out', assoc. travel	51	49	58***	56	56	44	60**
Visits to friends' houses, being visited	53	54	46*	46	43	61	50*
Playing sports, walks, outings	26	26	25	30	26	22	24
Telephone calls	9	9	11**	6	9**	11	15**
Hobbies, games, etc.	12	12	12	10	11	13	13
Radio, TV, video, etc.	157	163	135**	178	144**	151	121**
Reading newspapers, books, magazines	28	29	27	32	24**	26	30
Doing nothing, other	21	22	18	23	18	20	17
Computer games, etc.	4	3	9**	5	13**	1	4**
Email, browsing the Web	5	0	24**	0	28**	0	18**
Study, paid work, other, on the computer	10	6	26**	9	31**	4	20**
Missing	8	8	7*	7	6	9	8
	1,440	1,440	1,441	1,438	1,441	1,439	1,438
N	2,294	1,841	453	791	258	1,038	190

Note
T-test for difference between means: *$p < 0.05$, **$p < 0.005$.

3   Some of the remaining differences between users and non-users may still
    not be consequences of the net-use, but relate to other interpersonal dif-
    ferences which have not been measured, and indeed might in principle
    not be measurable at all ('unobserved heterogeneity').

We can deal with the first two of these problems by adopting a rather more
formal regression modelling strategy. And, indeed, the third problem has a
straightforward solution in the panel analysis to which we turn in the next
section.

There are three different categories of right-hand-side variable in the
regression models presented in Table 9.2. First, there are the straightforward
sorts of categorical and other classificatory information. Second are those
time-use elements that might be expected to be closely associated with
'causally prior third variables'. In the models, I have used paid work and
unpaid work ('contracted and committed activities' in the conventional
time-diary analysis terms: Aas, 1978) as right-hand-side predictor variables,
where they can both act as proxies for categories of employment status and
household responsibility, and also provide appropriate cross-sectional elasticity estimates – so as to deal with the 'crowding' problem.

Third, there are the predictor variables which are of direct interest to our
analysis, connected with Web-use. Web-use is itself a time-use category, so
we enter it as a scalar quantity rather than as a classificatory category. And
highly correlated with Internet use are the two other sorts of home computer
use (playing games and applications for work or study), which are also
entered as scalar quantities. For the moment we will simply estimate Equation 1 for each of the time-use categories not mentioned on the right-hand-
side of the regression.

Equation 9.1
Time use $= f$(age, age squared, gender, date of survey)
        $+ f$(time in: contracted, committed, games, other PC, Internet)

This produces a table of results with three pleasing characteristics:

1   The effects of the various categorical and other classificatory character-
    istics sum, across the full set of time-use variables not included on the
    right-hand-side of Equation 9.1, to exactly zero, since, whatever the
    characteristics – age, female gender, year of measurement – there are
    always exactly 1,440 minutes in the day; more time spent by a person
    with any given characteristic in one activity must be exactly compen-
    sated for by less time spent in the other activities.
2   The effects of the right-hand-side time-use variables must sum, for just
    the same reasons, to -1 (since the regression coefficients tell us, for each
    left-hand-side time-use category in turn, the effect of spending one extra
    unit of time on the right-hand-side variable).

Table 9.2 A cross-sectional time-use model (pooled data 1999–2001) (minutes per day)

	Personal	Going out	Visits	Sports, etc.	Phone	Hobbies	TV, etc.	Reading	Nothing	Missing	Total
Age	−3.15**	−0.81*	−0.03	0.94**	−0.21*	0.06	1.59**	0.11	1.34**	0.15*	0.00
Age squared	0.04**	0.00	−0.01	−0.01**	0.00*	0.00	−0.01*	0.01**	−0.02**	0.00	0.00
Women	21.76**	−3.80	11.60**	−8.02**	5.12**	1.96	−25.07**	−3.73*	−2.14	2.33**	0.00
Wave two	1.01	2.24	−0.61	4.83*	1.23	−1.26	−6.93	0.06	1.27	−1.85**	0.00
Wave three	1.76	−0.41	−1.10	1.36	0.38	−0.40	−1.21	−2.27	5.68	−3.80**	0.00
Paid work time	−0.25**	−0.08**	−0.14**	−0.07**	−0.01**	−0.02**	−0.25**	−0.05**	−0.13**	−0.01**	−1.00
Unpaid work time	−0.16**	−0.15**	−0.13**	−0.06**	−0.01**	−0.02**	−0.27**	−0.05**	−0.14**	0.00	−1.00
Computer games	−0.30**	−0.21**	−0.09	−0.07	−0.01	−0.04	−0.11	−0.01	−0.16	−0.01	−1.00
Other home PC	−0.10*	−0.10*	−0.14**	−0.06*	−0.01	−0.03	−0.45**	−0.02	−0.10*	0.01	−1.00
Internet time	−0.31**	0.16*	−0.22**	0.02	0.06**	0.02	−0.53**	−0.07	−0.12	−0.01	−1.00
(Constant)	760.14**	136.56**	122.10**	41.36**	14.61**	16.03**	247.00**	32.67**	64.56**	4.96**	1,440.00
Adjusted R^2	0.35	0.13	0.12	0.07	0.05	0.04	0.29	0.26	0.08	0.06	

Note
* $p < 0.05$, ** $p < 0.005$.

3   The intercepts sum to exactly one day's worth of the time units (since they represent the condition where all the right-hand-side variables are set to zero).

Thus Table 9.2 gives us the evidence we require: the effect of spending time on the Internet, controlling appropriately for the effects of all the other measured, relevant variables. It appears, on this basis, that each extra minute on the Internet is associated with about one-third of a minute reduction in personal care time, one-fifth of a minute less visiting, half of a minute less watching television – but, to pick a result that does not apparently accord well with the Net-nerd hypothesis, nearly one-fifth of a minute of extra time devoted to 'going out' – eating or drinking in a public place, going to the theatre or cinema. Not necessarily what we would initially associate with our nerds.

It should immediately be said that even this formally specified regression model is still not the correct way to consider the general problem. In fact, the elasticities we are estimating here are not really elasticities in the sense of changes consequential on the variation of the right-hand-side scalar variables. All we have so far are, in fact, cross-sectional differences; we are in effect attempting to simulate change by comparing people who have at some point changed. We have, for the moment, different people, perhaps people who differ in ways that are not yet included in the model, perhaps even differing in ways that are not measured in the survey instrument. There is really only one way to see effects of change: to take repeated measures of the behaviour patterns of the same individuals. We can only ultimately identify change by measuring it directly. We need, to get at Nie's Net-nerds, the sort of natural experiment provided by the diary panel, which looks at the consequences of people changing their Net use.

Before we turn to the evidence from our natural experiment, there is one other thing we might note from Table 9.2. This concerns the block of coefficients relating the right-hand-side independent time-use variables to the various left-hand-side dependent time-use categories. They are virtually all negative. This is not at all surprising: these are, after all (something like) time-use elasticities, in the context of a fixed-length day. What should surprise us is where these coefficients are positive. A positive coefficient indicates that something is really going on, that there is some sort of complementarity between the independent and the dependent variable.

Longitudinal consequences of Net-use

Now we can start to use the diary panel study as a panel. In this section we pool year-on-year changes, putting together pairs of years. We can model change over this period using essentially the same regression models as on page 126 for the pooled cross-section data. So Equation 9.1 becomes the pair of equations:

Equation 9.1a

Time use $t_1 = f$(age, age squared, sex, survey date at t_1)
$\quad\quad + f$(time in: contracted, committed, games, other PC,
Internet at t_1)

Equation 9.1b

Time use $t_2 = f$(age, age squared, sex, survey date at t_2)
$\quad\quad + f$(time in: contracted, committed, games, other PC,
Internet at t_2)

Now, our research question concerns change in the left-hand time-use variables, so we have to estimate a new regression equation derived by subtracting Equation 9.1a from Equation 9.1b. However, some of the right-hand-side variables estimated in the original Equation 9.1 are time-invariant. Sex, for example, does not change, and when we subtract 9.1a from 9.1b, constants disappear altogether. Age advances by exactly the same amount for all cases between each wave of data collection, so subtraction produces a new constant which must be dropped from the equation; we therefore also drop age squared. So we find ourselves estimating the straightforward Equation 9.2:

Equation 9.2

Time use change $t_2 - t_1$
$= f$(contracted time at t_2 − contracted time at t_1,
committed time at t_2 − committed time at t_1,
computer games time at t_2 − computer games time at t_1,
other PC time at t_2 − other PC time at t_1,
Internet time at t_2 − Internet time at t_1)

which has only time-use variables on both sides. This is genuinely an elasticity equation; it is estimated from panel data, with repeated measurements of the same respondents, and shows us directly the effect of changes in time use, on time use!

Now, if over some period we spend more time in one activity, we must necessarily spend less time in some other activity – a simple matter of time displacement. So, by default, we would expect that all the regression coefficients should be negative. And if we do not find negative coefficients relating one of the right-hand variables to a particular left-hand variable, then we may be entitled to conclude that there is some kind of complementarity between those variables. Consider Tables 9.3 and 9.4.

My expectation, on the basis of time displacement, is that in each case the coefficients will be negative. And, indeed, we do find that virtually all of the coefficients are negative. But not quite all of them. The effect of spending more time on the Internet on 'going out' is substantial (and, we might note, quite a bit bigger than the equivalent coefficient in the cross-section-based

Table 9.3 Modelling change in time use

	Personal	Go out	Visits	Sports	Phone	Hobbies	TV, etc.	Reading	Nothing	Missing	Total
Change in:											
Paid work	−0.23**	−0.10**	−0.23**	−0.06**	−0.01**	−0.02*	−0.19**	−0.05**	−0.11**	−0.01	−1.00
Unpaid work	−0.14**	−0.16**	−0.17**	−0.06**	−0.01*	−0.03*	−0.24**	−0.06**	−0.11**	−0.01*	−1.00
Computer games	−0.26	−0.36**	−0.04	0.03	0.02	−0.05	−0.39*	0.11	−0.07	0.02	−1.00
Other home computer	0.03	−0.17*	−0.23*	−0.10*	0.00	−0.13**	−0.20*	−0.04	−0.17*	0.01	−1.00
Internet time	−0.16	0.23	−0.20	−0.11	−0.02	−0.18*	−0.43*	−0.03	−0.13	0.03	−1.00
(Constant)	4.67*	0.72	−1.15	−0.52	0.72	−0.85	1.11	−1.52	−0.24	−2.95	–
Adjusted R^2	0.14	0.09	0.12	0.04	0.01	0.02	0.14	0.04	0.06	0.01	–

Note
* $p < 0.05$, ** $p < 0.005$.

Table 9.4 Modelling change in time use: women only

Change in:	Personal	Go out	Visits	Sports	Phone	Hobbies	TV, etc.	Reading	Nothing	Missing	Total
Paid work	−0.20**	−0.11**	−0.23**	−0.06**	−0.01	−0.03*	−0.18**	−0.06**	−0.11**	−0.01	−1.00
Unpaid work	−0.12**	−0.20**	−0.17**	−0.07**	−0.02**	−0.04*	−0.20**	−0.06**	−0.11**	−0.01	−1.00
Computer games	−0.68	−0.21	0.76	0.05	−0.05	0.06	−0.44	0.07	−0.64	0.08	−1.00
Other home computer	−0.23	−0.29*	0.09	−0.19*	0.02	−0.11	−0.03	−0.08	−0.22	0.03	−1.00
Internet time	0.02	0.51*	−0.46	−0.07	0.07	−0.60**	−0.77**	0.25	0.08	−0.02	−1.00
(Constant)	6.26	0.48	−3.67	−1.78	1.03	−1.01	4.59	−1.31	−1.61	−2.98**	0.00
Adjusted R^2	0.10	0.16	0.12	0.05	0.01	0.03	0.11	0.05	0.05	0.00	–

Note
* $p < 0.05$, ** $p < 0.005$.

estimate). According to our model, for each extra minute spent logged onto the Internet, there is something like fourteen seconds (0.23 of a minute) extra time spent going out. The coefficient is not significant – but if we look at the women in the sample alone (Table 9.4), the coefficient is even larger; an extra minute devoted to the Internet is associated with more than thirty seconds of extra time spent eating, drinking, going to the cinema. And this coefficient is statistically significant. In both cases, other sorts of socialising time do reduce: time spent visiting other people's homes declines at about the same rate that 'going out' increases. But if we sum these two types of 'out of home socialising', we still see that the increase in Internet time does not lead to a reduction of socialising time. (Note, incidentally, that the change coefficients in Table 9.4 are generally quite similar to the cross-sectional 'elasticity' effects in Table 9.2: this tells us that cross-sectional observations in this case are not in fact misleading – but panel observations are nevertheless needed as confirmation.)

There is a potential statistical objection to modelling change in the way I have done in Tables 9.3 and 9.4, in that there may be an inherent correlation between the level of the dependent variable and its rate of change. (Among possible substantive, as opposed to merely econometric, reasons for this, might be 'barriers to entry' to the activity, such that those already engaged in it find it easier to increase the time devoted to it, than do those who have not yet started.) One simple way of dealing with this problem is to enter the initial level of the dependent variable as an additional predictor on the right-hand-side of the regression equation. Table 9.5 compares the coefficients from the Table 9.3 estimations (model 1) with those using the alternative approach (model 2); there is a small change to the estimate of the

Table 9.5 Two alternative models of effects of the Internet on sociability

Model	Going out		Visits	
	1	2	1	2
Going out (wave p)	–	−0.54**	–	–
Visiting (wave p)	–	–	–	−0.68**
Change in:				
Paid work	−0.10**	−0.08**	−0.22**	−0.15**
Unpaid work	−0.16**	−0.12**	−0.16**	−0.10**
Computer games	−0.36**	−0.28*	−0.04	−0.10
Other home computer	−0.17*	−0.14*	−0.23*	−0.18*
Internet time	0.23	0.29*	−0.20	−0.24
(Constant)	0.71	26.85**	1.15	34.43**
Adjusted R^2	0.092	0.311	0.12	0.435

Note
* $p < 0.05$, ** $p < 0.005$.

Internet effect, but the same conclusion emerges. Indeed, we now see a significant positive relationship between Internet use and 'going out', as in Table 9.3, approximately balanced by a (a slightly smaller, non-significant) negative association with visiting. Overall, we are left with the same conclusion: increasing Internet usage has either a positive (on the narrow 'going out' definition) or a neutral (on the broader definition) effect on time devoted to sociability with non-household members.

I will speculate, in a moment, on the meaning of this result in the light of the neo-functionalist analysis that I introduced earlier. But it is worth reiterating the implication of this finding. We expect to find negative coefficients, on a straightforward time-displacement argument. If, as in the case of the relation of growth in Internet time to out-of-home socialising, we do not find negative coefficients, something must be counteracting the time displacement. There may be something, in the use of the Internet, that actively complements 'going out'. The coefficients are not strongly significant. But, to put it formally in the cumbersome language of statistical inference, the Nie Net-nerd proposition implies the hypotheses that significant negative coefficients relating Net-use to sociability are to be expected – and this hypothesis is not supported. To paraphrase Wellman *et al.* (2001: 450) on a parallel finding: 'This is one of those few situations in social science where a lack of statistical association is a meaningful result.'

What we know, and do not know, about the IT revolution, and how to find it out

It is not of course at all surprising that, once we model this process correctly, using time-diary measurement techniques, controlling appropriately for other sources of variation, and checking the cross-sectional 'difference' evidence against longitudinal change, the apparent association between Internet use and unsociable behaviour should disappear. Perhaps in the 1980s and 1990s some people corresponded to the Nie–Erbring stereotypical Net-nerd – reclusive, obsessive and often located behind a computer screen. We would expect the stock of computer-users in 1998 to include a fair number of such people. But this is not to say that the diffusion of Net use leads to such behaviour. It is, ultimately, only when we distinguish the sort of person who had a computer in 1998, from the consequences of acquiring a computer, or an Internet connection, at that particular historical juncture, that we can establish the effect of the Internet. The panel design allows us to do this. And a time-diary panel study, which provides adequate and stable measurement of time allocation, at successive points in history, allows us to construct proper time-use elasticity models which show, at least, the time-use correlates of growth in Internet usage.

But this does not provide an interpretation for our findings. Why is Internet use positively (or at least, contrary to our 'time-displacement' expectations, not-negatively) associated with sociability?

I started by discussing the conceptualisation of technical change as change in the chains of activity associated with the provision of particular final services. New technologies are used in chains of provision that satisfy particular wants. So, how (apart from my own work-related obsessions) do I use this technology? I use it to find out what is on at my local cinema, to book tickets on trains and aeroplanes, to buy routine groceries and arrange delivery as an alternative to shopping (hence, freeing time for leisure activities), and to contact my friends to arrange to meet them. In short: I use the technology at least in part as a means of organising and promoting my social life.

The complementarity of Internet time with sociability may be unexpected, particularly if we set out expecting to find Net-nerds, but nevertheless the findings are reasonably clear. They might, furthermore, be explained in terms of my own sorts of applications of the technology. We might reasonably – if entirely speculatively – associate this finding with the second of the categories of impact of technical change on time use listed on page 121: of a service function subject to elastic demand. The Internet can be used to search for and gather together information and compare different sorts of out-of-home leisure activity from a wide range of current sources, to make arrangements, pay or reserve speculatively, and so on. It can allow us to do all of these things with much more flexibility, immediacy, certainty, than was possible with the preceding technologies (post, telephone, fax). In short, it makes going out more efficient – potentially at least, more pleasant, and more sociable, better focused on our particular wants and preferences. And so, 'at the margin' we might be tempted to do more of it.

But the connection of the Internet/going-out complimentarity to the innovation is still, at this point, just speculation. Establishing an elasticity still falls well short of establishing causal priority. We can be certain that Internet use and social life vary together to some extent. But we cannot on the current evidence say definitively that the former causes the latter. It is still possible that there is yet another process going on – it may be, for example, that there is a personal process of 'opening out to the world' going on among computer users and that the increase in Internet usage and 'going out' are both reflections of this prior phenomenon.

Where to go from here? We need more evidence. We should continue to monitor time use on a panel basis, and this ought to be complemented by qualitative, observational work (e.g. by Silverstone *et al.*, 1991; Anderson and Tracey, 2001). We will only discover what the actual 'chains of provision' are by asking, and seeing, what people are actually using the Net for – by observing directly how the technology is embodied in the chains of provision for the various final services we consume.

Note

1 For reviews on the social impact of the Internet, see DiMaggio *et al.*, 2001; Wellman *et al.*, 2001.

References

Aas, Dagfinn (1978) Studies of time use: problems and prospects. *Acta Sociologica*, 15(2), 333–355.

Anderson, Ben and Tracey, Karina (2001) Digital living: the impact (or otherwise) of the Internet on everyday life. *American Behavioural Scientist* 45(3), 456–475.

Berger, Peter L. and Luckman, Thomas (1967) *The Social Construction of Reality*, London, Penguin Books.

DiMaggio, Paul, Hargittai, Eszter, Neumann, W. Russell and Robinson, John P. (2001) Social implications of the Internet. *Annual Review of Sociology*, 27, 307–366.

Gershuny, Jonathan (1978) *After Industrial Society? The Emerging Self-service Economy*, London, Macmillan.

Gershuny, Jonathan (1984) *Social Innovation and the Division of Labour*, Oxford, Oxford University Press.

Gershuny, Jonathan (2000) *Changing Times: Work and Leisure in Post-industrial Society*, Oxford, Oxford University Press.

Harvey, Andrew S. and Elliott, David H. (1983) *Time and Time Again: Explorations in Time Use*, Volume 4, Ottawa, Employment and Immigration Canada.

Hoffman, Eivind (1981) Accounting for time on Labour Force Surveys. *Bulletin of Labour Statistics*, 1, Geneva, ILO.

Juster, Francis T. (1985) A note on recent changes in time use. In Juster, F.T. and Stafford, F. (eds) *Time, Goods and Well-Being*, Ann Arbor, Institute for Social Research.

Kestenbaum, Meyer, Robinson, John P., Neustadtl, Alan and Alvarez, Anthony (2002) Information technology and social time displacement. *IT & Society* 1(1), 21–37.

Kraut, Robert, Patterson, Michael, Lundmark, Vicky, Kiesler, Sara, Mukophadhyay, Tridas and Scherlis, William (1998) Internet paradox: a social technology that reduces social involvement and psychological well-being? *American Psychologist*, 53(9), 1017–1031.

Lacohee, Heather and Anderson, Ben (2001) Interacting with the telephone. *International Journal of Human–Computer Studies*, 53(5), 665–699.

Laurie, Heather and Gershuny, J.I. (2000) Couples, work and money. In Berthoud, R. and Gershuny, J. (eds) *Seven Years in the Lives of British Households*, Bristol, The Policy Press.

Linder, Staffan (1970) *The Harried Leisure Class*, New York, Columbia University Press.

Nie, Norman and Erbring, Lutz (2000) *Internet and Society: a Preliminary Report*, Stanford Institute for the Quantitative Study of Society. Online, available at: www.stanford.edy/group/siqss/Press_Release/Preliminary_Report.pdf.

Niemi, Iiris (1983) *Time Use Study in Finland*, Finland, Central Statistical Office.

Robinson, John and Godbey, Geoffrey (1997) *Time for Life: The Surprising Ways Americans Use their Time*, University Park, Pennsylvania State Press.

Silverstone, Roger, Hirsch, Eric and Morley, David (1991) Listening to a long conversation: an ethnographic approach to the study of information and communication technologies in the home. *Cultural Studies*, 5(2), 204–227.

Szalai, Sandor (1972) *The Use of Time*, The Hague, Mouton.

Taylor, Mark, Brice, John, Buck, Nicholas H. and Prentice, Elaine (2000) *BHPS User Manual, Volume 2*, Wivenhoe, ISER. Online, available at: www.iser.essex. ac.uk/bhps/index.php#BHPSdoc.

Wellman, Barry, Haase, A.Q., Witte, J, and Hampton, K. (2001) Does the Internet increase, decrease, or supplement social capital? *American Behavioural Scientist*, 45(3), 436–455.

10 Telework transitions and the quality of life

Ben Anderson and Birgitte Yttri

Introduction

Chapter 17 by Brynin and Haddon outlines some of the current controversies and debates surrounding the definition and prevalence of telework. They have rather neatly developed a categorisation of telework that makes use of elements of location and technology to demonstrate the breadth of work practices that could in some sense be considered 'telework'. They go on to show that there are different types of people within each of the different forms of telework, suggesting that at least some forms of telework reflect historical occupational divisions and structures.

By contrast, in this chapter we are more interested in social outcomes associated with moving between different forms of work and telework over the two years of the e-Living panel survey. We go beyond Brynin and Haddon's prevalence analysis and use the longitudinal nature of the e-Living data to provide a descriptive analysis of telework churn. In this we are, we believe, providing a unique analysis. Recent studies have shown that there has been relative stasis in the proportions of the labour force occupying a range of telework definitions, at least in the UK (Felstead *et al.*, 2005). However, one of the crucial questions for policy as well as organisations considering telework procedures, is not just what the 'levels' are, but how many workers stay in a specific category and how many switch to another. Whilst an analysis of the possible reasons for and indicators of such churn is outside the scope of this chapter, we use this analysis of transitions as a background for presenting an analysis of the effect of switching between different forms of work on overall life satisfaction and on job satisfaction.

Our primary reason for doing this is the ongoing debate about the social consequences of telework for the individual in terms of lifestyle choice (although, as a number of commentators have suggested, such choice may be heavily constrained), quality of life and social interactions. All of these have been presented as potential individual benefits of telework which may have spillover effects that make them socially beneficial in the wider societal context (Gottleib *et al.*, 1998; Huws, 1999; Bailey and Kurland, 2002; CEC, 2002). In fact, we can find two quite different views of the effects of teleworking in the literature. One expects a beneficial outcome through the belief that telework reflects a preference for more control over, and freedom in, working patterns, whilst the other sees negative outcomes. The latter derives from the idea that telework might often be imposed by the employer, might be associated with new forms of control and household intrusion, and therefore might reflect constraint rather than increased individual control over work patterns or lifestyle.

Of course, neither of these viewpoints need be true in isolation. It is likely that a complex interaction of these effects takes place; telework is often a pragmatic response to changing conditions (both at work and at home) and, at the aggregate level, it may be primarily neutral. In this chapter we seek to test the extent to which aspects of these different views of the significance of telework are supported by the data to hand.

Transitions in and out of telework

Before turning to our analysis of social outcomes, we present two versions of the same phenomenon – transitions in and out of different work styles. In the first instance, we use a simple definition of work according to main location, and in the second we use Brynin and Haddon's categorisation system. In each case we analyse the 'transition paths' from 2001 (wave one) to 2002 (wave two).

Table 10.1 shows the transitions in and out of particular work locations for all six e-Living countries pooled. We can see that the top-left to bottom-right diagonal (i.e. no change) produces the largest cell value for the first three categories, although only just over half of all those who worked mainly at home at wave one were still doing so at wave two, whilst nearly one-third had switched (back?) to being mostly work-premises based. In contrast, 91 per cent of those who were based mainly at work premises were still there. As we progress across the table, we see increasingly more variation. For example, only just over 50 per cent of those who at wave one were 'driving or travelling' were still doing so in wave two, with equal proportions having switched to work premises and 'one or more other places'. Those workers with multi-sited work (as opposed to travelling) were most likely to have reverted to premises-based work.

Table 10.2 shows the transitions in and out of Brynin and Haddon's telework categories with the exception of 'mobile reliant' workers, who could not be so coded at wave two, as Brynin and Haddon note. These workers have been subsumed into the other categories as appropriate. Here again there is considerable churn, except for those who never work at home. Of most interest here is that some 24 per cent of those who did home-based work using the Internet at wave one now only use a PC, and 17 per cent of them no longer use a PC or Internet for this work at all. Some 25 per cent of those who used a PC for home-work now no longer do any work at home at all, and the figure is larger for non-ICT-using home-workers (39 per cent)

Table 10.1 Transitions in and out of location of work categories (all countries pooled)

W 2: main place of work	W 1: main place of work					
	At home	At work premises	Driving or travelling	At one or more other places	Other	Total
At home	52.41	1.6	2.39	2.06	8.7	3.96
At work premises	30.34	91.69	21.05	41.15	45.65	80.45
Driving or travelling	4.14	2.04	53.59	14.81	6.52	6.29
At one or more other places	11.03	3.83	21.05	37.04	21.74	7.82
Other	2.07	0.84	1.91	4.94	17.39	1.48
N	145	2,744	209	243	46	3,387

Table 10.2 Transitions in and out of Brynin and Haddon's telework categories (all countries pooled)

W 2: telework category	W 1: telework category					
	Any Internet-based work	Any PC-based work	Home – day work, no ICT	Home – evening work, no ICT	No work at home	Total
Any Internet-based work	43.2	9.92	8.62	6.95	0.92	6.57
Any PC-based work	24.4	41.73	10.95	11.76	4.49	11.6
Home – day work, no ICT	17.2	15.78	34.47	18.72	8.94	14.96
Home – evening work, no ICT	4.8	6.62	7.36	20.32	3.86	5.7
No work at home	10.4	25.95	38.6	42.25	81.79	61.18
N	250	393	557	187	2,070	3,457

and again for non-ICT-using evening workers (42 per cent). It should be emphasised that unlike in Table 10.1, these categories denote *any* work in the indicated form, rather than that this is the *main* form of work. The idea here is that much work at home, whether telework or not, is supplementary to other work. However, this also implies that shifts towards more (or less) telework express a preference for more (or less) work of that sort.

Overall, we can see that churn is probably the norm across the various definitions of telework and other work practices we have examined. Whilst there may be slowly rising trends or even stasis in the size of some of these categories within the workforce (Felstead *et al.*, 2005), these data suggest that something much more dynamic is happening beneath the surface.

Telework and quality of life

Teleworking might be influenced by personal or family demands for greater control over the use of time (Gottleib *et al.*, 1998). Indeed, unless it benefits the individual, it is difficult to see why teleworking should ever take off to a significant extent. However there are only a few studies on the potential link between telework and quality of life. Van Sells and Jacobs see quality of life as 'a global evaluative term that summarises a person's reactions to the experiences in his or her life' (1994) and separate quality of life from quality of work life. The latter is reflected in variables such as productivity, creativity, turnover and absenteeism in the organisation – and if and how individual employees identify with or feel alienated from the organisation. Van Sell and Jacobs conclude their study by suggesting the need for more research on the effects of telecommuting on individual quality of life at work and away from work. This was taken up by a more recent European study (Akselsen, 2001). This used a mixture of survey and qualitative data to assess the subjective quality of life of teleworkers, their families and their colleagues in the context of stress, management style and so on. They found that there was a weak, though significant and positive, relationship between the number of days worked at home by an employee and their subjective quality of life. Moreover, the partner of the teleworker was negatively affected by teleworking (when the latter was measured as the number of days worked in the home). This may be due to the blurring of traditional boundaries (in both space and time) between home and work.

For those in work, it is widely held that hours worked, pay levels, control of work, place of work and work–life flexibility all contribute both to perceived quality of work life and to overall quality of life in general (Van Sell and Jacobs, 1994; Warr, 1999; Akselsen, 2001). They are also therefore taken to be indicators of objective quality of life. Using 1994–1997 ECHP[1] data, Kaiser (2002) shows that, in general, fixed-term contracts are associated with lower job satisfaction, whilst job satisfaction is highest for those with a permanent part-time job. Similarly, Bardasi and Francesconi (2003), using the first ten waves of the British Household Panel Survey (BHPS: 1991–2000), find that:

> atypical employment does not appear to be associated with adverse health consequences for either men or women, when both health and employment are measured at the same time. However, there is evidence that job satisfaction is reduced for seasonal/casual workers and is higher for part-timers. . . . In addition, very few employment transitions appear to be consequential for a worsening in health outcomes, which tends to be observed in the case of job satisfaction.

Earlier results from the e-Living project (Brynin *et al.*, 2002) suggested that, across the six surveyed countries, the self-employed were likely to have a higher perceived quality of work life than those who work flexibly or at home, and that there was also a particularly strong positive effect for those who use the Internet as part of their home-working (Brynin *et al.*, 2002). The results also suggested a small negative relationship between both hours worked and commute time (UK and Israel only) and overall life satisfaction. It is therefore possible that the assumption that increasing telework reduces commute time and thereby leads to more satisfactory work conditions might not hold, though it is difficult to generalise from the limited nature of the finding.

Research questions

We can derive the following questions from the preceding discussion:

1 Does switching to a range of work locations have a significant effect on satisfaction with work when socio-demographic differences, other life events and changes in work status are controlled?
2 Does switching to different forms of telework have a significant effect on satisfaction with work when socio-demographic differences, other life events and changes in work status are controlled?
3 Are the same (or different) effects found for overall life satisfaction?

Answering these questions properly requires the use of longitudinal data that allow us to analyse change over time by comparing 'before' and 'after' satisfaction levels. In addition, we can control for both constant and changing socio-demographics and work factors that may have a confounding effect in the case of overall life satisfaction. If, as we have suggested above, telework is often a pragmatic, contingent response to changing conditions, whether at work or at home, then we would expect little change in job or life satisfaction as a result.

Data

In the analysis that follows, we use both waves of the e-Living survey and analyse each country separately. We use the lagged endogenous approach to examine the effects of a range of variables on the wave-two satisfaction scores, whilst controlling for satisfaction at wave one as well as for a range of other confounding transitions and background variables. We can therefore interpret significant coefficients as indicating a significant (positive or negative) effect on the quality of life outcome being modelled.

The quality of life outcomes are:

1   Job satisfaction as measured by a five-point (strongly disagree ↔ strongly agree) Likert scale in response to the statement:

In most ways my working life is close to ideal.

2   Overall subjective quality of life as measured by a similar Likert scale response to the statement:

Overall the conditions of my life are excellent.

As a general household survey with an ICT focus, the e-Living data does not provide a wide range of work-related variables which are generally considered important to quality of work life such as stress, workload, flexibility and concentration (Akselsen, 2001). It is unlikely therefore that the models we can produce will be highly predictive of quality of work life. However since our aim is to assess the relative significance of forms of home-working rather than to develop good predictive models of quality of working life, this is not a significant problem. We can also make use of a range of other employment or work-related variables to control for effects such as moving in and out of self-employment, contractual transitions (temporary, permanent) and work schedule control.

Results

With the transitions discussed above as background, we can use some of them to examine the effect of moving between work styles on social outcomes, in particular on aspects of perceived quality of life. The significance of this churn lies in the implication that the concept of telework, at least if defined in terms of part-time engagement in it, denotes not a form of work as such but a *style* of work. It is a work style in a similar sense to lifestyle, and might be fitted in with the latter. If it is a pragmatic response to possibly shifting needs and preferences, it may not therefore be associated with any substantial change in job or life satisfaction.

As we can see from Figure 10.1 some forms of home and teleworking are associated with both higher job satisfaction and higher overall life satisfaction in the six countries surveyed by e-Living – although, of course, these

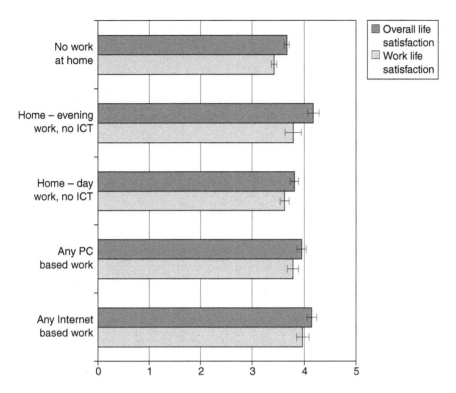

Figure 10.1 Mean life and work satisfaction scores by teleworker category (e-Living wave one, all countries pooled, n = 5,740, weighted for non-response, error bars are 95 per cent confidence intervals for the mean).

are simply indicators of particular kinds of people, as Haddon and Brynin (this volume, Chapter 17) show. The differences, though, are slight and need to be examined in more detail.

We have developed two simple multivariate models to test the effect that moving from one form of work to another might have on work-life satisfaction. The first tests the effects of work location transitions on perceived work-life satisfaction and is reported in full in Table 10.3 for each country. The second tests the effects of transitions between Brynin and Haddon's telework categories on perceived work-life satisfaction and is reported in full in Table 10.4 for each country. Note that we have not included pay as an explanatory variable in these models due to serious item non-response over the two waves of the e-Living survey which would have reduced the effective sample in all countries by up to 50 per cent.

As we can see from Table 10.3, and unsurprisingly, the best predictor of work-life satisfaction this year is work-life satisfaction last year. As we might also expect, we see a positive effect for becoming permanently

Table 10.3 Effects of work location transitions on work satisfaction (values are beta standardised coefficients)

	UK	Italy	Germany	Norway	Bulgaria	Israel
W 1: my working life is close to ideal	0.44***	0.50***	0.43***	0.43***	0.38***	0.51***
W 2: age	0.02	−0.41	−0.07	−0.05	0.15	0.27
W 2: age squared	0.03	0.41	0.04	0.08	−0.11	−0.27
W 2: gender	0.11**	0.00	0.07	−0.02	0.02	0.09*
Wave 1–2 changes						
Became permanently employed	−0.01	−0.03	0.06	0.02	0.02	0.09*
Became seasonally/temporarily employed	−0.06	−0.05	−0.02	0.00	−0.02	−0.07
W 1 did not set own schedule, now does	0.07*	0.03	0.00	0.00	0.11*	−0.06
W 1 set own schedule, now does not	−0.02	0.00	−0.06	−0.04	−0.05	0.00
Change in hours worked	−0.08*	0.03	0.01	−0.01	0.04	−0.10*
Difference between W 1 and W 2 work travel time	0.04	0.05	0.01	−0.02	0.04	−0.01
Now working mainly at home[1]	0.05	0.03	0.03	0.01	0.05	0.04
Now working mainly at work premises	−0.03	0.02	0.06	−0.04	−0.03	0.00
Now working travelling	0.00	−0.01	−0.04	−0.02	−0.05	−0.02
Now working at many places	0.06	−0.08*	0.03	0.06	0.03	−0.03
Was employed, now self-employed	0.02	0.04	−0.04	−0.01	0.04	0.05
Was self-employed, now employed	−0.01	0.01	−0.05	0.02	−0.02	−0.05
Adjusted R^2	0.212	0.250	0.178	0.179	0.145	0.287
N	621	487	539	712	352	449

Notes
1 Compared to not changing work location and all other.
$* = p < 0.05$, $** = p < 0.01$, $*** = p < 0.005$.

Table 10.4 Effects of telework transitions on work satisfaction (values are beta standardised coefficients)

	UK	Italy	Germany	Norway	Bulgaria	Israel
W 1: my working life is close to ideal	0.45***	0.50***	0.42***	0.44***	0.39***	0.52***
W 1–W 2: moved from office to telework	0.06	0.03	0.01	0.02	0.06	0.06
Adjusted R^2	0.21	0.25	0.18	0.19	0.15	0.29
N	631	491	547	721	374	451

Note
$* = p < 0.05$, $** = p < 0.01$, $*** = p < 0.005$.

employed, although this is statistically significant only in Israel, and also for gaining control over the job schedule in the UK and Bulgaria. Increasing work hours decreases job satisfaction in the UK and Israel. Only in Italy, for those who switch to working in many places, do we see any significant effect of changing work location on work satisfaction, and this is negative.

The model for telework transitions or, more specifically, the transition from office-based to any form of telework (excluding those who work at home at weekends and evenings), is reported in Table 10.4. Given that its specification is identical to the one above, we show only the lagged wave-one variable and the new telework transition indicator. As we might expect, the overall result has similar properties to the one for work location. More interestingly, we find no support for the hypothesis that changing from office-based work to telework has any substantial effect on work satisfaction and the coefficient is positive in all countries, so it is unlikely to be associated with reduced work satisfaction. This alone tells us that telework is generally unlikely to be an imposition or constraint.

Looking now at overall life satisfaction, we can see from Table 10.5 that switching work location has no statistically significant effect on overall life satisfaction at all. Indeed, the only employment-related variables that make any difference are becoming permanently employed, and only in Israel, where the effect is negative, perhaps implying a conflict between job and life satisfaction if we compare the two tables; becoming seasonally employed (Italy, negative); and becoming self-employed (UK, Israel, both negative).

Finally, our model of the effect of telework transitions on overall life satisfaction is reported in Table 10.6. As above, we do not include the variables that are identical to the previous model except for the lagged wave-one satisfaction variable. Again we can see no evidence that the transition from office-based work to any form of day-time telework has any significant effect on overall life satisfaction.

Table 10.5 Effects of work location transitions on overall life satisfaction (values are beta standardised coefficients)

	UK	Italy	Germany	Norway	Bulgaria	Israel
W 1: overall life satisfaction	0.50***	0.35***	0.41***	0.40***	0.26***	0.48***
W 2: age	-0.13	-0.28	-0.09	-0.24	-0.23	-0.07
W 2: age squared	0.16	0.25	0.06	0.29	0.30	0.06
W 2: gender	0.03	-0.02	0.00	0.03	-0.04	0.03
Wave 1–2 changes						
Became married	0.03	0.08	-0.01	0.00	-0.07	0.02
Became a co-habitee	-0.01	0.01	0.05	-0.05	-0.06	0.07
Couple split	-0.01	0.01	-0.03	-0.05	-0.02	-0.01
Widowed	0.07*	-0.09*	0.06	-0.12***	0.07	-0.05
Acquired children	-0.02	0.00	-0.02	0.06	0.03	-0.01
Became permanently employed	0.02	-0.01	0.00	-0.07	-0.05	-0.09*
Became seasonally/temporarily employed	0.02	-0.12*	-0.01	0.01	-0.04	-0.07
W 1 did not set own schedule, now does	0.01	-0.06	0.05	0.03	0.05	-0.04
W 1 set own schedule, now does not	0.07	0.01	-0.02	-0.02	0.01	-0.05
Change in hours worked	0.00	-0.08	-0.06	0.04	0.04	0.00
Difference between W 1 and W 2 work travel time	0.02	0.03	0.04	-0.02	-0.03	-0.02
Now working mainly at home[1]	0.03	0.04	0.00	0.03	-0.02	0.00
Now working mainly at work premises	0.04	-0.04	-0.01	0.01	-0.04	-0.04
Now working travelling	0.00	-0.03	0.03	-0.02	-0.05	0.03
Now working at many places	-0.04	0.00	0.04	-0.03	0.00	0.06
Was employed, now self-employed	-0.08*	0.00	-0.04	0.00	0.00	-0.10*
Was self-employed, now employed	0.01	0.00	-0.06	0.02	-0.03	-0.05
Adjusted R^2	0.244	0.140	0.161	0.177	0.044	0.246
N	623	485	540	712	375	456

Notes
1 Compared to not changing work location and all other.

Table 10.6 Effects of telework transitions on overall life satisfaction (values are beta standardised coefficients)

	UK	Italy	Germany	Norway	Bulgaria	Israel
W 1: overall life satisfaction	0.51***	0.35***	0.41***	0.40***	0.28***	0.48***
W 1–W 2: moved from office to telework	−0.06	0.03	0.02	0.00	0.07	0.02
Adjusted R^2	0.245	0.146	0.151	0.180	0.071	0.235
N	630	489	548	721	398	459

Note
$* = p < 0.05$, $** = p < 0.01$, $*** = p < 0.005$.

Conclusions

It will be apparent from the preceding results that, using this particular data, there is very little evidence linking transitions into telework or into other forms of work to changes in either job satisfaction or overall life satisfaction. Indeed, the only employment-related effects we have been able to isolate are ones we would have expected from the literature, such as switching from temporary to permanent employment, increases in hours worked and gaining greater autonomy at work.

There are perhaps two main alternative reasons for these results:

1   The data collected in the e-Living survey and used in this analysis are too sparse or constrained to provide the variables which might show an effect. Such variables might include flexibility, stress, workload, management style, trust, concentration and pay. Further, the effects of switching into various forms of work are so rich and varied at the personal level that, in the aggregate, there are few generalisable effects at all.
2   Telework is itself not a mode but a *style* of work. Certainly people do or do not telework at a particular point in time, but apart from the core cadre of full-time teleworkers who form an extremely small and seemingly stable proportion of all teleworkers, 'teleworkers' as such do not exist as a mode of worker. Therefore we should not expect substantial effects on quality of life from switches in and out of telework.

Whilst explanation one is certainly true, it is not clear that including any additional variables would have substantially altered our results without a very substantial increase in sample size to test all the possible causal relationships that the new variables would create. We accept the difficulty of assessing the effects of change given small numbers and only one transition, especially in view of the subjective nature of quality of life (which is difficult to measure and will therefore contain a significant random element) and of the likelihood that changes in this will work with a lag. Nevertheless, the extremely limited effects we observe are surprising in the light of the importance of work in people's lives.

This leads us to explanation two – if telework is a *style* rather than a mode of work, then we should not expect to see significant effects. Indeed, we are not alone in drawing this conclusion. A recent review of the literature also finds little clear evidence for a link between telework and higher job satisfaction (Bailey and Kurland, 2002). Here, it is worth returning to our figures of churn (Table 10.1 and Table 10.2). Sizeable numbers of people switched work locations and/or telework forms between the two waves of the e-Living survey. In particular, between 48 per cent and 90 per cent of workers in the various 'work at home' categories had moved out of these categories by wave two (in the main, into work premises or office-based work). Given the lack of positive effects for telework and home-work on aspects of quality of life analysed here, it is tempting to conclude that we are seeing small proportions of the labour force adopting telework or home-based work practices either in response to their own inclinations or their employers' workplace policies, but quite rapidly switching back out, either because the hoped-for quality of life effects fail to materialise (whether for themselves or for other household members), or simply because the shifts in and out of telework are pragmatic responses to changing circumstances (Akselsen, 2001). If this is the case, then there is a strong likelihood that, at some point, the proportions of the labour force who can thus experiment due to work-type/occupation, organisational or personal constraints will be saturated by those who have tried it and either found it not to their taste or simply do not need to continue to telework for the immediate job tasks to hand. At that point, the slow growth in these work practices will stop, due not as some may suppose, to technological constraints, but fundamentally to social and organisational constraints.

Note

1 European Community Household Panel.

Bibliography

Akselsen, S. (2001) *Telework and Quality of Life: Basic Concepts and Main Results*, Heidelberg, EURESCOM.

Bailey, D.E. and Kurland, N.B. (2002) A review of telework research: findings, new directions, and lessons for the study of modern work. *Journal of Organizational Behavior*, 23, 383–400.

Bardasi, E. and Francesconi, M. (2003) The impact of atypical employment on individual wellbeing: evidence from a panel of British workers. *Working Papers of the Institute for Social and Economic Research*, Colchester, University of Essex.

Brynin, M., Anderson, B. and Yttri, B. (2002) Homeworking and teleworking: a cross-sectional analysis. *e-Living Project Report*, Colchester, ISER, University of Essex.

CEC (2002) *eEurope 2005: an Information Society for All – an Action Plan.* Brussels, Belgium, Commission of the European Communities.

Felstead, A., Jewson, N. and Walters, S. (2005) The shifting locations of work: new statistical evidence on the spaces and places of employment. *Work, Employment and Society*, 19, 415–431.

Gottleib, B., Kelloway, E. and Barham, E. (1998) *Flexible Work Arrangements: Managing the Work–Family Boundary*, Chichester, John Wiley & Sons.

Huws, U. (1999) *Teleworking and Local Government: Assessing the Costs and Benefits*, London, Employers' Organisation for Local Government.

Kaiser, L.C. (2002) Job satisfaction: a comparison of standard, non-standard, and self-employment patterns across Europe with a special note to the gender/job satisfaction paradox. *EPAG Working Paper* 27, Colchester, University of Essex.

Van Sell, M. and Jacobs, S.M. (1994) Telecommuting and quality of life: a review of the literature and a model for research. *Telematics and Informatics*, 11, 81.

Warr, P. (1999) Well-being and the workplace. In Kahneman, D., Diener, E. and Schwarz, N. (eds) *Well-being: the Foundations of Hedonic Psychology*, New York, Russell Sage Foundation.

11 Informal social capital and ICTs

Rich Ling

Introduction

There is currently great interest in the topic of social capital, and the literature has grown dramatically during the past decade. Sparked more than anything by Putnam's 1995 article *Bowling Alone* (Putnam, 1995) and his subsequent book (2000), the use of this concept has been applied to a wide range of situations during the last decade, including the potential for Third World development (Fox, 1996), community governance (Bowles and Gintis, 2000), social and economic outcomes (Woolcock, 2001), self-rating of health (Kawachi *et al.*, 1999) and children's maths skills (Morgan and Sorensen, 1999). The question for this chapter is: do ICTs play into the way social capital is experienced in society? If so, what types of social capital (participation in formal groups, informal groups or in friendships) are in play?

After discussing some of this background theoretical and empirical development, this chapter examines the interaction between ICTs and *informal* social interaction that is seen as a proxy for a dimension of social capital. The analysis here tests a connection (though not a causal connection) between age, gender and SMS use on the one hand, and informal social interaction on the other, using material from the e-Living project and building on earlier work that concentrated on more formal group membership (Ling *et al.*, 2003).

I use this analysis to then develop an argument about the development of social capital through informal social interactions in contemporary society. The analysis also points to the ways that mobile communication plays into flexible group interaction. Where some communication via the Internet (perhaps excluding email and instant messaging) might be appropriate for formal groups since it provides a repository for freely accessible information of interest to the group (meeting calendars, committee membership, bylaws etc.), informal social groups rely on quickly arranged meetings. Given the suggested trend towards more informal socialising, mobile communication is a technology that passes easily into this type of interaction.

Finally, it is possible to speculate from these findings that the group ethic that, for example, arose out of being the member of an organisation is being replaced by an ethic – or perhaps ideology – that is developed within the group (Gergen, 2005). To use Putnam's concept, there may be a balkanisation of social interaction wherein groups are more inwardly focused and less interested in interaction with those who are generally outside the group. If this is the case, then we should see a negative relationship between informal and formal social activities.

Social capital – why this is important

Social capital arises from relationships between individuals embedded within a group, and is developed, maintained, or dispersed as a result of inter-personal and group processes. There is a basic distinction within the discussion of social capital between the so-called bonding (internal sense of belonging to a group of similar individuals) and bridging (links between dissimilar individuals and groups) dimensions of the concept. The former concept refers to the internal characteristics of the social group (the strength of the ties between in-group members) while the latter describes the links between groups.

When considering the analysis of social capital, there are several major contributors to the field. Pierre Bourdieu (1985) introduced the concept, outlining its distinction from human, cultural and economic capital and arguing that it is

> ... the aggregate of the actual or potential resources which are linked to possession of a durable network of more or less institutionalized relationships of mutual acquaintance and recognition – or in other words, to membership in a group – which provides each of its members with a type of collective backing, a 'credential' which entitles them to credit, in the various senses of the word.
>
> (1985: 248–249)

James Coleman (1988) elaborated the 'bonding' dimension while Mark Granovetter (1973) and Robert Burt (1998, 1999, 2000, 2001) developed the importance of the 'bridging' or weak ties. Robert Putnam (2000) added a historical dimension and more than the others has popularised the concept and finally, Portes has looked into the effects and negative consequences of social capital (1998).

According to Portes, Bourdieu's focus is, in many ways, an instrumental one. He is looking at the 'investment strategies' and the benefits that come to the individual as a result of their participation in various groups. Thus, while it is a social phenomenon, Bourdieu's concept clearly focuses on the individual and their social relationships and their access to social resources of various types.

Coleman's analysis focused on the mechanisms that generated social capital, the consequences of its generation and the general context in which it could be found. It is in Coleman that we encounter the more fully developed concepts of reciprocity, network closure, trust and gifting that form central dimensions of social capital (1988, see also John *et al.*, 2003). In addition, there is a discussion of the outcomes of social capital.

Coleman develops the idea that the more completely connected the social network, and the greater the number of connection types (common church, neighbourhood, business and/or free-time interests), the greater the social capital.

A paradox here is that were society made of these intense but closed groupings, information would be poorly distributed. Romantic relationships would be highly endogenous. Meaning and attitudes would be locally produced and not cosmopolitan to any serious degree. This hypothetical society would be highly balkanised. Indeed, Putnam cites work showing that in networks that are over-configured and where there is a lack of so-called weak ties, there is preservation of impoverishment since one literally does not receive information about possible job opportunities.

The key work here was done by Mark Granovetter who described how 'bridges' or 'weak ties' provide for the efficient diffusion of information regarding the availability of different resources (1973). He says that it is far more efficient for information to move through weak ties that are more spurious. Putnam uses social capital as a tool to better understand the shifts and changes in American civil life. He draws on a large number of different data sources in order to examine the flux in our willingness to exert energy in the public sphere, participate in politics, civic interaction, religion, at work, in informal settings, and in volunteer and altruistic groups (2000). Almost without exception he finds that Americans have lower rates of participation in the public sphere in the kinds of activities he measures.

Based on this, he examines some of the reasons for the changes in these social institutions. According to Putnam, the reasons include increased working hours, suburbanisation, generational changes and an element that is most relevant for the work here, the absorption of time watching TV.

Putnam has been critiqued in that he does not pay enough heed to informal interaction. Rather, he sees a demise of social capital largely, but not exclusively, from declining participation in formal organisations. Costa and Kahn, for example, note that Putnam understates the influence of women's increased participation in the workforce. According to their analysis, this factor weighs heavy in the reduction in social capital (2001). In addition, in the UK researchers such as Hall (1999) have found that social capital has been stable in the UK, although subsequent re-analyses have also suggested that the stability is largely found in the middle and upper classes, and not among the working classes (Grenier and Wright, 2001). Regardless, Putnam's contribution has been to add a historical dimension to the discussion and, more than any other person, to popularise the concept.

As we can see, there is tension between the individual and the group when viewed through the prism of social capital. On the one hand, the individual is perhaps drawn into social groups through the desire for group identity vis-à-vis ritual interaction (Durkheim, 1954; Collins, 1994; Ling *et al.*, 2003). A second – perhaps declining – force that supports social capital is the accumulation of obligations and the resulting implications for reciprocity. It may be, however, that people seek the latter without the constraints of the former. That is, we seek bonding without the attendant constraints on our individualism. Several authors have noted this drift in society (Beck, 1994; Giddens, 1994; Lash, 1994; Bauman, 2001). Beck and Beck-Gernsheim speak of the institutionalisation of individualism (2002), whilst Wellman *et al.*, in the context of ICTs, refer to the concept of networked individualism to emphasise our continued embedding in social networks of choice rather than of culture (2003). Indeed, Castells *et al.* suggest that mobile communication plays into a tendency towards autonomy in society (Castells *et al.*, 2004). An issue taken up by Portes is that informal groupings may become over-configured, resulting in a form of bounded solidarity (1998). Given this tendency, the informal clique develops its own internal structure and ideology that, because of a lack of bridging ties, operates as an autonomous entity. Just as a society with too many anomic individuals is a social problem, the growth of too many overly configured cliques with too few ties to the broader social order is also problematic, not least for themselves.

Social capital and information and communication technologies

One of the impacts of mobile telephony may be that it supports the development of a bounded solidarity in some social groups (Ling, 2004a, 2004b). Thus, mobile telephony may reduce the threshold for communication to such a degree that the peer group exists in a state of more or less continual contact (Ito, 2003; Rivere and Licoppe, 2003; Licoppe, 2004) that can have both logistical and ideological components (Gergen, 2003, 2005). Results in this direction are found, for example in the *Ung i Norge* (*Young in Norway*), where it was found that intensity of SMS-use amongst a sample of 9,902 Norwegian teenagers was significantly higher for teens who had tight friendship bonds. At the same time, there is a low correlation between number of SMS and the number of friends (Ling, 2005a). Another indication comes from the work of Reid and Reid who show that, for example, greater use of text messaging corresponds to the improvement of existing relationships along with more closeness in those groupings, but that it also results in a preference for smaller groups (Reid and Reid, 2004). These findings may point to the suggestion that mobile communication encourages a type of intense bounded social capital without the corresponding weak links.

Analysis

The focus of the analysis reported here is on the role of ICTs in informal social interaction as measured by the frequency of participation in informal social events (visits to cafés, theatre, meeting friends, informal sports participation and participation in activity groups). All the elements in the question battery loaded onto a single factor[1] that was used as the dependent variable in the regression analyses described below. The data comes from the e-Living survey which has been described in Chapter 1. In this chapter, I take these elements as a proxy for the concept of informal social capital, although in previous work from the e-Living project, the role of ICTs has been examined in formal groups and among friendship groups (Ling *et al.*, 2003). That research found that there was a weak relationship between ICT use and participation in formal social groups (see also Heres and Thomas, this volume, Chapter 13).

My hypothesis is that, as people are more active socially, they will rely more on ICTs to support this activity. Thus, social activity at these various levels, it is hypothesised, will co-vary positively with the use of ICTs.

To provide the reader with some of the texture of the leisure time variables, a simple descriptive analysis of the individual indicators was done where the items were simply summed, and this variable had a range of zero to thirty-five. Looking at the informal social activities variables (without the group activities element) we see from Table 11.1 that men report slightly higher levels of activity here than do women. Males reported a mean score of 17.65 and females reported a mean score of 16.28. In addition, younger respondents reported higher levels of activity. Those in the sixteen-to-nineteen-year age group reported a score of about twenty-two, where those in the oldest age group (those over sixty-seven years of age) reported a mean score just under fourteen.

In terms of country differences, Italy and the UK had the highest levels on the informal social activity index, while Bulgaria has a far lower reported score on this variable.

Table 11.1 Mean activity level by age and gender

Age group	Males	Females
16–19	22.79	21.29
20–24	21.26	19.91
25–34	19.36	17.66
35–44	17.79	16.71
45–54	16.06	15.60
55–66	15.36	14.86
>67	13.98	11.77
Total	17.65	16.27

Cross-sectional regression analysis

However, such descriptive analysis does not point out the most significant indicators of high or low informal social activity. For this, I developed a regression model (Table 11.2) that uses socio-demographic and quality of life variables, as well as variables describing ICT use, and in particular those describing telephony to predict the level of informal social activity.

The demographic variables included the standard items of income, age, gender and educational attainment and working status. In addition, there was a variable describing the proclivity to join formal organisations. Quality of life was measured using a battery of four questions (see Anderson, this volume, Chapter 12) and countries were included as dummy variables to control for potential national and/or cultural differences. The ICT variables related to telephony use (both mobile and landline), the frequency of using of email and duration of television viewing. These variables were included with the thought that the more channels of communication you employ, the greater likelihood that you are enmeshed in a social network, and vice versa. Several variables describing the use of telephony were used. These included the use of the traditional landline telephone, the use of voice mobile telephony and the use of texting. In addition, a variable describing the respondents' reliance on the telephone was included. Respondents were asked on a scale of 1 (Disagree strongly) to 5 (Agree strongly) how much they agreed with the following statements:

1 'I enjoy speaking to people on the phone.'
2 'I could spend hours on the phone given the chance.'

Table 11.2 Specification of the model used for the analysis of leisure activity

Item name
Household income (grouped into quintiles)
Age
Gender
Highest achieved educational level
Number of text or SMS messages sent a day
Reliance on and enjoyment of using the telephone (factor score)
Minutes using the PSTN telephone per day
Minutes using mobile telephone per day (wave two)
Number of people outside family can really count on
Proclivity to join formal organisations
Perceived quality of life
Minutes used watching TV per day
Number of private email messages sent and received per week (wave two)
Minutes using PC per day (wave two)
Minutes using the Net per day (wave two)
Country

3   'I only use the phone when I have to.'
4   'I need the phone to organise my everyday life.'

These four elements were subjected to a factor analysis which showed that they loaded onto a single factor. The resulting factor score was used in the regression analysis reported below.

The reported time spent using the PC and also the Internet[2] were included in the analysis. The hypothesis here is that as one commits more time to the 'stand-alone' use of the PC or the Internet, that one may reduce the amount of time that is available for social interaction (Nie, 2001). In addition the more 'social' activity of time spent sending and receiving emails was included to identify any complementation or substitution effects between online and offline social activity rates. Finally, we included time spent viewing TV. Putnam points to this activity as being particularly disturbing vis-à-vis the maintenance of social capital (Putnam, 2000). The results are shown in graphical form in Figure 11.1.

Aside from the influence of the individual countries, the model shows that the major influence on the informal social activity was age (negative, that is the younger one is, the more the informal social interaction). In addition, gender (being a female was negatively associated), one's perceived quality of life (positive), use of SMS (positive) and proclivity to join formal organisations (positive) were also strong elements in the model.

A third tier of variables made significant contributions to the model. At this level, one finds the variables describing: reliance on the telephone; time used viewing the TV; and income (all three were negative). Positive indicators were the use of email, use of the landline telephone, the number of persons outside the family upon which one can rely and use of voice mobile telephony. Contrary to Nie's claim, there is no evidence that greater Internet use is associated with decreased informal social activities.

Looking at the influence of the various countries, Italy was the country that did the most to contribute to the model – i.e. being an Italian, compared to the others, indicates increased social activity. Repeating the analysis on a country-by-country basis (not shown) shows that the model 'fits' best for Germany,[3] and rather well in Italy and Israel. The model has its poorest fit in Bulgaria and Norway.[4]

In many respects this is an appropriate result. The situation of Germany and Italy perhaps represents a more 'normal' situation in the European context than does that of either Bulgaria or Norway, that exist on the periphery of the continent both geographically and socially. In the case of Bulgaria, the strongest positive indicators are the proclivity to join formal organisations and time spent on the Internet. In addition, the use of email and age were negative. In the case of these variables, the situation in Bulgaria is quite different than that of the other countries in the project. Indeed, the contribution of the proclivity to join variable is almost three times as strong for Bulgaria as for the next strongest country (Israel).

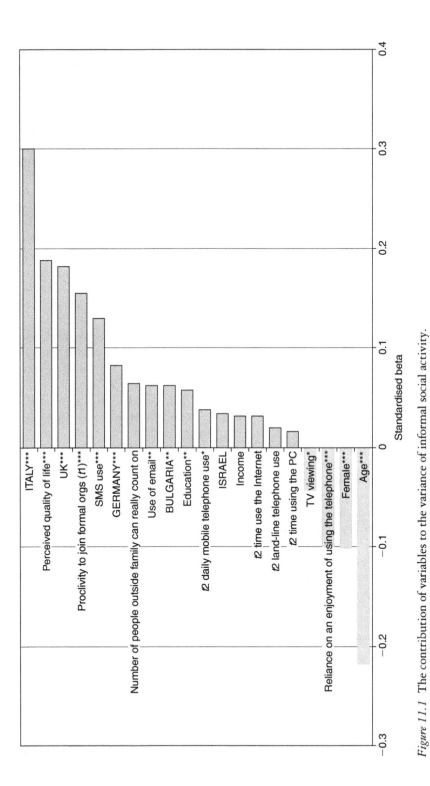

Figure 11.1 The contribution of variables to the variance of informal social activity.

Notes

OLS, all countries pooled, adjusted $R^2 = 0.254$, $* = p < 0.05$, $** = p < 0.01$, $*** = p < 0.005$.

Where mobile telephony makes a relatively strong contribution in other countries, it seems that face-to-face interaction is a central motor in the generation of informal social interaction in Bulgaria. It is interesting to note the adoption of landline telephony and the strong influence of age in this case. It points, perhaps, to a different approach to social activity in the coming generation when compared to those who are somewhat older.

Conclusion

Aside from the influence of the national differences, the analysis shows that the major influences on informal social activity for these countries were: (1) age; (2) the proclivity to join formal groups; (3) gender; (4) perceived quality of life; and (5) of special interest here, use of SMS even when age is controlled. In line with the findings of Putnam, we found that time spent watching the TV is negatively associated with this form of social capital. However Putnam's fear of balkanisation is not supported since those with informal activities also had high levels of activities.

We also found that use of the telephone had a positive association, and this is especially true for mobile telephony and for SMS even when age (young people did this more) and gender (young men did this more) are controlled. Thus, it may be the case that mobile communication, and in particular SMS, is supporting informal social activities and thus some forms of social capital.

If we extrapolate somewhat from these findings as well as those reported from others, SMS use occurs with a casual type of social interaction among a relatively limited group of persons. The focus is more often than not the planning and coordination of social interaction (Ling, 2005b). Indeed, the number of persons with whom one interacts with regularly via SMS is usually only five-to-ten (Ling, 2004a). The use of SMS (person-to-person interaction) and its relatively strong relationship to informal activity and the limited number of persons with whom we interact point to a shift in the way that we go about populating our social lives. There is a growing sense that social interaction for some portions of society is becoming more bounded. Licoppe describes mobile-phone induced 'connected presence' in France (2004); Ito and Okabe see lightweight interaction over the phone in Japan (2005); Reid and Reid report the rise of smaller, more intimate peer groups co-varying with SMS use (2004); and my own work from Norway raises the question of bounded intimacy (Ling, 2004a).

Taking this line of thought one step further, material from focus groups carried out by Telenor indicate that informal social interactions among teens and young adults often start as being vague and go through refinement, evaluation and reformulation before they take place. That is, they are perhaps loosely planned, weighed against other potential involvements, recast and changed as other opportunities come onto the social radar. All of this is different from the planning style of more restrictive formal groups – that, indeed, are also a part of the picture here. Informal social interaction is not based on obeisance to the collective as seen in the formal group, but perhaps more on individual need. So long as the informal group is a comfortable situation, we will continue to meet and to interact. The low threshold for interaction means that the social group has immediate access to each other and that planning can be a naturalistic interaction as alternatives and barriers rise and fall.

However, the small informal group often does not have the same reservoir of alternative groupings that one finds in, for example, a club or organisation where, if one does not like one committee or grouping, they can still seek out generally like-minded persons in another portion of the organisation. Just as modern marriage is more precarious as it is not usually supported by a broad community but, rather, the determination of the couple to make it work (Berger and Kellner, 1964), the small social group is also precarious. As with marriage, the ultimate measure of an informal group's relevance to our interests is our individual satisfaction with the marriage/social group (Beck and Beck-Gernsheim, 2002). In addition to being precarious, the bounded group does not have the same access to weak ties (Granovetter, 1973) and the various social resources that they afford.

The results here indicate that mobile communication plays into this, since it seems to allow a more flexible form of coordination and the maintenance and perhaps concentration of in-group bonding. It allows one to fit sociation into the nooks and crannies of everyday life (Ling and Yttri, 2002) and possibly obviates the need for social contact in the context of other, more formal institutions which bring access to weak ties. However the tendency towards participation in formal groups shown in the results may form a bulwark against the isolated clique of an over-configured social network. Perhaps a balance is being achieved. Nonetheless, as the fate of social capital ebbs and flows with the introduction of new technologies, the material also points towards a shift in society that bears watching.

Notes

1 All variables factored onto a single dimension that had an eigenvalue of 2.30. The factor weights ranged from 0.53 to 0.70.
2 The data here comes from the actual questionnaire. In addition a time use diary was included in the second wave of the survey. However, the material from this analysis produces roughly the same results as the reported use statistics.
3 The adjusted R^2 in $t2$ was almost 0.30 for Germany.
4 The adjusted R^2 in $t1$ was just below 0.1 for Bulgaria. It rose however to 0.17 for $t2$.

160   *Rich Ling*

References

Bauman, Z. (2001) *The Individualized Society*, Cambridge, Polity.

Beck, U. (1994) The reinvention of politics: towards a theory of reflexive modernization. In Beck, U., Giddens, A. and Lash, S. (eds) *Reflexive Modernization: Politics, Tradition and Aesthetics in the Modern Social Order*, Cambridge, UK, Polity.

Beck, U. and Beck-Gernsheim, E. (2002) *Individualization: Institutionalized Individualism and its Social and Political Consequences*, London, Sage.

Berger, P. and Kellner, H. (1964) Marriage and the construction of reality. *Diogenes*, 45, 1–25.

Bourdieu, P. (1985) The forms of capital. In Richardson, J.G. (ed.) *Handbook of Theory and Research for the Sociology of Education*, New York, Greenwood.

Bowles, S. and Gintis, H. (2000) Social capital and community governance. *The Economic Journal*, 112, 419–436.

Burt, R.S. (1999) The social capital of opinion leaders. *Annals of the American Academy of Political and Social Science*, 566, 37–54.

Burt, R.S. (2000) The network structure of social capital. In Sutton, R.I. and Staw, B.M. (eds) *Research in Organizational Behavior*, Greenwich, CT, JAI Press.

Burt, R.S. (2001) The social capital of structural holes. In Guillien, M.F., Collins, R., England, P. and Meyer, M. (eds) *New Directions in Economic Sociology*, New York, Russell Sage.

Castells, M., Fernandez-Ardevol, M., Qiu, J.L. and Sey, A. (2004) *The Mobile Communication Society: a Cross-cultural Analysis of Available Evidence on the Social Uses of Wireless Communication Technology*, Los Angeles, Annenberg research network on international communication.

Coleman, J. (1988) Social capital in the creation of human capital. *American Journal of Sociology*, 94, 95–120.

Collins, R. (1994) *Four Sociological Traditions*, New York, Oxford.

Costa, D.L. and Kahn, M.E. (2001) Understanding the decline in social capital 1952–1998. Boston, MIT/Tufts University.

Durkheim, E. (1954) *The Elementary Forms of Religious Life*, Glencoe, IL, The Free Press.

Fox, J. (1996) How does civil society thicken? The political construction of social capital in rural Mexico. *World Development*, 24, 1089–1103.

Gergen, K. (2003) Self and community and the new floating worlds. In Nyri, K. (ed.) *Mobile Democracy: Essays on Society, Self and Politics,* Vienna, Passagen Verlag.

Gergen, K. (2005) Comments on the psychological dimensions of mobile use. In Katz, J. (ed.) *Mobile Communication and the Networked Society*, San Francisco, Morgan Laufman.

Giddens, A. (1994) Living in a post-traditional society. In Beck, U., Giddens, A. and Lash, S. (eds) *Reflexive Modernization: Politics, Tradition and Aesthetics in the Modern Social Order*, Cambridge, UK, Polity.

Granovetter, M. (1973) The strength of weak ties. *American Journal of Sociology*, 78, 1360–1380.

Grenier, P. and Wright, K. (2001) Social capital in Britain: update and critique of Peter Hall's analysis. *ARNOVA Conference*, Miami.

Hall, P. (1999) Social capital in Britain. *British Journal of Politics*, 29, 417–461.

Ito, M. (2005) Mobile phones, Japanese youth and the replacement of social contact. In Ling, R. and Pedersen, P. (eds) *Front Stage/Back Stage: Mobile Communication and the Renegotiation of the Social Sphere*, London, Springer.

Ito, M. and Okabe, D. (2005) Intimate connections: contextualizing Japanese youth and mobile messaging. In Harper, R., Palen, L. and Taylor, A. (eds) *The Inside Text: Social, Cultural and Design Perspectives on SMS*, Dordrecht, Netherlands, Springer.

John, P., Morris, Z. and Halpern, D. (2003) Social capital and causal role of socialization. *ESRC Democracy and Participation Conference*, University of Essex, March 17–19.

Kawachi, B., Kennedy, B. and Glass, R. (1999) Social capital and self rated health: A contextual analysis. *American Journal of Public Health*, 89, 1187–1193.

Lash, S. (1994) Reflexivity and its doubles: structure, aesthetics and community. In Beck, U., Giddens, A. and Lash, S. (eds) *Reflexive Modernization: Politics, Tradition and Aesthetics in the Modern Social Order*, Cambridge, UK, Polity.

Licoppe, C. (2004) 'Connected' presence: the emergence of a new repertoire for managing social relationships in a changing communications technoscape. *Environment and Planning*, 22, 135–156.

Ling, R. (2004a) *The Mobile Connection: the Cell Phone's Impact on Society*, San Francisco, Morgan Kaufmann.

Ling, R. (2004b) Where is mobile communication causing social change? In Kim, S.D. (ed.) *Mobile Communication and Social Change*, Seoul, South Korea.

Ling, R. (2005a) Mobile communications vis-à-vis teen emancipation, peer group integration and deviance. In Harper, R., Taylor, A. and Palen, L. (eds) *The Inside Text: Social Perspectives on SMS in the Mobile Age*, London, Kluwer.

Ling, R. (2005b) The socio-linguistics of SMS: an analysis of SMS use by a random sample of Norwegians. In Ling, R. and Pedersen, P. (eds) *Mobile Communications: Renegotiation of the Social Sphere*, London, Springer.

Ling, R. and Yttri, B. (2002) Hyper-coordination via mobile phones in Norway. In Katz, J.E. and Aakhus, M. (eds) *Perpetual Contact: Mobile Communication, Private Talk, Public Performance*, Cambridge, Cambridge University Press.

Ling, R., Yttri, B., Anderson, B. and Deduchia, D. (2003) Mobile communication and social capital in Europe. In Nyri, K. (ed.) *Mobile Democracy: Essays on Society, Self and Politics*, Vienna, Passagen Verlag.

Morgan, S. and Sorensen, A. (1999) Parental networks, social closure, and mathematical learning: a test of Coleman's social capital explanation of school effects. *American Sociological Review*, 64, 661–681.

Nie, N.H. (2001) Sociability, interpersonal relations, and the Internet: reconciling conflicting findings. *American Behavioral Scientist*, 45, 420–435.

Portes, A. (1998) Social capital: its origins and applications in modern sociology. *Annual Review of Sociology*, 24, 1–24.

Putnam, R. (1995) Bowling alone: America's declining social capital. *Journal of Democracy*, 6, 65–78.

Putnam, R. (2000) *Bowling Alone: the Collapse and Revival of American Community*, New York, Touchstone.

Reid, D. and Reid, F. (2004) Insights into the social and psychological effects of SMS text messaging. *160 Characters*. Online, available at: www.160characters.org/documents/SocialEfffectsOfTextMessaging.pdf.

Rivere, C. (2005) Mobile camera phones: a new form of 'being together' in daily interpersonal communication. In Ling, R. and Pedersen, P. (eds) *Mobile Communications: Renegotiation of the Social Sphere*, London, Springer, 167–186.

Wellman, B., Quan, B., Haase, A., Boase, J., Chen, W., Hampton, K., Isla De Diaz, I. and Miyata, K. (2003) The social affordances of the Internet for networked individualism. *Journal of Computer-Mediated Communications*, 8.

Woolcock, M. (2001) The place of social capital in understanding social and economic outcomes. *Printemps*, Spring, 11–17.

12 Social capital, quality of life and ICTs

Ben Anderson

Introduction

The conclusions of the European Council's Lisbon summit of 2000 clearly state that a shift to a knowledge-based economy will not only be a powerful engine for growth, competitiveness and jobs, but 'in addition ... will be capable of improving citizens' quality of life...' (FP6 IST WP2003-4, paragraph 8).

In addition, the e-Europe 2005 agenda document states:

> The information society has much untapped potential to improve productivity and the quality of life.... New services, applications and content will create new markets and provide the means to increase productivity and hence growth and employment throughout the economy.
>
> (CEC, 2002: 2)

This statement, on which much of the subsequent e-Europe 2005 agenda depends, is intended to show how ICT investment can support the Lisbon objectives of increased productivity and quality of life (QoL) through increased economic participation.

However, there is growing evidence that one of the key characteristics of the information and communications technology revolution is not so much access to knowledge, information or work, but access to other people, as the explosion in, and revenues generated by, person-to-person communication services attests. It has also long been recognised that resources accessed through inter-personal and community-based social relationships (known as 'social capital') can be critical energisers of social and economic regeneration and contributors to overall quality of life, as we discuss below.

To bring this analysis into an ICT context, Ling *et al.* (2002) introduced the idea that social capital, perceived quality of life and usage of ICTs might be linked.

Their conceptual model is as follows:

> A person's [perceived] QoL score depends on a range of variables including several types of social capital, socio-economic situation, life stage/lifestyle, personality and attitudes. Some ISTs may mediate some

of these variables. Thus the ISTs themselves are not necessarily significant factors, but they may enhance behaviours that are associated with increased QoL.

(2002: 25)

Clearly this is a very simple model of the components of quality of life. However, it draws attention to the fact that the e-Europe agenda focuses excessively on economic (employment growth) considerations, and even where it refers to quality of life it ignores many related aspects, such as human and social capital. This chapter seeks to address this imbalance by making clear the conceptual and empirical relationships between ICTs, quality of life and social capital in order to ground the policy debates in concrete evidence.

The link between quality of life, social capital and technology

What precisely do we mean by 'quality of life' and also by 'social capital'? Unfortunately there is no clear and unequivocal definition of either.

A search of one of the most complete academic literature databases[1] for 'quality of life' produces 17,689 separate journal articles published over the last forty years. With such a body of work, it is little wonder that those seeking to review and assimilate the field have concluded that it is no longer possible to do so (Cummins, 1997). On the one hand, subjectivists believe that QoL is only a meaningful concept when subjectively described by individuals within their life context. Such indicators might include perceptions of an individual's own sense of community, safety, happiness, general life satisfaction, sex life and quality of relationships. One of the strongest criticisms of the subjective approach has been that what is being measured may well be determined by the individual's adaptation to their life experiences. To avoid this problem, objectivists believe that quality of life can only be sensibly measured independently of an individual's life experience. As Fahey *et al.* note (2003b), following Cummins (1997), it must be best to combine the two when speaking of quality of life, and this would surely apply to the social aspects of quality of life where we can measure both the amount of communication with friends and subjective factors such as feelings of loneliness.

Whilst there is not space here to provide a wide-ranging account of all aspects of QoL (the interested reader is directed to a recent review: Ling *et al.*, 2004), we should note that there is an emerging consensus that QoL indicators should include measures of objective and subjective material resources (Diener *et al.*, 1999; Frijters *et al.*, 2002); education (Fahey *et al.*, 2003a) and employment (Clark and Oswald, 2002; Blanchflower and Oswald, 2004); age, family (Adams, 1999) and household factors (Helliwell, 2003); health (Diener *et al.*, 1999), housing and environment (Stewart,

2003); the political and cultural context (Frey and Stutzer, 2000); leisure (Wendel-Vos *et al.*, 2004) and social relationships.

Given our interest in the social aspects of QoL, it is to these that we now turn. Following Bourdieu (1986), we suggest that an individual can draw upon resources based on whom they know (social capital) as well as what they possess. It has long been recognised that resources accessed through inter-personal and community-based social relationships can be critical energisers of social and economic regeneration and contributors to overall QoL (see also Ling, this volume, Chapter 11). For example, Putnam finds evidence of positive associations between well-being and higher social cohesion in terms of civic activities (2000), though Michalos and Zumbo (2000) find very little effect for a range of measures of the heterogeneity of social networks, racial prejudice and ethnicity on reported life satisfaction. Using country-level data, Helliwell (2003) shows that well-being is positively linked to a range of social capital indicators, including social trust and membership of associations. Of course we should note that such cross-sectional analyses does not prove causation – there is, as yet, rather little longitudinal analysis to confirm these effects over time.

Other studies show that increases in social participation can have significant mediating effects on mental and physical health (Myers, 1999), especially for those not in work and for women, although there is little evidence that increasing social capital can negate more fundamental structural inequities in health (Pevalin and Rose, 2003).

Recent British research using the British Household Panel survey (Li *et al.*, 2003) found that those in disadvantaged positions are more likely to obtain help through informal neighbourhood relations and especially kinship (bonding) ties, whilst those more advantaged tended to rely on non-localised social networks and civic engagement (bridging ties). They also found that some aspects of social capital have strong associations with social trust and QoL and, perhaps most importantly of all, that informal forms of social capital (neighbouring, family and friends networks, etc.) have a significantly greater explanatory power in explaining differences in QoL than formal types of social capital such as civic engagement or formal 'participation'. Here then is a hint that ICT policies focusing on civic participation may be misplaced. Clearly Helliwell and Putnam's thesis that declining civic participation and, in particular, formal participation threatens well-being is but half of the picture, since this perhaps underestimates the continuing role of informal personal social networking, a concept central to the analysis we present below.

Turning to the links between ICTs and social capital in the context of QoL, recent studies of individuals have focused on the use of ICTs to support those who are home based through economic, age, health (i.e. lack of mobility) and household situations such as single mothers with no resources for alternative childcare (Haddon, 2000). These have shown the importance of communications technologies in combating individuals' feelings of isolation.

Historically this has been the telephone, but the mobile telephone is being increasingly used for local interaction, and email is increasingly important to the maintenance of more distant, difficult to synchronise or international relationships.

Research questions

For the purposes of this chapter, we focus on subjective aspects of QoL (happiness/satisfaction) rather than on objective measures. In essence we are interested in what causes changes in satisfaction at the individual level and the extent to which these changes can be associated with ICT acquisition and use and changes in indicators of QoL and social capital. Given our interest in understanding how ICTs mediate aspects of social capital and QoL, we therefore pose the following questions:

- To what extent is overall subjective QoL at one time predicted by a previous score? In other words, how much real variation is there that policy actions could affect?
- What difference do changes in other aspects of QoL make?
- What difference do informal social activities make?
- What difference do formal social activities make?
- What difference do ICTs make?

The rest of this chapter reports analysis of these questions using a relatively simple longitudinal lagged regression model.

Data considerations

The research uses both waves of the e-Living dataset. The e-Living QoL scale comprises five different elements with which respondents were asked to agree/disagree via a Likert scale:

1   Overall the conditions of my life are excellent.
2   I have enough free time to do what I want.
3   The environmental conditions in my area are good.
4   I have good communications with friends.

And for those in paid work only:

5   In most ways my working life is close to ideal.

These items were repeated unchanged in wave one and wave two providing a constant measure of perceived QoL. We focus here on items 1 to 4, and in particular on 1 and 4. Item 1 provides an overall QoL score to which the next three items might be expected to contribute. We focus then on item 4 as it reflects an element of QoL that most closely relates to social capital and also, by considering the part of ICTs in communication, to ICTs as well. Item 5 is discussed elsewhere with respect to flexible and telework (Anderson and Yttri, this volume, Chapter 10).

It should be noted that this two-wave sample is not ideal for these purposes. For example, apparent changes in QoL scores over a single twelve-month period may be measurement error, rather than any sort of real change or trend and it is not possible to distinguish between the two. As a result we may not find consistent effects. This clearly calls for a longer-term study than the two-wave survey analysed here.

However, the data does provide scope for an initial and unique analysis of the longitudinal components of QoL with respect to social capital and ICT use.

We present a simple longitudinal model of changing QoL. Using the wave one and wave two data, we analyse the effect of changing QoL elements (items 2 to 4 above) as well as a range of social capital and ICT indicators on changing overall QoL (item 1). This analysis enables us to see which elements have the strongest effect on overall perceived QoL. The models use lagged (i.e. wave one) scores for overall QoL to control for QoL level effects (Finkel, 1995), and difference or transition effects for the explanatory variables. The full model is described in Table 12.1.

Results

We have run this model for each of the six e-Living countries separately using ordinary linear regression.[2] Table 12.2 shows the results of running a simple model where only wave one QoL is used to predict wave two QoL. This gives some indication of the year-to-year variation in overall QoL. Table 12.3 shows the results for the QoL, social capital and ICT variables in the full model. Both tables report un-standardised coefficients.

These results can now provide some answers to our key questions.

To what extent is overall subjective QoL at one time predicted by a previous score?

Overall subjective QoL is very well predicted by previous scores in some countries. Considering Table 12.2 we find that as much as 21 per cent (Israel) of current score is predicted by the same score last year, but this falls to as low as 13 per cent in Bulgaria. In other words, if the year-to-year variation is largely non-random, then there may be considerable scope to alter perceived QoL scores through policy actions.

Table 12.1 Longitudinal model specifications (W 1 = wave one only, W 1 & 2 = both waves)

	Variable	Meaning
Bonding capital	W 1 close friends	Number of friends you can count on if you need to talk
	W 1 & 2 leisure activity	Frequency of: • playing sport, keep fit or go walking; • going to cinema, concert, theatre or watching live sport; • having a meal in a restaurant, cafe or going for a drink to a bar or club; • meeting with friends. Actual index used is the *average* of these scores for each respondent.[1]
Bridging capital	W 1 social group activity	Number of the following groups a member of: • social groups (sport, gym, etc.); • voluntary groups (church and volunteering); • political groups (such as unions and other political campaign groups); • other groups. Actual index used is the *sum* of these scores for each respondent.
	W 1 & 2 social group activity	Frequency of attending: • activity groups such as evening classes.
Objective quality of life	W 1 & 2 wealth	Change in number of household electronic goods.
	W 1 & 2 access to car	Lost/gained (coded as 0 for non-changers).
	W 1 & 2 work status	Lost job/gained job/retired/became homemaker (coded as 0 for non-workers).
	W 1 & 2 work hours	Change in work hours (coded as 0 for non-workers).
	W 1 & 2 work control	Change in ability to control own work schedule (coded as 0 for non-workers).
	Number rooms per adult	Number of rooms per adult (overcrowding measure often used as indicator of socially deprived neighbourhood).
Subjective quality of life	W 1 & 2 satisfaction	Change in any of the QoL items: • overall the conditions of my life are excellent; • I have enough free time to do what I want; • the environmental conditions in my area are good; • I have good communications with friends.
ICT variables	W 1 & 2 ICT events	• Got mobile phone. • Got Internet access.

	W 1 & 2 ICT usages	Change in:
		• frequency of emailing friends and family;
		• number emails sent from home;
		• minutes spent online;
		• minutes spent on telephone (fixed line);
		• frequency of telephoning friends and relatives;
		• usage of Internet for specific purposes (started to shop online; started to bank online; started to use library services; started to use travel info; started to use educational services; started to use health info; started to look for environmental info; started to look for job info; started to do 'other' things online).
Control variables	W 1 structural variables	• Gender
		male (0)
		female (1)
		• Education
		None
		Age 16 (UK GCSE equivalent)
		Age 18 (UK A-level equivalent)
		Degree
		• Age categories:
		16–29
		30–59
		60–74
		75+
	Transition variables (dummies)	• Now living with partner/as couple.
		• Now married.
		• Was in a couple, now split.
		• Widowed.
		• Acquired children.
		• Became unemployed.
		• Became a homemaker.
		• Retired.
		• Gained a job having been non-working.

Note
1 A principle components analysis produces only one component, so averaging across the items is acceptable.

Table 12.2 Overall life satisfaction – simple model (regression coefficients shown)

	UK	Italy	Germany	Norway	Bulgaria	Israel
W 1: overall life satisfaction	0.434***	0.360***	0.394***	0.380***	0.373***	0.411***
Adjusted R^2	0.215	0.163	0.198	0.184	0.128	0.214
N	1,137	1,138	1,147	1,208	1,412	1,040

Note
* $p < 0.05$, ** $p < 0.01$, *** $p < 0.001$.

What difference do changes in other aspects of QoL make?

Increasing satisfaction with free time made a difference in some countries (Norway, Israel); increasing satisfaction with environmental conditions made a difference in all countries except Italy; and increasing satisfaction with communications with friends made a difference in all countries except Bulgaria and Israel.

What difference do informal social activities make?

In general, the number of close friends is associated with higher overall QoL although there is only a statistically significant result in Israel. Changes in informal leisure activities have mixed effects and again the only statistically significant result is for Israel, where it is positive.

What difference do formal social activities make?

Membership of formal groups is, in general, negatively associated with overall QoL, although the only statistically significant result is for Germany where the effect is positive. Changes to the frequency of engaging in such activities also has a generally negative effect, although no statistically significant results were found.

What difference do ICTs make?

As with our social capital indicators, we can also see that ICTs have rather few effects on overall life satisfaction. One that is notable is that the change in time spent on the Internet is positively associated with change in QoL in all countries except the UK, and the result is statistically significant in Italy and Bulgaria.

Table 12.3 Overall life satisfaction – part of full model (regression coefficients shown)

	UK	Italy	Germany	Norway	Bulgaria	Israel
W 1: overall life satisfaction	0.439***	0.369***	0.399***	0.362***	0.311***	0.405***
W 2–W 1: satisfaction with free time	0.022	0.028	0.023	0.054***	0.01	0.045*
W 2–W 1: environmental satisfaction	0.109***	-0.001	0.088***	0.206***	0.067*	0.086***
W 2–W 1: good communications with friends	0.095*	0.074*	0.091**	0.112**	0.012	0.045
W 1: bonding capital (number friends can talk to)	0.009	0.003	0.009	0.005	-0.004	0.010**
W 2–W 1: bonding capital (leisure)	-0.02	-0.004	0.016	0.009	-0.001	0.055*
W 1: bridging capital (number of groups)	-0.1	-0.038	0.058*	-0.018	-0.352	0.049
W 2–W 1: bridging capital (activity groups)	-0.009	-0.01	-0.002	-0.012	0.034	0.004
W 1: number mobile calls made per day	-0.013	0.026	0.028	0.016	-0.005	0.059*
W 1: number texts per day	-0.011	0.003	0.036	-0.006	0.023	0.004
W 2–W 1: frequency emailing friends and relatives	-0.007	-0.002	0	0.015	-0.116***	-0.004
W 2–W 1: frequency of emailing from home	0.068	0.064	0.017	-0.029	-0.073	0.062
W 1–W 2: get a mobile	-0.015	-0.021	0.019	-0.021	0.032	0.025
W 2–W 1: frequency of phoning friends and relatives	0	0	-0.001	0	0.002	-0.001
W 2–W 1: minutes on phone per day	-0.001	-0.002*	0	-0.001	0.003	0
W 1–W 2: get Internet at home	0.013	0.116	0.021	-0.121	0.23	0.107
W 2–W 1: Internet minutes	-0.208	0.217*	0.11	0.175	0.524*	0.074
W 1–W 2: started to shop online	0.005	-0.201	0.038	0.049	0.186	-0.062
W 1–W 2: started to bank online	-0.146	-0.166	-0.085	-0.01	-0.414	-0.01
W 1–W 2: started to use library services	0.041	0.056	0.053	0.032	0.137	-0.034
W 1–W 2: started to use travel info	0.088	-0.068	-0.005	0.011	0.854	-0.022
W 1–W 2: started to use educational services	-0.098	-0.072	-0.018	0.077	0.252	0.025
W 1–W 2: started to use health info	-0.135	-0.185	0.007	-0.377**	0	0.13
W 1–W 2: started to look for environmental info	0.116	-0.005	0.022	0.08	0.444	0.035
W 1–W 2: started to look for job info	-0.233	-0.277*	-0.175*	0.131	-0.501	-0.025
W 1–W 2: started to do other things	0.198	-0.068	-0.107	-0.093	0.224	0.1
Constant	2.494***	2.499***	2.120***	3.083***	1.747***	1.714***
Adjusted R^2	0.222	0.163	0.229	0.213	0.11	0.245
N	967	998	1,034	1,115	812	890

Notes
Only QoL, social capital and ICT variables shown; *$p < 0.05$, **$p < 0.01$, ***$p < 0.001$.

Conclusions

As we have seen, uptake and usage of ICTs makes little difference to overall perceived QoL and this is not surprising since there is little reason to suppose that they would have *direct effects*. However, the positive relationship between changes in Internet time and overall QoL adds to the growing body of evidence showing that heavier Internet use does not lead to reduced social interactions and, in this case in particular, to reduced QoL as some have suggested (Kraut *et al.*, 1998; Nie, 2001).

Our results are therefore cautious as to the direct effects of ICTs on well-being. They must also be cautious as to the effects of social capital, as measured here, on overall QoL, since significant effects were few. However, the lack of an effect for the bridging capital indicators and, indeed, the possible indication of overall negative effects should make us wary of assuming that investing ICT-development euros in civic 'e-participation' will pay off.

Nevertheless, as this chapter has shown, satisfaction with social interaction and with the environment, whether or not mediated in some way by ICTs, contributes significantly to perceived QoL. The role of ICT policies must therefore be to focus on second order or indirect effects on overall QoL via their mediation of these stronger effects.

Indeed this supports the UK Government's position, which has concluded that 'the greatest impact on satisfaction came from factors that the government was among the least qualified agencies to influence – social relationships' (UK Cabinet Office, 2002).

This may be the case with respect to direct measures, but it is fairly clear that social interaction in Europe is strongly supported by a significant industrial sector – telecommunications. There might therefore be an argument to be made for investment in research and development activities with the specific intent of generating new telecommunications products and services to support and enhance informal social interaction. This clearly is policy action, but not of the legislative kind.

Overall, then, we have shown in this chapter how complex the relationships between social capital, ICTs and QoL might be. We have shown the significance of at least the satisfaction with social relationships for QoL and raised the possibility, with mixed empirical support, that ICTs may play a future role in mediating the relationship between social capital and QoL. Certainly current policy foci on e-inclusion would do well to consider the explicit role of ICTs and social capital in well-being.

Acknowledgements

This research was funded by the European Commission funded Framework 5 project e-Living (IST-2000-25409) and the Framework 6 funded project SOCQUIT (IST-2002-507753).

Notes

1 British Library ZETOC journal abstracting service.
2 Using strata's regress command.

Bibliography

Adams, V.H. (1999) Predictors of African American well-being. *Journal of Black Psychology*, 25, 78–104.

Blanchflower, D.G. and Oswald, A.J. (2004) Well-being over time in Britain and the USA. *Journal of Public Economics*, 88, 1359–1386.

Bourdieu, P. (1986) The forms of capital. In Baron, S., Field, J. and Schuller, T. (eds) *Social Capital – Critical Perspectives*, Oxford, Oxford University Press.

CEC (2002) *eEurope 2005: an Information society for All – An Action Plan*, Brussels, Belgium, Commission of the European Communities.

Clark, A.E. and Oswald, A.J. (2002) A simple statistical method for measuring how life events affect happiness. *International Journal of Epidemiology*, 31, 1139–1143.

Cummins, R.A. (1997) Assessing quality of life. In Brown, R.I. (ed.) *Quality of Life for People with Disabilities: Models, Research and Practice*, Cheltenham, Stanley Thornes.

Diener, E., Suh, E.M., Lucas, R.E. and Smith, H.L. (1999a) Subjective well-being: three decades of progress. *Psychological Bulletin*, 125, 276–302.

Dolton, P. and Vignoles, A. (2000) The incidence and effects of overeducation in the UK graduate labour market. *Economics of Education Review*, 19, 179–198.

Fahey, T., Layte, R., Smith, E., Whelan, C. and Fisher, K. (2003a) *Quality of Life in Europe: an Illustrative Report*, Dublin, European Foundation for the Improvement of Living and Working Conditions.

Fahey, T., Nolan, B. and Whelan, C. (2003b) *Monitoring Quality of Life in Europe*, Dublin, European Foundation for the Improvement of Living and Working Conditions.

Finkel, S. (1995) *Causal Analysis with Panel Data*, Thousand Oaks, CA, London, Sage.

Frey, B. and Stutzer, A. (2000) Happiness, economy and institutions. *Economic Journal*, 110, 918–938.

Frijters, P., Haisken-Denew, J. and Shields, M. (2002) The value of reunification in Germany: an analysis of changes in life satisfaction. *IZA Discussion Paper*, Bonn, IZA.

Haddon, L. (2000) Social exclusion and information and communication technologies. *New Media & Society*, 2, 387–406.

Helliwell, J. (2003) How's life? Combining individual and national variables to explain subjective well-being. *Economic Modelling*, 20, 331–360.

Kraut, R., Lundmark, V., Patterson, M., Kiesler, S., Mukopadhyay, T. and Scherlis, W. (1998) Internet paradox: a social technology that reduces social involvement and psychological well-being? *American Psychologist*, 53, 1017–1031.

Li, J., Pickles, A. and Savage, M. (2003) Social capital dimensions, social trust and quality of life in Britain in the late 1990s. *ISER Seminar Paper*, Colchester, UK, University of Essex.

Ling, R., Anderson, B., Døffler, W. *et al.* (2004) Report of literature and data review, including conceptual framework and implications for IST (D6). In Heres, J. (ed.) *SOCQUIT Project Deliverable*, Delft, TNO-STB.

Ling, R., Yttri, B., Anderson, B. and Diduca, D. (2002) Age, gender and social capital: a cross-sectional analysis. *e-Living Project Report*, Oslo, Telenor R&D.

Myers, D.G. (1999) Close relationships and quality of life. In Kahneman, D., Diener, E. and Schwarz, N. (eds) *Well-being: the Foundations of Hedonic Psychology*, New York, Russell Sage Foundation.

Nie, N. (2001) Sociability, interpersonal relations, and the Internet. *American Behavioural Scientist*, 45, 420–435.

Pevalin, D. and Rose, D. (2003) *Social Capital for Health: Investigating the Links Between Social Capital and Health Using the British Household Panel Survey*, London, UK, Health Development Agency.

Putnam, R.D. (2000) Social capital: measurement and consequences. *Proceedings of an OECD/HRDC Conference*, Ottawa, Quebec, HDRC and OECD.

Stewart, K. (2003) Monitoring social inclusion in Europe's regions. *Journal of European Social Policy*, 13, 335–356.

UK Cabinet Office (2002) What do we know about life satisfaction? Workshop summary. *SU Strategic Futures Seminar Series*, London, Strategy Unit, UK Cabinet Office.

Wendel-Vos, G.C., Schuit, A.J., Tijhuis, M.A. and Kromhout, D. (2004) Leisure time physical activity and health-related quality of life cross-sectional and longitudinal associations. *Quality of Life Research*, 13, 667–677.

13 Civic participation and ICTs

Jeroen Heres and Frank Thomas

In the last decade there has been an increasing awareness of the relevance of involving societal aspects in the development of new ICTs by both policy and commercial stakeholders in Europe. Instead of focusing on technological innovation or, worse still, technology determinism, there is the vision of a knowledge society (or market) in which the use of new ICTs is embedded in its social context (Ling *et al.*, 2004).

In the period before 1995, the focus was mainly on economic aspects and sector-specific issues such as the de-regulation and privatisation of the telecommunications sector. This left little room for focusing on societal aspects such as social capital or the quality of life of individuals and communities. Since 1995 this has changed, not least because of the influence of the High-Level Expert Group (HLEG) report, *Building the European Information Society For Us All* (1997) which gave a strong stimulus to integration of social and ICT policy.

More recent activities have been based on the implementation of the Lisbon strategy (CEC, 2005) via the e-Europe and i2010 initiatives. These aim to translate Internet and other ICT use into increased economic productivity, quality of life, social cohesion and economic/social participation. Moreover the European Commission acknowledges the relevance of concentrating on e-inclusion and social capital in their most recent activities (van Bavel *et al.*, 2003).

As part of this awareness, the promise of a knowledge society that contributes to people's well-being is becoming commonplace. For example Viviane Reding, the current Commissioner of the Information Society Directorate at the European Commission has said:

> Ultimately, the development of new technologies must be to the benefit of citizens and of their welfare. It is therefore essential to move towards a more people-centred approach where technologies are used by and for citizens. Three aspects are fundamental here: combating the digital divide, stimulating the quality of life and encouraging participation.
>
> (European Commission, Autumn 2004)

Statements such as these express a vision in which ICT developments are driven by the aim to improve people's quality of life. Despite the great number of references to quality of life in policy documents, its precise meaning is never clear, and Anderson (this volume, Chapter 12) shows the broad range of interpretations of the concept. As Ling (this volume, Chapter 11) and Anderson (this volume, Chapter 12) note, the opportunities for ICT to provide access to information, connecting individuals with their social networks and supporting the acquisition of knowledge and skills could enhance personal development as well as emotional well-being. Sectors such as healthcare, education or finance could enable more efficient and effective service provisioning by the use of ICT. Such improvements in the manner services are delivered could benefit citizens in indirect (through improved care or reduced costs) rather than direct ways.

Despite the large number of policy references to the positive effects of ICT on people's lives, few of these claims are supported by empirical research. Furthermore, there is also literature reporting negative effects of ICTs on people's well-being. Many studies suggest that the use of ICT could have a negative effect on people's social lives (Kraut *et al.*, 1998, 2002; Nie and Erbring, 2000; Nie, 2001). However, these results have been disputed (Franzen, 2000, 2003; Wellman *et al.*, 2001; Gershuny, 2003). The latter suggest that the societal impact of ICT is more complex, diverse and less self-evident than is sometimes assumed.

Ling (this volume, Chapter 11) suggests that the concept of social capital helps to better understand the way ICT impacts on quality of life. As he notes, social capital refers to the social resources individuals can rely on to improve their socioeconomic position and the quality of their lives. These social resources play an important role in emotional and social well-being, but also influence personal development and economic position. Research suggests that even physical health depends on people's social relationships. Ling draws attention to a distinction between two forms of social capital: 'bridging' social capital, referring to relation-ships and networks of people who are differing from each other (hetero-geneous social groups), and 'bonding' social capital, referring to relationships and networks of individuals who share the same interests and backgrounds (homogeneous social groups). ICT use could have an impact on both kinds of social capital. On the one hand, ICT could help people to find people outside their current social network (bridging social capital) and to build new relationships, like, for example, in chat rooms. On the other hand, ICT is used to sustain and strengthen relation-ships within people's current social network (bonding social capital), for example, use of mobile telephony for communication between family members or teens.

In summary, the effects of ICT on social interactions can be differentiated into three distinct forms:

- *ICT strengthens social interaction*
  Example: The Internet provides a cheap and simple way to maintain relationships with others. People can contact each other based on shared interests, not hindered by the limitations of time and space.
- *ICT weakens social interaction*
  Example: Just like television was assumed to do, ICT draws people away from real-life contacts with family and friends. Furthermore, by facilitating global communication and involvement, it can reduce the interest in local community.
- *ICT supplements social interaction*
  Example: People use ICT to maintain existing social contacts by adding electronic contact to telephone and face-to-face contact. In addition, it adds an online social dimension to existing social networks in the offline world. In this sense the Internet gives an additional impulse to existing patterns of social contact and civic involvement.

However ICT use is not only affecting social capital, it is becoming apparent that the effects are reciprocal. On the one hand, ICT use influences social capital, and on the other, social capital influences ICT use. ICT not only provides a means for people to build and sustain social relationships, but it also shapes the way people make use of ICT and plays a role in different stages in its diffusion.

Bridging capital comes into play when an innovation is transferred to a new area and the technology becomes diffused between and within social networks. Early adopters, with their openness to new ideas, have far-flung contacts and create strong bridging capital through 'weak ties' that link between social strata, countries or cultures (Granovetter, 1973).

Bonding capital largely helps in rapidly diffusing an innovation as the social homogeneity facilitates rapid propagation once an opinion leader of a network has accepted the innovation. When the adoption of a new ICT leaves its first niche markets of technology-oriented users and touches mainstream society, the early majority ask neighbours and friends (i.e. use their bonding capital to call on opinion leaders) for advice and guidance about a new ICT (Rogers, 1995).

Conceptual framework

Following Ling (this volume, Chapter 11) and Anderson (this volume, Chapter 12) we have developed a more detailed conceptual framework to describe the inter-relationships between quality of life, social capital and ICT. As shown by Figure 13.1 the framework hypothesises that the effect of ICT use on quality of life is, for an important part, mediated through the ICT effects on social capital. Social capital effects quality of life by definition as it refers to the social resources individuals can rely on *to improve the quality of their lives*. Therefore this framework starts with an understanding of the

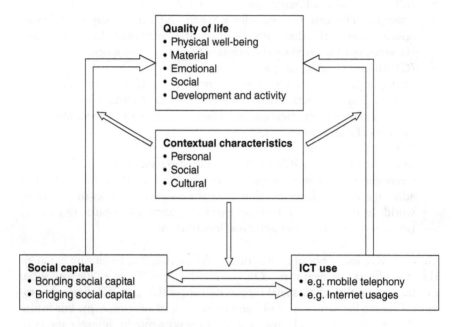

Figure 13.1 Conceptual framework.

processes by which ICT use and social capital are mutually shaping each other. These insights provide a better understanding of the contribution of ICT to quality of life.

The causality of the relationships between social capital, quality of life and the use of communication technologies are not straightforward. Longitudinal research could help to identify these causalities but, unfortunately, there is hardly any cross-national longitudinal data available that covers all the conceptual clusters specified in the framework. The e-Living survey is one of the few examples that gets close, and Anderson (this volume, Chapter 12) uses it to good effect to study the relationship between ICTs and quality of life.

The conceptual framework also makes clear the importance of the personal, social as well as societal contexts. This context needs to be taken into account to understand the social embedding of ICT use and the links with social capital that we discuss below.

Understanding the cultural context of ICT use

The largely overlooked differences in social structure, national culture or in the welfare regime of countries can create social and cultural differences between countries that may influence the way people use ICTs (Thomas, 2004). There are therefore national communication cultures, besides transnational or European traits, that have to be explicitly introduced into the analysis. For this reason, the results of US or Japanese communication studies cannot simply be transferred to the European context. In the following section, the importance of the cultural context is shown empirically.

These national differences are particularly visible in two dimensions of social capital – civic engagement and social trust. Civic engagement, such as membership in a formal association or volunteering, can be understood as a more formal type of bridging capital, whereas contact with acquaintances, colleagues or neighbours are its informal components. Civic engagement is viewed by Putnam as the glue that holds society together (Putnam, 2000). Social trust is understood as the central result of social capital but, as Norris (2002) showed, trust and engagement should be distinguished, as there are societies with high civic engagement and low social trust. She explains variations between countries by the fact that the dominant religious culture of a country and its cultural traditions influence both civic involvement and interpersonal trust, with the highest levels in countries with a Protestant culture, like Scandinavia. The link with interpersonal trust can favour ICT use as trust can reduce transaction costs. Thus interpersonal trust facilitates meeting strangers on the Internet or using e-commerce applications and, as a result, helps Internet diffusion (Huang, 2003).

In the following we focus on a specific link between ICTs and their social uses: the mutual relationship between Internet use and civic engagement. The European Commission did not explicitly mention civic involvement in its i2010 strategy proposal, but it believes that one of its political objectives in particular, an inclusive society, could be attained by civic engagement (European Commission, 2005).

The idea is that people can be empowered, and community building and e-inclusion can be attained, if formal associations can be acculturated at all levels of society in addition to informal networks. Therefore, active involvement in an association (participating in meetings, taking responsibilities) and not only mere nominal membership should be taken as an indicator for a socially inclusive way of life, a strong bridging capital, and thus a strong quality of life.

Ling's analysis of levels of nominal membership in associations and ICT use based on the e-Living data from 2001 covers a large array of ICTs (TV, land-line telephone, PC, Internet at home, mobile phone calls, text messages) and of usage intensity measures (Ling *et al.*, 2002). In all of the countries, social class correlated with involvement, as did age and gender in a majority of them. In Norway and the United Kingdom, countries with higher diffusion levels, an intensive use of emails correlated with a higher number of memberships, in Israel, with its lower Internet diffusion level, the same effect was seen with an intensive use of the mobile phone. However his analysis is necessarily limited to the six e-Living countries and we address this limitation below.

In previous work, the link between ICT uses and bridging capital (limited to civic engagement in formal associations) has been examined using the longitudinal British Household Panel Survey (Stoneman and Anderson, 2006). In this research the use of email and the Internet were strong indicators of civic engagement, even when potential confounding influences of the respondents' socio-demographics were controlled.

Of interest here is whether this result is related to the well-known British tradition of charity and volunteering, or whether it could also be shown in other countries, albeit with cross-sectional data. To test the link between ICT use and bridging capital, the analysis was adapted and repeated with the eighteen countries covered in the European Social Survey in 2002/2003.[1] These countries cover a large diversity of societal conditions which can be regrouped into the well-known welfare regimes developed by Esping-Andersen (1990) and extended by Fenger (2005) to include East European countries. Thus, there are five regimes:

- The social-democratic welfare states in Scandinavia with their strong public administration, high interpersonal trust, and intense social integration.
- The liberal regimes in the United Kingdom and Ireland, with a traditionally weak social welfare balanced by a strong civil society.
- The corporatistic regimes in Continental Europe, which base interventions in social policy on a mix of large charities, a weak public welfare and strong families.
- The Mediterranean regime, with a weak welfare state which has to be balanced by strong families.
- The East European transformation regimes which mix the traditions of state communisms with elements of the social democratic regime and whose civil society is still in its early phase.

We therefore extend Ling's initial e-Living analysis of formal group activities (Ling *et al.*, 2002) to a wider range of countries, classified according to the extended Esping-Andersen typology but with more limited ICT usage data.

Model and empiricial results

The analysis presented here is based on the European Social Survey 2003 data because of its large geographical coverage, the representative sampling, the extensive socio-demography, and the large array of information on civic engagement, combined with the fact that the European Social Survey asks a question about Internet and email use which the comparable European Values Study does not ask (Hagenaars *et al.*, 2003).

To be sure that there is a link between civic engagement (operationalised as having an active membership in at least one of twelve engagement domains) and Internet and email use (at least every week in 2002/2003), we developed a logistic regression model that tested the relative effects of the following independent variables:

- socio-demography and social class;
- geography of the social network: its stability (length of residence in the area) and the geographical profile of the community;
- bonding social capital: frequency of informal socialising, the importance of family contacts and of contacts with friends;
- bridging social capital: informal volunteering (in self-help groups, ad-hoc, single issue networks, etc.), and regularly attending religious services;
- social trust and norms: interpersonal as well as trust in institutions, the perception of volunteering as a social norm;
- ICT use: operationalised as regular, i.e. at least weekly, private use of email and the Internet.

At a country level, a clear correlation ($r = 0.86$) appears between the national levels of civic involvement and Internet use (Figure 13.2). However, the position of the countries does not completely mirror the pattern of the welfare regimes.

The main result from the logistic regression (Table 13.1) is that, in a large majority of European countries, the effects of ICT Internet use on civic

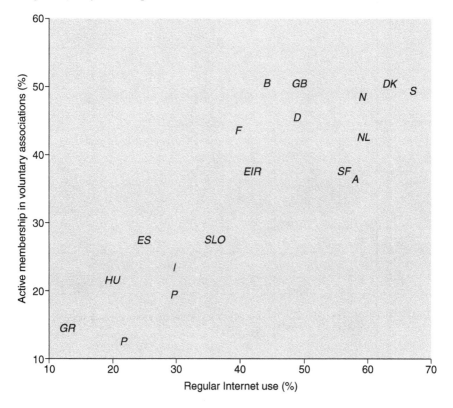

Figure 13.2 Internet use and civic engagement in eighteen European countries (source: European Social Survey 2002/2003).

Table 13.1 Results from logistical regression on civic engagement in eighteen European countries

	Welfare regimes (odds ratios) Social-democratic				Liberal		Corporatistic					Mediterranean				Transformation countries		
	Denmark	Finland	Norway	Sweden	Great Britain	Ireland	Austria	Belgium	Germany	France	Netherlands	Spain	Greece	Italy	Portugal	Hungary	Poland	Slovenia
Socio-demographic context																		
Age group (−29 yrs) ref.																		
30–49 yrs	0.70	1.02	1.342[a]	0.98	1.02	1.05	1.578[a]	0.91	1.09	1.11	0.817	0.748	0.757	0.691	0.788	1.237	1.151	1.16
50–60 yrs	1.33	1.11	1.41	0.80	1.05	0.74	1.50	0.84	0.92	0.99	0.864	0.701	1.180	0.787	0.471[a]	1.071	1.110	1.635[a]
61+ yrs	1.55	1.37	2.101[c]	0.96	0.88	0.80	1.27	0.72	1.08	1.08	0.990	1.248	0.758	0.799	0.319[c]	0.866[c]	1.559	0.85
Gender (male)	0.90	0.86	0.83	1.399[c]	1.352[b]	1.565[a]	1.354[a]	1.292[a]	1.13	1.15	0.808[a]	1.774[c]	1.676[c]	1.128	1.553[c]	1.189	1.108	1.895[c]
Educational attainment																		
Secondary education	1.822[c]	1.30	1.14	1.07	1.608[c]	1.20	1.549[c]	1.559[c]	1.28	1.599[b]	1.252	1.222	0.982	1.443	1.271	1.160	1.761[b]	0.96
Tertiary education, degree	1.718[b]	1.30	1.42	1.716[c]	1.996[c]	1.30	1.741[b]	2.248[c]	1.474[a]	2.191[c]	1.735[c]	2.725[c]	1.676[a]	2.250[a]	2.181[a]	1.797[a]	2.519[c]	1.03
Income																		
2nd quartile	0.97	0.96	1.01	0.99	1.06	1.16	1.12	1.609[b]	1.437[a]	0.93	1.174	1.380	1.436	0.700	1.046	0.902	1.338	1.18
3rd quartile	1.28	0.98	1.343[a]	0.98	1.04	1.19	1.26	1.482[a]	1.16	1.29	0.985	1.396	1.858[a]	0.817	1.075	1.450	1.470	1.51
4th quartile	1.22	0.90	1.27	1.01	1.34	1.19	1.29	1.670[b]	1.19	1.42	1.053	1.851[a]	1.715	1.101	0.958	1.244	1.92[a]	1.45
Gainful activity	1.07	1.06	1.15	1.09	1.13	1.09	0.89	0.87	1.07	0.89	1.554[c]	1.73[b]	1.152	1.696[a]	0.551[b]	1.147	1.161	1.35

Type of community																		
Town or small city	0.88	0.98	1.06	1.12	0.705[b]	1.631[a]	0.718[a]	1.36	1.315[a]	1.08	1.323	0.57[a]	1.216	0.873	1.352	0.719	1.072	1.27
Village, countryside	0.85	1.13	1.463[c]	1.450[c]	0.76	1.10	0.87	1.545[c]	2.403[c]	1.30	1.494[c]	1.004	0.723	0.33[c]	1.717[a]	1.131	0.720	1.623[b]
Local residence																		
11–20 yrs	1.15	1.374[a]	0.88	1.14	1.471[b]	1.19	1.34	0.97	1.19	1.915[c]	1.262	1.368	1.153	1.045	1.261	0.909	1.178	0.92
21+ yrs	0.78	0.95	0.98	1.391[a]	1.14	1.06	1.22	0.99	1.16	0.87	1.167	1.270	1.102	0.899	1.188	0.962	0.985	1.07
Social capital: bonding capital																		
Informal socialising	1.31	0.93	1.819[c]	1.404[c]	1.25	1.08	1.712[c]	1.11	1.524[c]	1.466[b]	1.164	1.171	1.669[c]	1.222	2.185[c]	1.732[c]	1.538[c]	1.30
Importance of family	0.91	3.005[b]	2.383[a]	0.91	0.74	1.21	0.90	1.25	1.03	0.96	1.050	0.429	1.829	0.667	3.550	0.785	0.873	1.25
Importance of friends	0.98	0.84	1.09	1.38	1.849[c]	1.00	1.19	1.575[a]	1.48[a]	0.89	1.668[b]	1.171	1.795	0.972	0.928	2.763[c]	1.164	1.18
Social capital: bridging capital																		
Informal volunteering	1.13	1.17	1.21	0.97	0.98	1.18	1.511[c]	1.24	1.16	1.26	1.147	1.599[a]	2.187[c]	1.258	1.477	1.121	1.859[c]	1.30
Religious attendance	0.74	1.885[b]	2.772[c]	2.666[b]	4.044[c]	1.286[a]	1.03	1.40	2.327[c]	1.44	2.039[c]	1.191	0.971	1.97[c]	2.049[c]	3.895[c]	0.944	1.02
Trust and norms																		
Interpersonal trust	1.00	1.11	1.11	1.17	1.374[b]	0.90	1.13	1.11	1.561[c]	1.31	1.195	1.139	1.457[a]	1.114	0.925	1.067	1.455[a]	1.32
Trust in institutions	1.00	1.325[b]	1.05	1.19	1.03	1.03	1.25	1.27	1.231[a]	0.88	1.407[c]	1.053	0.805	1.226	0.842	0.958	0.994	1.00
Volunteering a norm	1.291[a]	1.801[c]	1.400[c]	1.846[b]	1.435[c]	1.475[c]	1.448[b]	1.954[c]	2.186[c]	2.188[c]	1.264[a]	1.877[c]	3.056[c]	0.956	2.237[c]	1.867[c]	1.877[c]	1.373[a]
ICT																		
Regular private Internet use	1.608[c]	1.677[c]	2.302[c]	1.656[b]	1.609[c]	1.331[a]	1.33	1.520[c]	1.476[c]	1.592[c]	1.288[a]	1.176	1.237	1.414	2.004[c]	2.215[c]	1.612[a]	1.603[b]
Sample size	1.225	1.731	1.907	1.733	1.717	1.529	1.281	1.247	2.188	1.193	1.947	843	1.575	578	865	1.212	1.507	1.093
Nagelkerke R^2	0.070	0.058	0.142	0.111	0.183	0.068	0.103	0.141	0.169	0.186	0.102	0.168	0.185	0.148	0.168	0.230	0.151	0.109

Source: European Social Survey 2002/2003.

Note
Table shows odds ratios, a = $p < 0.05$, b = $p < 0.01$, c = $p < 0.005$.

engagement remain significant after having controlled for confounding effects.

In the Scandinavian welfare states, with their high levels of active engagement and of Internet penetration (see Table 13.1) the common pattern is that people see volunteering as a social norm and that the appropriation of ICTs correlates with a strong civic involvement.[2] Other than in Norway, where active engagement is higher for the elderly, there is no significant effect of age. Compared to the positive impact of strong bonding with the family and proximity with the Church and its social life, the effects of social class in these relatively homogeneous societies appear limited. In Sweden, an intense civic involvement can be found in rural communities with a sedentary population. However, due to the general high levels of interpersonal trust and trust in institutions, the influence of these variables is either no longer significant or weak.

In the liberal regimes, civic engagement is a question of social class, (male) gender, an intense informal social life with friends, but also a question of religious practice and civic values. The social segregation of civic engagement is a long-standing trait of British social life (Bott, 1957; Li *et al.*, 2003). Whereas, in Britain, strong civic involvement is more of an urban phenomenon, in the Irish Republic it is more concentrated in the provincial cities. Frequent ICT use correlates in both countries with intense civic involvement.

In the countries with a corporatist welfare regime, an active involvement is sustained by social class (in particular university education), the acceptance of civic engagement as a norm and regular ICT use. However demography exercises contrasting effects: in Austria civic engagement is a question of being of the age of economically active men, whereas elsewhere age plays no role. In the Catholic countries of Austria and Belgium, being male favours involvement; in the historically Protestant Netherlands, it is the women who are actively engaged. In Austria, civic involvement is an urban phenomenon, contrary to the other countries. Length of residence does not play a role, except in France. Here the family is a weaker indicator of civic involvement than friends, although intense informal socialising goes along with intense formal engagement, as religious involvement does in Germany (Offe and Fuchs, 2002) and the Netherlands. Interpersonal trust links to civic involvement in Germany only. Trust in institutions is a strong indicator in Germany and in the Netherlands, but not in the other countries.

In the Mediterranean countries, with their low trust and weak public welfare regimes, civic engagement is a question of (upper) social class and of culture. Active membership in an association is linked to urban places, to the *notabile*, as well as to the economically active. The influence of culture shows up in the importance of attending religious services. In all of these countries, an active engagement is more or less linked to youth, to being male and to living in the city (except in Portugal). Having an intense social life with family and friends mirrors social engagement, as does an engagement in informal help networks, but these links do not exist in all of the Southern countries. Interpersonal trust goes with an active engagement in Greece, but surprisingly, given Putnam's analysis, not in Italy. In these countries with their low level of formal active involvement (see Figure 13.2), the Internet is not linked to a strong integration into civil society. However, in this country group, the analysis is particularly impaired due to missing data.

In the transformation countries we meet contrasting patterns again. In Hungary, an intense civic involvement is foremost a question of middle-class, religious individuals who maintain a strong networks of friends and who have appropriated the Internet. In Poland, civic engagement is strongly class-oriented but also linked to intense informal contacts and support, to trust in others, to norm orientation and to ICT use. In Slovenia, the richest of the three countries and culturally more close to Austria, civic engagement correlates with employment, living in rural communities, norm orientation and use of the Internet and email.

Overall, the patterns of explanation vary between countries, but the classification of the societal context of social capital and communication seems to be useful. However, one may also ask whether Esping-Andersen's classification of welfare regimes, which had some success in explaining national patterns of social capital (Scheepers *et al.*, 2002; Van Oorschot and Arts, 2004) and in describing electronic communications (Räsänen, 2004), could be further adapted to integrate the value structure of a society and economic and policy context of ICT infrastructure and services build-up.

In summary, the analysis shows that the positive effect of Internet use on social capital posited in theory can largely be confirmed by empirical evidence. The effect is robust as it shows up after a multivariate analysis of confounding influences. This is even more impressive as the cultural and institutional conditions of the countries studied vary significantly.

The analysis has unfortunately been hampered by the lack of adequate data. The relative value of longitudinal and cross-sectional data has been discussed elsewhere in this book, and we will not repeat it here. Whilst the pan-European survey with the highest sampling quality, the European Social Survey, provides questions on social capital and quality of life, it lacks a set of more in-depth questions on ICT use. On the other hand, the European Commission's bi-annual Eurobarometer surveys cover nearly all of Europe and regularly carry modules on ICT use, but do not integrate social capital questions into the same waves. In addition, we have found from personal experience that the long embargo periods for data from the ICT questions in the Eurobarometer are an effective obstacle for any policy-relevant research. There is clearly a need for more, better and more timely data.

Conclusion

Following Ling (this volume, Chapter 11) and Anderson (this volume, Chapter 12), we have developed a more detailed model of the relationships between social capital, ICT and quality of life which describes the complexity of their inter-relationships.

In contrast, however, we have provided empirical analysis of the effects of Internet use on bridging capital (active membership in associations), using part of the multi-country 2002/2003 European Social Survey data. We find that, in all European countries studied, the strongest common indicators of active involvement can be found among individuals who think that being a good citizen implies volunteering, who belong to the well-educated, are male, who regularly attend religious services, and who have integrated the Internet into their daily lives. Those who can be characterised as having highest bonding capital are also to be found amongst the actively engaged in activity that develops bridging capital, although the intensity of the relationship can vary with the national context. The effects of social geography and length of residence can play a varying, though limited, role.

As ICT is developing more and more into the direction of a social network and communication technology, the role of ICT in social processes increases. However, the effects of ICT on social interactions can be very complex, and in the preceding analysis it was shown how the Internet and emailing is a strong indicator of bridging capital. Much more research is needed before we can conclude that the link is causal.

This analysis has several implications for policy. ICTs can clearly support an inclusive society, but to achieve this aim, policy should target the less educated and the socially isolated to prevent those with the highest social resources simply acquiring more in comparison to the ICT disengaged. Policy should capitalise on the understanding that civic engagement makes a good citizen to expand its popularity and motivate people to actively engage in associations and informal networks. However, for the time being, a certain part of the population will continue to refrain from using ICTs (Anderson, 2005), and, indeed, it is not clear if the relationship between ICT use and civic engagement is causal. If it is, then an inclusive multi-channel delivery should mix the Internet, the telephone and traditional paper media to ensure 'access for all'.

Finally we note that ICT-focused social policy is, in Europe at least, now acknowledging that the development of the knowledge society is a social as well as a technological process. Even though our analysis of policy documents shows a certain progress in this respect, current European policy is still mostly based on assumptions that do not fully take the complex inter-relationships between ICT and people's social life in consideration. A deeper insight into the inter-relationships between ICT use, social capital and quality of life will support a European ICT policy that makes the social promises of an inclusive and innovative knowledge society considerably more likely.

Acknowledgements

With thanks to Rich Ling, Ben Anderson, Jo Pierson and Valerie Frissen. This research was funded by the Framework 6 funded project SOCQUIT (IST-2002-507753).

Notes

1 Switzerland and the Czech Republic had to be excluded as they did not ask for membership in associations, and Luxembourg due to too many missing data for income.
2 Significant effects are shown in bold.

References

Anderson, B. (2005) The value of mixed-method longitudinal panel studies in ICT research: transitions in and out of 'ICT poverty' as a case in point. *Information Communication & Society*, 8, 343–367.

Bott, E. (1957) *Family and Social Network*, London, Tavistock.

CEC (2005) Working together for growth and jobs: a new start for the Lisbon Strategy. *Communication to the Spring European Council*, Brussels, Commission of the European Communities.

Franzen, A. (2000) Does the Internet make us lonely? *European Sociological Review*, 16, 427–438.

Franzen, A. (2003) Social capital and the Internet: evidence from Swiss panel data. *Kyklos*, 56, 341–360.

Gershuny, J. (2003) Web use and net nerds: a neo-functionalist analysis of the impact of information technology in the home. *Social Forces*, 82, 141–168.

Hagenaars, J., Halman, L. and Moors, G. (2003) Exploring Europe's basic values map. In Arts, W., Hagenaars, J. and Halman, L. (eds) *The Cultural Diversity of European Unity*, Leiden, Brill.

HLEG (1997) *Building the European Information Society for Us All*, Brussels, High-Level Expert Group – INFSOC.

Huang, H., Keser, C., Leland, J. and Shachat, J. (2003) Trust, the Internet and the digital divide. *IBM Systems Journal*, 42, 507–518.

Kraut, R., Kiesler, S., Boneva, B., Cummings, J., Helgeson, V. and Crawford, A. (2002) Internet paradox revisited. *Journal of Social Issues*, 58, 49–74.

Kraut, R., Lundmark, V., Patterson, M., Kiesler, S., Mukopadhyay, T. and Scherlis, W. (1998) Internet paradox: a social technology that reduces social involvement and psychological well-being? *American Psychologist*, 53, 1017–1031.

Li, Y., Pickles, A. and Savage, M. (2003) *Social Capital Dimensions, Social Trust and Quality of Life in Britain in the late 1990s*, Colchester, UK, University of Essex.

Ling, R., Anderson, B., Døffler, W. *et al.* (2004) Report of literature and data review, including conceptual framework and implications for IST (D6). *SOCQUIT Project Deliverable*, Delft, TNO-STB.

Ling, R., Yttri, B., Anderson, B. and Diduca, D. (2002) Age, gender and social capital: Deliverable 7.4. *e-Living Deliverables*, e-Living Consortium.

Nie, N. (2001) Sociability, interpersonal relations, and the Internet. *American Behavioural Scientist*, 45, 420–435.

Nie, N.H. and Erbring, L. (2000) *Internet and Society: a Preliminary Report*, Stanford, CA, Stanford Institute for the Quantitative Study of Society.

Offe, C. and Fuchs, S. (2002) A decline of social capital? The German case. In Putnam, R.D. (ed.) *Democracies in Flux: the Evolution of Social Capital in Contemporary Society*, Oxford, Oxford University Press.

Putnam, R.D. (2000) *Bowling Alone: the Collapse and Revival of American Community*, New York, Simon and Schuster.

Räsänen, P. (2004) Structural characteristics of 'communicative' Internet use in Europe. *Inequality and Stratification: Broadening the Comparative Scope of the Research.* Committee on Social Stratification (RC28) of the International Sociological Association. Rio de Janeiro.

Rogers, E.M. (1995) *Diffusion of Innovations*, New York, USA, The Free Press.

Scheepers, P., Te Grotenhuis, M. and Gelissen, J. (2002) Welfare states and dimensions of social capital: cross-national comparisons of social contacts in European countries. *European Societies*, 4, 185–207.

Thomas, F., Haddon, L., Gilligan, R., Heinzmann, P. and De Gournay, C. (2004) Cultural factors shaping the experience of ICTs: an exploratory review. In Haddon, L. (ed.) *COST Action 269: International Collaborative Research. Cross-cultural Differences and Cultures of Research*, Brussels, COST Office.

Van Bavel, R., Punie, Y., Burgelman, J.-C., Tuomi, I. and Clements, B. (2003) *ICTs and Social Capital in the Knowledge Society*. Report on a Joint DG JRC/DG Employment Workshop, 3–4 November. Sevilla, IPTS.

Van Oorschot, W. and Arts, W. (2004) The social capital of European welfare states: the crowding out hypothesis revisited. RC19 Conference *Welfare State Restructuring: Processes and Social Outcomes*, Paris.

Wellman, B., Haase, A.Q., Witte, J. and Hampton, K. (2001) Does the Internet increase, decrease, or supplement social capital? Social networks, participation, and community commitment. *American Behavioral Scientist*, 45, 436–455.

14 ICTs and growth potential

Jochen Dehio and Rainer Graskamp

Introduction

As a result of the rapid worldwide expansion and use of telecommunications networks, the Internet has broadened the potential of the exchange of information and goods significantly. Most of the entire economic and social system will be affected by this development (see, e.g., Bosworth and Triplett, 2000; Jorgenson and Stiroh, 2000; Oliner and Sichel, 2000; David, 2001; Nordhaus, 2001). In Germany, the Internet is becoming firmly established as a mass medium in a similar way as it is in the USA. This affects, on the one hand, the areas of communications (email, chats, etc.), information (news, databases, advertisements, etc.), as well as entertainment (music, videos, PC games, online casinos, etc.), and, on the other hand, 'electronic commerce'. E-commerce represents one of the most important applications based on information and communications technologies. Therefore, this chapter focuses on the overall economic effects of e-commerce and their implications for a long-lasting growth. This is also of prominent interest with respect to the bursting of the speculative bubble of the technology stock markets in 2000. In this context, the following questions needed to be answered:

- What role does e-commerce play in the optimisation of production processes, the reduction in transaction costs and, ultimately, in overall economic growth?
- Is Germany lagging behind in the use of new technology in comparison to other countries?
- If that were the case, which supporting macroeconomic policies to foster the future development of the use of ICT, and e-commerce in particular, should come into consideration?

Against this background, an international comparison between Germany and the USA, the leading nation in the world in the use of e-commerce, is carried out. Consequently, this chapter is structured as follows. First, a definition of e-commerce will be given. Then, some results of selected market studies and our own estimates with respect to the volume and effects of e-commerce are presented. In the subsequent sections, some proposals for policy interventions to support the use of e-commerce are discussed.

Definition of e-commerce

Generally, e-commerce is understood as the exchange of goods and services via electronic networks, mainly via the Internet. Along with online trade in goods, the provision of services via the Internet, such as online banking, online booking or online auctions fall into this category. For statistical purposes, e-commerce comprises all trade activities conducted via the Internet, regardless of whether the billing takes place online or not, and of how the respective product is delivered. This exceeds the mere electronic invitation of an online deal and the pure initiation of a transaction. These activities lead to the formation of more-or-less closed user groups, to a rising business volume, and to the formulation of standards for contracts and appropriate business conduct.

In principle, one can distinguish between three types of transactions:

- Business-to-Business (B2B): business relations between enterprises;
- Business-to-Consumer (B2C): business relations between enterprises and consumers;
- E-government: government services via electronic networks.

In B2B, interactions among enterprises via the so-called virtual 'market places' can be made online. Until now, B2B trade has been of greater importance, especially in branches with standardised products like electronics, cars and energy, as well as in the chemical industry, and in some service sectors (financial services, trade, etc.). An expansion into other branches is conceivable in the near future.

Besides the online sales of goods sent to the consumers (books, CDs, DVDs, hardware, software, cars, equipment, clothing, food, etc.), B2C also deals with a range of services (travel bookings, online banking, online stock brokerage, online auctions, etc.). B2C trade focuses on retail trading, as well as on areas of finance, communications and information. E-government aims to improve the information and data exchange within public administration. Furthermore, citizens are enabled to carry out certain administrative tasks via the Internet.

Results of selected market studies

To assess whether the introduction of e-commerce has led to additional economic activity, an overview of selected market studies will be given in the following paragraph.

Prices of PCs and Internet access are continuously declining because of the qualitative and quantitative expansion of content in the Internet, and the worldwide increased intensity of competition in the computer and telecommunications sector. Most forecasts conclude that these processes will lead to substantially enhanced growth rates. We have investigated the differences in the general labour productivity performance of the USA and Germany (see Table 14.1).

Various studies have provided different assessments of the worldwide e-commerce sales level. ActivMedia Research assumed that the sales worldwide are about 300 billion USD in the year 2001, whereas Goldman Sachs estimates the e-commerce sales at 1.2 trillion USD (NFO Infratest, 2001: 219). These differences arise because it is often disputable whether an activity should count as e-commerce or not. Nevertheless, the different studies give at least a rough impression of the quantitative importance of electronic trade.

Below, a study of eMarketer will be discussed in more detail (eMarketer, 2001; an overview of the results is given by NFO Infratest 2001). According to this study, worldwide e-commerce sales amounted to about 550 billion USD in the year 2001. With a share of 70 per cent, the USA has by far the highest share in worldwide e-commerce sales, though this share is decreasing. Asia and Europe score sales shares of 14 per cent and 12.5 per cent, respectively. In all regions of the world, B2B trade dominates the sales shares in this market. Consequently, the share of B2B trade in the whole e-commerce market in 2001 has even increased compared to the previous year, from just fewer than 80 per cent to approximately 82 per cent. Not only in the short term, but also in the long term the e-commerce growth will be dominated by B2B trade. The share of B2B in relation to the whole e-commerce market may rise to about 90 per cent in the medium term.

According to the calculations displayed in Table 14.2, in 2001 Germany was at the leading edge of the e-commerce market in Europe, with sales of about nineteen billion USD. The German share of worldwide e-commerce sales amounted to 3.5 per cent. Nevertheless, in relation to the gross output

Table 14.1 Productivity in the non-farm private business sector (annual average growth rates in per cent)

Growth rate	Germany		USA	
	Productivity		Productivity	
	Hourly	Labour	Hourly	Labour
1970–1980	4.0	2.9	1.9	1.2
1980–1990	2.9	2.1	2.0	1.3
1990–2000	2.7	2.0	2.0	1.6
1995–2000	3.0	2.1	3.2	2.5

Note
Author's computations; see Dehio *et al.* (2003).

Table 14.2 Projection of the trends in e-commerce sales until the year 2010

	2001	2010
E-commerce sales in USD		
Germany	19	700
USA	390	3,500
World	550	7,000
Share of worldwide e-commerce sales in per cent		
Germany	3.5	10
USA	71	50
E-commerce sales in per cent of gross national output		
Germany	0.6	14.5
USA	2.2	14.1
World	1.1	8.1
E-commerce sales per resident in USD		
Germany	230	8,650
USA	1,350	11,350
World	90	1,050

Source: Calculations of Dehio and Graskamp (2002).

per resident, as well as e-commerce sales per resident, Germany lags considerably behind the USA, which scored e-commerce sales of about 390 billion USD in the year 2001. Whereas in 2001 Germany's share of e-commerce sales in relation to total gross output amounted to a little bit more than one-half percentage point (230 USD per resident), the share of the USA was already over 2 per cent (1,350 USD per resident).

Even though the gap between the USA and Europe will no doubt decrease, it might take a long time to close completely.

Prospects for the e-commerce trends

The precondition for a comprehensive expansion of e-commerce is the supply of an appropriate infrastructure for Internet use and the provision of easy Internet access. In the coming years, the equipment of German households with Internet connections is likely to be characterised by fast growth, which will level off later. Eventually, the share of households with Internet connections will asymptotically approach the maximum equipment level of 100 per cent (Figure 14.1).

Below, the potential medium-term growth of the e-commerce market is estimated for the USA, Germany and the world up to the year 2010. The data for the year 2001 (see Table 14.2) are based on the estimate of e-commerce sales by eMarketer. Compared with other studies, this definition of e-commerce is relatively restrictive (for example, Goldman Sachs assumes that the total sales volume for the year 2001 is more than twice as

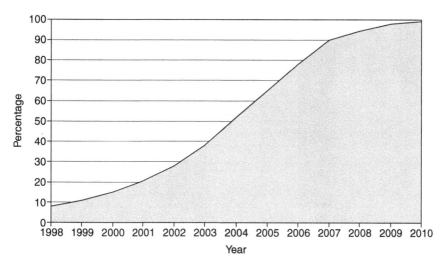

Figure 14.1 Projection of Internet use for Germany (share of households with Internet in per cent).

high; cited in NFO Infratest, 2001: 219). In the context of the projection, however, a lower annual growth rate than that assumed by various studies available is expected for some years. The projection takes into account some modified assumptions in comparison to several forecast studies of the e-commerce market, and relates these to population forecasts.

The results indicate that worldwide e-commerce sales could increase to seven trillion USD by the year 2010, which would mean an average annual growth rate of 28 per cent in the second half of the current decade. From 2001 to 2010, worldwide e-commerce sales will grow by one-third per year on average. The assumption of seven trillion USD in e-commerce sales in the year 2010 means that a sufficient coverage of broadband cable network must be available, through which the velocity in data transfer can be significantly increased. Moreover, it is assumed that the Internet will have attained high security standards so that one of the greatest factors inhibiting its use for e-commerce can be eliminated.

Furthermore, it is assumed that Germany's share of worldwide e-commerce sales will increase to 10 per cent by the year 2010, while the share of the USA will decrease to 50 per cent by 2010. Consequently, e-commerce sales in Germany will amount to 700 billion USD in 2010, while in the USA sales will amount to 3.5 trillion USD. Thus, by 2010, German e-commerce sales would increase much faster than in the USA, mainly due to different starting levels.

The share of worldwide e-commerce sales in world gross production value, according to the projection will amount to 8 per cent in the year 2010 (Figure 14.2). If one relates the e-commerce sales to the number of

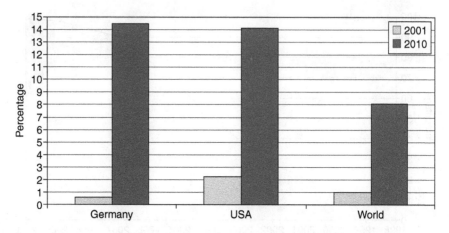

Figure 14.2 E-commerce sales in per cent of the gross output value.

residents – with the assumption of 1.1 per cent average annual growth in the world population – it becomes clear that per-capita sales in the next ten years will increase more than tenfold.

By world standards, however, e-commerce sales will only have relatively limited importance by the end of the current decade. On the other hand, in the industrialised countries, e-commerce will reach considerable proportions, even with respect to production as well as per-capita sales. In this context, it can be assumed that the rate of e-commerce sales will be higher in Germany than in the USA in the next few years, due to a catch-up process resulting from the less-advanced development of the German e-commerce market.

Overall economic effects of e-commerce

There is doubt, however, as to whether sales is a good indicator of e-commerce market trends, since the amount of sales does not permit any conclusions on the real national economic implications. However, even if it is difficult to predict the growth effects of e-commerce in particular, one can estimate the growth effects of ICT use in general. For that purpose, we estimate growth effects of ICT by assessing quantitatively the order of magnitude of the overall economic growth effects of B2B. With the help of input–output analysis, the effects of B2B trade on the growth rate of gross domestic product have been calculated for the period of 2000 to 2010 (Brookes and Wahhaj, 2001). The analysis is based on the assumption that the B2B trade will be one-third of the output by the end of the current decade. Furthermore, a calculation is made of the extent to which cost reductions result and are reflected in the corresponding reduction of input prices. The USA, Germany, Japan, France and Great Britain are included in this analysis.

For the period mentioned above, the contribution of B2B to GDP average annual growth rate was calculated in comparison to the contribution without B2B for all countries included in this analysis. For Germany, the result was an additional growth of 0.4 percentage points per year; for the USA, less than one-quarter of a percentage point, and for Japan, France and Great Britain, 0.3 percentage points per year. This is clearly not large. Nevertheless, e-commerce will probably exert a wide range of effects in the years to come, which might also influence growth positively, though in ways that are currently difficult to predict. Among the effects that are most likely are the opening-up of new markets, the optimisation of the cost structure, the increase in productivity, the intensification of competition and the improvement of market transparency. The basis of economic action in the future will no longer be the classical value-added chain (input supplier–intermediary–producer–distributor–dealer–final consumer), but a value-added-creation network (Urchs, 2000: 72). With this network, there will no longer be linear, but multidimensional relationships between the participating actors. The additional utility of such a network does not necessarily correspond to the increase in the number of users, but actual use may rise disproportionately. The resulting external network effects cannot be easily verified empirically.

Furthermore, many aspects of individual or social welfare, which may be enhanced by e-commerce, are difficult to quantify. These aspects comprise ease of information access, time savings in the ordering of goods, increased entertainment and communication possibilities, or positive ecological consequences caused by savings in the packaging of digitised products, etc. Consequently, they will not be reflected in the national accounts. Accordingly, the gross domestic product as an indicator of social welfare will provide an underestimation of the positive effects of the Internet and e-commerce.

The scope for policy interventions

There are causes for concern that the use of e-commerce by small and medium-sized German enterprises is too moderate at present. Many of them never use the Internet for the intermediate trade between enterprises (B2B) or as a channel of distribution (B2C). Obviously, there are still considerable impediments, such as:

- security problems (e.g. with online payment);
- implementation costs;
- the integration of e-business applications into existing IT-systems;
- shortfalls in know-how at both the management and the specialist level.

It may still take some time, therefore, before e-market forces alter the economy significantly. In the following areas, therefore, suitable conditions should be created to facilitate the acceleration of development.

Legal and tax hurdles are further problems. It is the primary task of the individual economic actors to create conditions in the areas that facilitate rapid market penetration of e-commerce (Scheuer *et al.*, 2003). The Government must act in the future to create greater legal security in order to facilitate dynamic growth in e-commerce sales. The European eCommerce Guidelines represent the legal framework for cross-border electronic trade. One of the essential regulations of these guidelines is the 'country of origin' principle. According to this, the activities of an enterprise on the Internet are subject to the legal provisions of the country in which it has its headquarters and its branch establishment. This provision is not without problems regarding Internet enterprises, because valid legal regulations in the destination country could possibly be dodged, since it is relatively easy for an Internet enterprise to move their servers to a country that offers relatively favourable legal framework conditions for the respective business purpose.

In respect to the payment of value added tax (VAT), it is not the country of origin principle, but rather the country of destination principle which is effective in the EU. According to this, taxes must be paid in the country in which the customer is residing. At present, third countries do not have to pay any VAT within the scope of B2C e-commerce. However, the EU intends to charge VAT in the future for such products of B2C online trade offered by suppliers from non-EU countries in order to reduce competitive disadvantages for EU countries. In this regard, the absence of tax harmonisation within the EU is problematic, with the consequence that the tax rates in the individual EU countries are different. However, in order to keep the bureaucratic expenditure for the taxation of online goods as low as possible, provisions in the EU are intended to oblige third countries in the future to choose a freely determinable EU country as a so-called country of registration through which VAT will be paid. The country of registration will then subsequently transfer the VAT to which each member country is entitled.[1]

Conclusions

For e-commerce success, one expects the development of new distribution and procurement channels, a reduction in transaction, distribution and marketing costs and therefore lower input and consumer prices. Consequently, it will lead to an increase in productivity, competitiveness, market transparency and, finally, in real income.

Depending on the particular data, worldwide e-commerce sales in 2001 amounted to just 1 or 2 per cent of world gross output value. However, the growth rate of e-commerce sales will be very high in the coming years. According to the results of our projection, the share of worldwide e-commerce sales in world production will be 8 per cent in 2010. Germany's share in worldwide e-commerce sales will increase considerably, since Germany already has a highly modern network infrastructure, it is a leader with respect to B2B-platforms, and has large growth reserves in the field of mobile communications. By the year 2010, Germany – according to our own projections – will further close the gap with the USA. Thus, for the period 2001 to 2010, the result for Germany was an additional growth of 0.4 percentage points per year on the one side, and for the USA less than a quarter of a percentage point on the other.

To meet the expected trends in e-commerce sales, especially successful integration of e-business applications in existing IT systems, more legal security in worldwide trade via the Internet, and the implementation of internationally accepted industry standards for online transactions are necessary preconditions.

Note

1 However, the problems in connection with the collection of value added tax for B2C e-commerce will probably only be solved satisfactorily after tax harmonisation within the EU has been accomplished.

Bibliography

Bosworth, B. and Triplett, J.E. (2000) *What's New about the New Economy? IT, Economic Growth and Productivity*, Brookings Institution, 1–31.

Brookes, M. and Wahhaj, Z. (2001) The economic effects of business to business Internet activity. *National Institute Economic Review*, 175(1), 95–108.

David, P. (2001) Productivity growth prospects and the new economy in historical perspective. *European Economic Growth: The Impact of New Technologies*, EIB-Papers, 6(1), 41–62.

Dehio, J. and Graskamp, R. (2002) Perspektiven der Internetwirtschaft. *RWI-Mitteilungen*, 53(1–4), 41–64.

Dehio, J., Döhrn, R., Graskamp, R. *et al.* (2003) *New Economy – The German Perspective*. RWI: Schriften 70, Berlin, Duncker & Humblot.

Jorgenson, D.W. and Stiroh, K.J. (2000) U.S. economic growth at the industry level. *American Economic Review*, 90(2), 161–167.

NFO Infratest (Hrsg.) (2001) *Monitoring Informationswirtschaft. 3. Faktenbericht 2001*, Band I, München.

Nordhaus, W.D. (2001) Productivity growth and the new economy. *NBER Working Paper 8096*, Cambridge, MA.

Oliner, S.D. and Sichel, D.E. (2000) The resurgence of growth in the late 1990s: is information technology the story? *Journal of Economic Perspectives*, 14(4), 3–22.

Scheuer, M., Dehio, J., Graskamp, R. and Rothgang, M. (2003) Allemagne, pénurie de specialistes en nouvelles technologies: la nécessaire réforme de la formation professionnelle. *Formation Emploi*, 82, 33–46.

Urchs, O. (2000) Von der Kommunikation zur eCommunication: Neue Trends im Online-Marketing. *Gesellschaft für Konsumforschung*, 59–73.

15 The relative gains from computer usage and skills

A gender perspective

Malcolm Brynin

Introduction

It is generally assumed that since roughly midway through the second half of the twentieth century, there has been a generally rising demand for high-level technical and management skills. This in turn raises the value of education and of technical skills (e.g. Bell, 1973: 144; Gallie, 1994; Green *et al.*, 2000). Information and communication technologies (ICTs) might play an important part here because of the huge take-up of all aspects of computer technology in production processes, but also through the widespread consumption of computer-based entertainment information and communication systems. OECD evidence suggests a strong link between ICT developments and national economic growth (OECD, 2003). Several researchers have shown that a wage premium accrues to users of computers at work (Krueger, 1993; Green, 1998; Arabsheibani *et al.*, 2004). Moreover, we need not assume this relates solely to the skills required to operate computers. For instance, desk-top publishing transfers the processes of organisation and design previously managed by a small number of highly skilled people to a wider set of users. The computer is merely the vehicle for this process. Even if the new skills are less than those of the specialist workers who are replaced, the new operators nevertheless need skills, both in the substance of what they are doing and in the operation of the computer itself.

Such technology-based change has major distributional implications. It offers new employment chances for many, but people who lack the requisite skills have highly reduced opportunities. In the case of gender, however, the balance is uncertain. It has been argued that traditional male control over the operation and maintenance of technology, as well as over the associated skills, puts women at a considerable disadvantage in employment (Cockburn, 1985). Computerisation might provide a further basis for this. It is, for instance, well known that men predominate in the more complex functions of the computer (Panteli *et al.*, 2001). Nevertheless, women are in a good position to benefit from the expansion of ICTs as they predominate in some sectors where computer usage is widespread. Does the growth of the new ICTs provide a chance for women to acquire and apply new skills, and thus reduce gender inequality, or does it serve to exclude women from good employment opportunities?

Gender and the computer premium

There are some empirical grounds for denying the 'technology bias thesis', as briefly described above. Increasing wage differentials in Britain and the USA are viewed as a response to growing demand for high skill levels and to persistent skill shortages (Nickell and Bell, 1995), but Nickell and Bell note that *only* in Britain and the USA was there a substantial fall in the relative wages of the unskilled, and then only during the 1980s (1995: 51). In a number of countries, the rise in skilled non-manual work has been matched by an increase in unskilled non-manual labour (Esping-Andersen, 1993). At the same time, there is a growing economics literature on the effects of educational inflation and overqualification (e.g. Borghans and de Grip, 2000). The more specific thesis of the computer premium has also been contested (DiNardo and Pischke, 1997; Entorf and Kramarz, 1997; Borghans and ter Weel, 2004). For instance, more skilled workers might be asked to use computers at work, so that any wage effect that appears to be associated with computer usage reflects the skills of the user. The same might apply to motivations or attitudes.

This last point would mean there is no skill enhancement from the use of computers at work but simply a new skill utilisation whereby more skilled or motivated workers are allocated work on (or alternatively are attracted to) computing work. However, whether or not the *use* of computers enhances wages, we should certainly expect this to be the case with computer skills, and in principle we should expect this to be equal for both men and women. That is, computers might attract more skilled workers, but these skills should attract the same wage enhancement for both men and women. There are good reasons to expect this. For instance, even if higher-level usage such as software design is predominantly male, the extent of traditional male control over technology has surely changed with computerisation. In general, skilled female work has risen relative to that of men (Esping-Andersen, 1993), while the more specific use of computers is spread relatively evenly across the genders (Wagner *et al.*, 2002; Brynin, 2006).

Are differences in attitudes to technology likely to be important in employment? Again, there is reason to think that computerisation should change this. It has often been argued that women are less in tune with technology than men (e.g. Turkle, 1984). Indeed, this is implicit and sometimes even explicit in Cockburn's critique of the male hold over the benefits of technological progress (1985). Thus, whatever the relationship between computer skills and wages, it is possible that skills are strongly correlated with attitudes to technology, so that any effect on wages that we observe really reflects the effect of attitudinal factors. If women fare worse, this could be because they have the wrong attitudes. However, I have argued elsewhere (Brynin, 2006) that attitudes to computer technology vary far more by experience with computers (whatever the nature of the causal relationship) than by gender. If there is a wage difference between men and women in respect of computer skills, this is not because of differential attitudes.

None of this need mean that women have gained from computerisation. It is possible that some uses of computers do not demand higher-level skills but, instead, serve to control or simplify labour processes. It is possible that women tend not to have access (or acquire the skills to access) the most productive technologies. Technological advance is often accompanied by increased job segregation and by a more intensive use of relatively cheap female labour in the affected sector (Goldin, 1990). When skilled 'making through' of garments was replaced by computer-assisted design and manufacture, the new operators – increasingly female – were constrained by the machine to perform relatively standardised tasks, rather than being able to use creative skills, which were now effectively redundant (Webster, 1996). In the case of the work computer, if women predominate in the more routine uses of this technology, then computerisation could have a negative effect on their wages. This suggests that, in respect of the computer-wage premium, the positive productivity argument has been treated at too general a level. Qualitative accounts pick out more clearly the considerable variation in complexity, and therefore in the implicit gains from this, of work with computers. In an early view, Albin and Appelbaum note that computerised systems have created 'multi-activity, skilled clerical positions' which can result in a 'para-professionalisation' of clerical work (1988: 144); but, at the same time, they observe that the use of computers to standardise work processes is likely to be associated with more casual use of labour, which in turn is likely to apply more to women than to men (1988: 151). Many studies suggest a wide variety of computer usages by women; some detract from the use of skills, some make little difference, others add to skills requirements (Kirkup, 1992; Webster, 1993; McLoughlin and Clark, 1994; Grint and Woolgar, 1997; Woodfield, 2000).

This does not mean that some women have not gained from the use of computers. Where these generate a productivity gain for employers, then the women who use them might also gain. However, this productivity could derive from the application of skills or from the intensification of labour. Those working in occupations where the latter is more likely to occur might gain relatively little, so that any advantages are occupationally skewed. As women are likely to be more concentrated in occupations characterised by a labour-intensive usage of computers, it is possible that many women either have limited opportunity to use computer skills or gain a limited return for whatever skills they have.

The data

What are women's computer skills relative to men, and how far do they gain from these, relative to men? This is tested here using data from the e-Living household panel survey. The survey, funded by the EU's IST Programme, was undertaken towards the end of 2001 and repeated in a second wave in 2002. Interviews were with one person per household (though some subsidiary interviews were undertaken with partners in wave two). The average response rate in wave one was fairly low, because telephone interviewing produces low response rates, at around 40 per cent across five countries (though considerably higher in Bulgaria, where the interviews were face-to-face). A high proportion of wave-one respondents, averaging over 65 per cent, were re-interviewed in wave two.

The survey included questions which asked specifically about computer skills. These were whether the respondent knows how to: download files from the Web, construct a Web page, email a file, cut and paste, reboot, or copy files to a floppy. This strategy of asking about specific computer skills is perhaps unique, though the British Skills Survey asks respondents a more general question – whether they are able to perform various computer functions effectively. The latter is a survey of those in work, while e-Living, being a general household survey, can be used to say something about the general distribution of computer skills.

In addition to the skills question, the survey asked about computer access and usage, both at home and at work, as well as questions on attitudes to computers. Through the latter, it is possible to establish a 'technophobia' score (where a high number indicates more negative attitudes). This measure is based on a scale of responses to five statements, asking how far people are in agreement with them. They include items like 'computers are intimidating to use' and 'I am interested in new technologies'.

Results

Computer skills and education

Table 15.1 shows that men have higher levels of computer skills, as measured above, than women do. It also shows these differences by levels of education (for three selected levels of educational achievement). Computer skills unsurprisingly vary by education. However, this relationship itself varies only slightly by gender. In some countries, those with no qualifications have hardly any computer skills, which seem to be acquired mostly at school (higher education adding only slightly to these, on average). The level of skills is high at all educational levels in Germany, though, which suggests that the educational system there is able to transmit these skills more effectively than in other countries. The main point to observe, however, is that gender makes little difference to these relationships. At all levels, men have higher skill scores. The differential equally does not seem to depend greatly on educational level.

Computer skills correlate with attitudes to computers, but not especially highly. The correlation ranges between 0.29 and 0.48 across the six

Table 15.1 Mean scores on PC knowledge at three levels of educational achievement (sample aged sixty or under)

Educational achievement		Britain	Italy	Germany	Norway	Bulgaria	Israel
None	Men	1.8	0.8	4.3	n/a	0.0	1.6
	Women	1.3	0.1	3.1	n/a	0.0	1.1
School-leaving	Men	4.8	3.9	4.8	3.8	0.8	3.0
	Women	3.3	3.2	3.4	2.9	0.6	2.5
Degree	Men	4.9	4.2	4.7	5.1	2.1	4.4
	Women	4.0	3.5	3.4	4.2	2.0	3.4

Note
Not applicable (n/a) indicates cell sizes too small.

countries for those in work, but from 0.38 to 0.54 for all those aged sixty or under. Thus, it cannot be assumed that having positive attitudes is associated with higher levels of skills, though it seems likely that those with higher skills must generally have positive attitudes.

The wage effects of computer skills

What is the gender distribution of computer skills in employment? Table 15.2 shows the average score for both men and women in each country: (1) for the entire sample in each country; (2) for those in work; (3) for those who use a computer at work; and (4) for those who use a computer either at work

Table 15.2 Mean scores on PC knowledge

		Britain	Italy	Germany	Norway	Bulgaria	Israel
1 All	Men	2.9	2.5	3.0	3.9	0.5^{ns}	2.7
	Women	2.0	1.5	1.8	2.7	0.6	2.1
2 In work	Men	3.3	3.0	3.5	4.3	0.7	2.9^{ns}
	Women	2.8	2.6	2.7	3.5	1.1	2.8
3 Work PC	Men	4.4	4.3	4.4	4.9	3.6	4.5
	Women	3.8	3.9	3.7	4.2	3.1	4.0
4 Work/home PC	Men	4.2	4.2	4.3	4.8	3.8	3.8
	Women	3.5	3.8	3.4	4.0	3.2	3.3

Notes
ns = gender difference not statistically significant at $p < 0.05$, all others highly significant.
Sample sizes vary by the specification: summed over the countries these are:

1 7,708 men, 10,014 women;
2 4,633 men, 4,819 women;
3 3,001 men, 3,298 women;
4 4,654 men, 5,230 women.

or at home. In virtually all cases, men score better. The difference is not always great, but it is nearly always highly statistically significant, and given the limited range of the scale (1–6, but including zeros in the first two specifications for those who do not use a computer), is substantively significant too. Men always seem to know more about computers than women do.

Having shown that men have, on average, higher computer skills, it seems reasonable to assume that men enter the labour market somewhat better armed in this respect. This is perhaps a practical more than a psychological advantage, as gender differences in attitudes are of little consequence. Does this practical advantage, whatever its cause, confer any real advantage in employment?

To test this, a regression analysis has been undertaken (using ordinary least squares) with wages as the dependent variable (in fact, the log of gross monthly wages). The models are quite simple. Explanatory variables are those which say something about the individual (age and education), those which say something about the job they do (occupation, industry, hours worked and the extent of job autonomy), plus the critical variable, computer skills. The aim is to see if the effect of these skills is, first positive, and second, whether it is higher for men or for women. Separate models are therefore run for each gender (though an alternative of including both plus an interaction term with skills is equally possible). This is done in two ways. The effects are tested in each of the six countries separately, but before this, a test with a bigger sample, pooling some of the countries, is undertaken. This is because non-response on wages (a universal problem) reduces the sample to quite small sizes in each country once we also divide by gender. However, only the four most culturally similar countries have been selected for this purpose, excluding Bulgaria and Israel, as it is possible that the relationship of the control variables with the dependent variable would be different in these cases. The results of the pooled analysis (treating Norway as the reference category) are shown in Table 15.3.

Taking all those in work first, it is possible to see that there is a small gender gap in the effects of computer skills on wages. This does not mean the differential is unimportant. As wages are expressed in log form, the coefficients can be read as roughly the percentage increase in wages derived from each increment in the skills scale. Each skill increment makes a 4 per cent difference in wages for men, 3 per cent for women. Cumulatively this difference is of note, as there are six increments to the scale. Moreover, as the standard errors are very small, it is unlikely that the estimates for men and women might overlap in practice. Having said this, the model does not demonstrate a fundamental gender divide. Moreover, the result conflates two things – the effect of having skills in the use of a computer, and the effect of using a computer at all. Most of those who do not use a computer at work will score zero on the skills scale. Thus zero does not mean really having low skills but, rather, not using a computer (although it is possible that non-use at work could be compensated for through familiarity with computers in other settings such as the home). For this reason, the analysis was re-run for

Table 15.3 OLS regression coefficients, showing effect of computer skills plus controls on log of monthly gross wages (four countries pooled)

	All in work		Those who use a work PC	
	Men	*Women*	*Men*	*Women*
Age	0.09***	0.05***	0.08***	0.05***
Age squared	−0.001***	0.000	−0.001***	0.000
Has degree	0.16***	0.20***	0.17***	0.20***
Managerial	0.30***	0.38***	0.18**	0.12
Technical	0.20***	0.27***	0.10	0.01
Clerical	0.13*	0.23***	−0.03	−0.04
Service	0.08	0.02	0.02	−0.13
Craft	0.13**	0.14*	0.04	−0.04
Production	−0.01	0.06	0.04	0.07
Trade	−0.10***	−0.11***	−0.04	−0.12***
Finance	0.05	0.03	0.05	0.04
Public	−0.14***	−0.04	−0.11**	−0.07*
Hours	0.01***	0.03***	0.01***	0.03***
Autonomy	0.11***	0.10***	0.12***	0.08***
Britain	−0.12***	−0.25***	−0.05	−0.19***
Italy	−0.62***	−0.69***	−0.55***	−0.67***
Germany	−0.25***	−0.41***	−0.16***	−0.32***
PC skills	0.04***	0.03***	0.04***	0.01(*)
Constant	5.05***	5.19***	5.46***	5.61***
R^2	0.53	0.63	0.47	0.57
N	2,204	2,162	1,478	1,495

Notes
*** $p < 0.001$, ** $p < 0.01$, * $p < 0.05$, (*) $p < 0.1$.
Reference category for occupation (managerial/professional-craft) is 'elementary' and 'other'; for industry (trade/transport-public) it is 'other'.

the group of workers who do use a computer at work. This result is shown in the second pair of columns.

This produces a fairly arbitrary sample – those in work and who happen to use a computer at work – which changes the coefficients for some occupations and industries, and also the coefficients for Germany, across the two models, quite substantially. Yet it does not change the skills coefficient for men. Thus, through dropping the zero values for skills, it seems that it is not so much using the computer at work which makes the difference for men but having skills. In the case of women, in contrast, there is a big diminution in the effect, and therefore a sizeable increase in the gender gap. It seems that it is precisely usage of a computer that makes the difference for women, not skills. Their work is probably either often in rather routine tasks requiring little in the way of skills, or in jobs where whatever skills are applied are regarded less highly than other skills.

Finally, the gender differences for each country are shown in Table 15.4, but excluding Bulgaria as a result of insufficient numbers and without showing all the controls.

In only one case, in Norway, do computer skills obtain a higher return for women than for men, but this applies more to use of a computer than to actual skills, as in the second specification the effect in Norway is reversed. At least in the first specification there is at least sometimes equality for women; in the second, though, we nearly always see inequality.

Conclusion

The expansion of ICTs encourages the learning of computer-related skills, whether out of curiosity, to satisfy other personal preferences, or to undertake paid work. Many jobs now require some familiarity with computers. It seems reasonable that these skills, because they usually generate higher productivity than the same work undertaken without the use of computers (otherwise, why use them?), should simultaneously generate some sort of wage premium; and, even if mere use of a computer does not, surely the skills required to use a computer must do. Indeed, the effect that is supposed to derive from the computer itself is disputed partly because it is indistinguishable from the effect of the skills the individual brings to the job. However, in the case of computers these skills must always be important because they cannot easily be applied elsewhere. They relate solely to use of a computer, even if they are correlated with other skills.

As the use of computers is fairly evenly spread by gender, it might be expected that women gain as much as men do from the use of the computer, but more particularly from the skills they as individuals bring to the computer. This perhaps would be the case if the types of work done by men and

Table 15.4 OLS regression coefficients, showing effect of computer skills on log of monthly gross wages in five countries

	All in work		Those who use a work PC	
	Men	Women	Men	Women
Britain	0.05***	0.01	0.04(*)	0.00
Italy	0.03*	0.03***	0.02	0.01
Germany	0.05***	0.04***	0.04***	0.03(*)
Norway	0.02**	0.03***	0.03*	0.02*
Israel	0.05*	0.05***	0.04	0.04**

Notes
*** $p < 0.001$, ** $p < 0.01$, * $p < 0.05$, (*) $p < 0.1$.
N, model 1: Britain 616 men, 658 women; Italy 343 men, 330 women; Germany 503 men, 450 women; Norway 815 men, 799 women; Israel 349 men, 625 women.
Model 2: Britain 392 men, 431 women; Italy 199 men, 212 women; Germany 317 men, 279 women; Norway 617 men, 612 women; Israel 176 men, 373 women.

women do not differ. It is possible that women tend to undertake more routine computer tasks than men, which would almost certainly be reflected in a lesser computer premium. Some of this would be reflected in the types of jobs women are likely to have, such as clerical work, but it might also be the case that what skills they have are under-rewarded. The analysis of data from six mostly European countries, which uses an innovative definition of computer skills, shows that women on average have somewhat lesser skills (though this appears not to be reinforced by any substantial differential in attitudes to computers). Yet the margin is not great, and is unlikely to explain the fact that women obtain a lower wage premium from their computer skills than men do. This differential applies even where only those who actually use a computer are included in the analysis. It means that every increment in skills that a man has earns a greater premium than the very same increment that a woman has. The skills are differentially rewarded.

Acknowledgements

The author is grateful to the IST Programme of the EU's Fifth Framework Programme for the grant for e-Living, which enabled both data collection and research based on this. The work reported above also forms part of a programme of research funded by the Economic and Social Research Council, whose assistance is gratefully acknowledged.

References

Albin, P. and Applebaum, E. (1988) The computer rationalization of work: implications for women workers. In Jensen, J., Hagen, E. and Reddy, C. (eds) *Feminization of the Labour Force: Paradoxes and Promises*, Cambridge, Polity, pp. 137–152.

Arabsheibani, G.R., Emami, J.M. and Marin, A. (2004) The impact of computer use on earnings in the UK. *Scottish Journal of Political Economy*, 51, 82–94.

Bell, D. (1973) *The Coming of Post-industrial Society: a Venture in Social Forecasting*, New York, Basic Books.

Borghans, L. and de Grip, A. (2000) *The Overeducated Worker? The Economics of Skill Utilization*, Cheltenham, E. Elgar.

Borghans, L. and ter Weel, B. (2004) Are computer skills the new basic skills? The returns to computer, writing and math skills in Britain. *Labour Economics*, 11, 85–98.

Brynin, M. (2006) The neutered computer. In Kraut, B., Brynin, M. and Kiesler, S. (eds) *Domesticating Information Technology*, Oxford, Oxford University Press.

Cockburn, C. (1985) *Machinery of Dominance: Women, Men and Technical Know-how*, London, Pluto.

DiNardo, J.E. and Pischke, J.S. (1997) The returns to computer use revisited: have pencils changed the wage structure too? *Quarterly Journal of Economics*, 112, 291–303.

Entorf, H. and Kramarz, F. (1997) Does unmeasured ability explain the higher wages of new technology workers? *European Economic Review*, 41, 1489–1509.

Esping-Andersen, G. (1993) *Changing Classes: Stratification and Mobility in Post-industrial Societies*, London, Sage.

Gallie, D. (1994) Patterns of skill change: upskilling, deskilling, or polarization? In Penn, R., Rose, M. and Rubery, J. (eds) *Skill and Occupational Change*, Oxford, Oxford University Press, pp. 41–76.

Goldin, C.D. (1990) *Understanding the Gender Gap: an Economic History of American Women*, New York, Oxford University Press.

Green, F. (1998) *The Value of Skills*, University of Kent.

Green, F., Ashton, D., Burchell, B., Davies, B. and Felstead, A. (2000) Are British workers becoming more skilled? In Borghans, L. and de Grip, A. (eds) *The Overeducated Worker? The Economics of Skill Utilization*, Cheltenham, E. Elgar, pp. 77–106.

Grint, K. and Woolgar, S. (1997) *The Machine at Work: Technology, Work and Organization*, Cambridge, Polity Press.

Kirkup, G. (1992) The social construction of computers: hammers or harpsichords? In Kirkup, G. and Keller, L. (eds) *Inventing Women: Science, Technology and Gender*, London, Polity Press, pp. 267–281.

Krueger, A.B. (1993) How computers have changed the wage structure: evidence from microdata, 1984–1989. *Quarterly Journal of Economics*, 108, 33–60.

McLoughlin, I. and Clark, J. (1994) *Technological Change at Work*, Buckingham, Open University Press.

Nickell, S. and Bell, B. (1995) The collapse in demand for the unskilled and unemployment across the OECD. *Oxford Review of Economic Policy*, 11, 40–62.

OECD (2003) *ICT and Economic Growth: Evidence from OECD Countries, Industries and Firms*, Paris, Organisation for Economic Co-operation and Development.

Panteli, N., Stack, J. and Ramsay, H. (2001) Gendered patterns in computing work in the late 1990s. *New Technology Work and Employment*, 16, 3–17.

Turkle, S. (1984) *The Second Self: Computers and the Human Spirit*, London, Granada.

Wagner, G., Pischner, R. and Haisken-deNew, J. (2002) The changing digital divide in Germany. In Wellman, B. and Haythornthwaite, C.A. (eds) *The Internet in Everyday Life*, Oxford, Blackwell, pp. 164–185.

Webster, J. (1993) Women's skills and word processors: gender issues in the development of the automated office. In Probert, B. and Wilson, B. (eds) *Pink Collar Blues: Work, Gender and Technology*, Carlton, Vic, Melbourne University Press, pp. 41–59.

Webster, J. (1996) *Shaping Women's Work: Gender, Employment and Information Technology*, London, Longman.

Woodfield, R. (2000) *Women, Work and Computing*, Cambridge, Cambridge University Press.

16 The use of ICTs in the workplace

Opening the black box

Bram Steijn and Kea Tijdens[1]

Introduction

So far, this book has argued that the use of information and communication technologies (ICTs) is paramount, in domestic as well as in work situations. In fact, its use has risen so dramatically that one may wonder whether the question, 'Do you use a computer at work?', is still an appropriate measure for the use of ICT at work. According to our research in the Netherlands, the percentage of ICT users – measured using the question, 'Do you use any kind of automated device in your work?' – increased from 74 per cent in 1994 to 80 per cent in 2000, and then to 84 per cent in 2001 and 89 per cent in 2002.

Measured in this way, computer use has not only ceased to be a real variable but, even more importantly, a wide range of different tasks and activities are obscured by such a crude indicator of computer use. Indeed, there is a huge difference between a checkout worker in a supermarket using an advanced scanner/terminal, a white-collar worker in a bank or office using a PC for word processing and the Internet, and a high-tech consultant involved with ICT applications: yet they all use a computer!

Limiting the concept of ICT to 'using or not using a computer' no longer seems to discriminate in a relevant way among various categories of workers. Further, in our view, a dichotomous variable of ICT use gives little insight into the *actual* use of ICT and its consequences: ICT use covers a range of hardware (not only the PC or laptop, but also the pocket computer, the mobile phone and – last but not least – computer guided production facilities and robots) and software programs (ranging from everyday word-processing or email applications to more complicated statistical programs and applications for production facilities). To get a more detailed understanding of the use of ICT in everyday working life, we therefore need to open the black box of the ICT concept. We approach this, in this chapter, by distinguishing three dimensions of ICT use: complexity, diversity and intensity. *Complexity* refers to the inherent difficulty of understanding or operating a distinct ICT hardware item or application. *Diversity* refers to the number of different pieces of hardware or applications workers use in their work situation. *Intensity* refers to the percentage of working time devoted to ICT use.

This chapter aims to gain a better understanding of the factors that drive ICT use at work with respect to these three dimensions. More precisely, our research aims to investigate which factors explain the differences in the complexity, diversity and intensity of ICT use. A greater insight into these factors will contribute to a better understanding of why different computer users might benefit in different ways from their use of the computer. It is probable, for instance, that people who work with more complex and more diverse computer applications will benefit to a greater extent from their use compared to less complex and more limited computer usages. In the next section we will discuss several factors that, according to our understanding of the literature, influence the use of ICT at work. The subsequent section gives details of the hypotheses we are investigating, the data used and how we measure the main concepts. The results of the analysis are discussed after this, followed by the major conclusions in the final section.

Factors explaining differences in ICT use at work

The analysis focuses on the effects of three different clusters of variables on computer use, namely: (1) individual; (2) job; and (3) workplace characteristics. Each cluster contains a range of variables. The following table lists all the variables we look at in our analysis, including the relationships we anticipate with ICT use.

Table 16.1 reveals the expected relationships, and are partly based on previous research. This has indicated that women use computers at work more intensively than men (Dolton and Makepeace, 2004; and also Andries *et al.*, 2002), but we also anticipate that women will generally use ICTs that are less complex and less diverse (Felstead *et al.*, 2002: 61 – findings from the UK). In a similar way, we also expect that older workers will use them in a less complex, less diverse but also in a less intensive way – although Andries *et al.* have shown that older workers are closing the gap with younger workers in

Table 16.1 Main variables and expected relationship with ICT use

Variables	ICT use
Gender	More intense, but less complex and diverse for women.
Age	Less complex, diverse and intense for older workers.
Educational level	More complex and more diverse for the higher educated.
Supervisory position	Less diverse and less intense for supervisory workers.
Labour contract	Less diverse and more intense for temporary workers.
Workplace size	More diverse and less intense in smaller workplaces.
Economic sector	Less complex, diverse and intense in social service sector.
Management practices/ production methods	Less complex, less diverse, more intense in organisations with less well-developed personnel management policies or where production is highly controlled.

computer use. As for job characteristics, ICT usage is different between workers with a permanent and those with a fixed-term contract (Felstead and Gallie, 2004). In the case of workplace characteristics, earlier research (Andries *et al.*, 2002) has shown a relationship between computer use and economic sector. Research has also revealed some effects of management practices and production concepts implemented within an organisation on the willingness of workers to acquire ICT competences, and on the actual level of these competences (Steijn and Tijdens, 2005; Tijdens and Steijn, 2005).

Hypotheses, sample, and operationalisation

This study investigates both the measurement and the determinants of ICT use at work. How can ICT use at work be characterised? Which factors determine it? The measurement of ICT use has to go beyond the common survey question, 'Do you use a computer at work?', because, today, more than 90 per cent of a workforce will probably say 'Yes'. Moreover, this question ignores the variety in ICT use at work. This is an issue of growing importance, given the rapidly increasing number of ICT users at work. The hypotheses formulated below therefore aim to detect which social factors influence this ICT usage.

Hypotheses

It is argued that ICT use can best be measured by taking into account the diversity of hardware and software used, the activities performed with the hardware and software, and the time spent on these activities. The following hypotheses will therefore be tested.

1   The heterogeneity of ICT use at work can be best measured using measures of the complexity, diversity and intensity of ICT use.

The discussion has indicated that a large number of factors could influence ICT use. These factors have been divided into three clusters of explanatory variables, notably individual characteristics, and job and workplace characteristics. Our main hypothesis is that all three types of variables are relevant in explaining differences with respect to the complexity, diversity and intensity of ICT usage. In other words, we expect that:

2   Differences in ICT use can be explained by differences in demographic, job and workplace characteristics.

With respect to workplace characteristics, we are, as discussed above, especially interested in the possibilities that organisations have to influence the complexity, diversity and intensity of the computer use of their workers. This leads to our third hypothesis.

*3　Within organisations with a Tayloristic, or highly controlled,
production structure, or with a less well-developed human resource
management (HRM) strategy, ICT usage will be less complex, less diverse
and more intense.*

These issues are important because they tell us a lot about the potential
welfare implications of computer usage. In general, a more complex, more
diverse and less intense computer usage will be characteristic for a more
favourable work situation. Clearly, computers are not an unequivocal sign of
the 'knowledge society'. They might allow the use of higher skills but they
might also be oppressive in terms of work routines. We can begin to unravel
some of these issues through a clearer focus on the three aspects of usage
described above.

Sample

For the analysis in this chapter, results from a Telepanel survey were used.
Designed to measure ICT use at work, this is a database of more than 2,000
households that are surveyed weekly through a computer connection (see
also Tijdens and Steijn, 2005). However, the sample is not biased in favour
of computer users, since non-computer-users either receive a computer or
use their television screen for completing the questionnaire so that they can
be fairly represented in the panel. The panel is managed by the CenERdata
Panel at the University of Tilburg, the Netherlands. Although Telepanel
emphasises the representative character of the panel, in reality the respondents' average educational level and job level appear to be relatively high
(Tijdens and Steijn, 2002: 6). Weighting factors have been introduced to
correct for this bias, using labour force data from Statistics Netherlands for
age, education and industry. The Statistical Department of the Dutch Social
and Cultural Planning Office carried out the actual weighting.[2] The data, as
used in this chapter, should therefore be representative of the employed
labour force in the Netherlands.

The survey analysed here was conducted in January 2002. The respondents – individuals in waged employment aged between fifteen and sixty-
four – were asked approximately fifty questions. A total of 938 respondents
(597 men and 341 women) answered the questions about ICT use at work,
their competencies, their jobs, the HRM policy and other characteristics of
their workplace.

In total, 89 per cent of the sample used a computer or other computerised
equipment at work. This is a very high percentage, and appears to be somewhat at odds with other studies (such as Andries *et al.*, 2002; Dolton and
Makepeace, 2004). It is possible that this has to do with our survey sample,
although the fact that we use weighted data makes this less likely. It can
more probably be explained by the specific question posed: 'Do you use any
kind of automated device?' Affirmative answers to this question will include

workers at the supermarket checkout who would probably say 'No' if asked whether they use a computer. The same holds true for conductors on the train who – at least in the Netherlands – now use a pocket computer (PDA) to obtain travel information for travellers. In fact, we believe the implication of our figures, that only a few workers do not use any automated device at all, is correct. The answer to the question of what they do with it is, of course, a totally different issue, and precisely the topic of this chapter.

In total, our dataset includes 834 respondents who use some form of automated device, of whom 819 supplied valid values for all the variables used in the analysis. Of these, the men were, on average, 41.3 years of age, and the women 38.0. On average, the men worked 37.7 hours per week and the women 29.3 hours.

Measurement of the dependent variables

Our aim is to see under what circumstances relatively creative uses of computers at work will arise, and from which the operators can benefit. Our basic view is that complexity denotes depth of skills, diversity denotes range of skills (but not necessarily depth), while intensivity indicates the reverse of these.

The three dimensions of ICT use at work (complexity, diversity and intensity) form the dependent variables for the analyses. The survey had a number of questions for measuring ICT use at work. The use of hardware and software was questioned, each with multiple answer categories. In addition, questions addressed the time spent on computerised activities. In the question about hardware, asking which 'automated systems' were used at work, respondents could choose from a list of eleven categories, including PCs, PDAs, Cad-Cam, robots and other items. A text box allowed respondents to add other equipment. Next, they were asked to indicate the three systems they most frequently used at work. Then, the respondents were asked to indicate which computer programs they used. Here, they could choose from a list of twenty categories of software applications, ranging from word processing to email applications and ERP packages.

The *complexity* of ICT use at work is a composite variable, based on our judgement of the complexity of both the ICT equipment and the programs reported as being used by the respondents. Initially, this variable was used to divide the sample into four categories:

a   non-ICT users (13.4 per cent);
b   users of simple ICTs, defined as users who only use simple automated hardware such as scanners in supermarkets or automated box office systems in cinemas, and who do not use any software applications (6 per cent);
c   users of basic ICTs, defined as users who use 'ordinary applications' such as word processing, programs for simple book-keeping, Internet applications, etc. (50.4 per cent);

d   users of complex ICTs, defined as users of more advanced hardware such
     as robots or software such as statistical packages (30.3 per cent).

As the analyses are focused on computer users, we have excluded the group
of non-users from further analysis. Moreover, our analyses showed that a
binary variable, comparing (d) to a combination of groups (b) and (c), is a
good proxy for *complexity* of ICT use at work.

The *diversity* of ICT use at work was measured by the total number of
hardware and software applications that are reportedly used. In theory, the
respondents could indicate twenty-three applications, i.e. twenty software
packages and three hardware applications. On average, the respondents
reported using 5.4 applications, albeit with a wide distribution (standard
deviation 3.7). Only 4 per cent used only one ICT application; 30 per cent
used five to seven applications, and almost 10 per cent claimed to use ten or
more applications.

Intensity was measured as the percentage of the working day that involved
ICT use. We calculated this by adding the number of hours per day spent on
the three most-used ICT hardware applications and dividing by the number
of working hours per day. The results indicate a high intensity of ICT use at
work. Excluding workers who do not use ICT at work, ICTs are used, on
average, during 70 per cent of a typical working day (SD 0.33). Some 53 per
cent of ICT users spend more than 80 per cent of their time working with
computers, and only 24 per cent spent less than 40 per cent.

So far, the data summaries have involved the whole sample. However,
from now on, since the detailed analyses are limited to ICT users, only the
819 ICT users in the sample with valid values for all variables will be considered. After weighting, this results in 790 ICT users. Table 16.2 shows
that 35 per cent of these employ complex forms of ICT. Diversity of ICT use

Table 16.2 Descriptive statistics: dependent variables

Descriptives	Minimum	Maximum	Mean	Standard deviation
Complexity of ICT use	0	1	0.35	0.48
Diversity of ICT use	1	17	6.27	3.28
Intensity of ICT use	0	1	0.70	0.33
Correlations	Complexity	Diversity	Intensity	
Complexity of ICT use	–	–	–	
Diversity of ICT use	0.296***	–	–	
Intensity of ICT use	0.175***	0.475***	–	

Source: AIAS/EUR, 2002.

Notes
Weighted data $N = 790$ (unweighted $N = 819$), ***$p < 0.001$.

has a mean of 6.27; intensity, a variable that ranges from 0 to 1, has a mean of 0.7. Complexity significantly correlates with diversity and intensity, but the correlation coefficient is low. Intensity and diversity however are significantly and substantially correlated with a coefficient of 0.48.

Measurement of the independent variables

Educational level is measured as a five-category quasi-interval variable, using the international ISCED classification. Here, this ranges from category 1, 'basic education', to category 5, 'first stage of tertiary education'. *Supervisory position* ('no' versus 'yes') is a dichotomous variable, as is *type of employment contract* (permanent versus other types). *Economic sector* is included using dummy variables for construction, wholesale and retail trade, commercial services, public administration, education and health and social work, with manufacturing used as the reference category. However, we report but do not show the results for these industry controls.

In general, *HRM practices* can be defined as the instruments used by employers to enable their employees to work better. Following Guest (2000: 12), who has stated that 'the greater the number of practices, the greater the impact on workers', we formed a scale (later found to have a Cronbach's alpha of 0.74), based on five HRM practices (performance, salary, career possibilities, training and the functioning of the supervisor).

Turning to the *production concept*, a measure was used derived from Steijn (2001). Three dummy variables were included to indicate various types of work organisation or production concepts: (a) the traditional Tayloristic organisation, (b) a professional organisation – characterised by a high degree of individual autonomy, (c) a sociotechnic team organisation (characterised by teamwork plus a high degree of autonomy); plus (d) a lean team organisation (characterised by teamwork but with a relatively low degree of autonomy) used as the reference category. Finally, *workplace size* was included using ten size categories.

Explaining ICT use at work

The aim of the research is to test the factors that are associated with different types of ICT usage at work. In particular, we are looking for social factors determining more favourable usages and, in particular, we want to know whether there are management policies which influence such favourable usages. We therefore look at the factors associated with each form of usage in turn – controlling for various, more economic related background factors.

Explaining the complexity of ICT use

The complexity of ICT use is defined using a binary variable, indicating basic or complex use, as explained above. Therefore a logistic regression analysis is appropriate. The analysis is performed for the individual factors first, then including the job characteristics, and finally including workplace-related characteristics. The chi-square is low for the first two models, but increased with the third model.

Table 16.3 shows that complex usages of ICTs are more common amongst men and amongst the highly educated, even when we control for other factors. Mostly these (e.g. contract type or supervisory level) have little significant effect (other than that employees in manufacturing are more likely to use complex ICTs than those in other industries – which broadly applies also to diverse and less intensive uses, even if the differences are not always statistically significant, and which we will therefore not discuss further). Thus complex usages are most strongly correlated with individual characteristics such as gender.

Explaining the diversity of ICT use

Diversity in ICT use is measured on a scale ranging from 1 to 17, indicating the number of software and hardware options used at work. Ordinary least squares regression is therefore appropriate. Explanatory power is again low with the first two models but, as before, increases for the third model.

Individual characteristics again matter (Table 16.4). Female workers are far less likely to have a diverse use of ICT than are male workers. Highly educated employees are more diverse users. Other factors are also important, though. Supervisory workers use more diverse ICTs, as do workers experiencing well-developed HRM practices. The style of work organisation also affects diversity of ICT use; in professional organisations and in teamwork organisations, employees use a greater number of diverse ICTs. Workplace size also has a significant impact: in larger workplaces, workers use more diverse ICTs. In sum, certain types of work organisation are especially important to more diverse usage of ICTs at work.

Explaining the intensity of ICT use at work

Intensity in ICT use at work is measured on a scale ranging from 0 to 1, reflecting the proportion of working time spent using ICT. This again enables the use of OLS regression. Once again, explanatory power is very low for the first two models, but increases substantially for the third model.

The findings are partially similar to those for diversity, but obviously in reverse, as we assume that intensive usage is unfavourable. Gender is again prominent, with female workers using ICTs more intensively than their male colleagues. Surprisingly, education is positively associated with intensive use, though the effect is small (presumably reflecting the work of higher-level computing specialists). Also of note is that while, in line with expectations, supervisors and also workers in the professions use ICT less intensively than non-supervisors, ICTs are used more intensively in those

Table 16.3 Explaining the complexity in ICT use through three clusters of factors (using logistic regression)

	B	Standard error	Significance	B	Standard error	Significance	B	Standard error	Significance
Individual characteristics									
Age	−0.003	0.008	ns	−0.002	0.008	ns	0.002	0.009	ns
Gender (0 = male, 1 = female)	−1.316	0.175	***	−1.303	0.177	***	−0.985	0.192	***
Education (1–5)	0.284	0.082	**	0.284	0.082	**	0.374	0.095	***
Job-related characteristics									
Permanent contract (0, 1)	–	–	–	−0.270	0.337	ns	−0.474	0.347	ns
Supervisory position (0, 1)	–	–	–	0.105	0.162	ns	0.155	0.175	ns
Workplace-related characteristics									
HRM practices (0–5)	–	–	–	–	–	–	0.077	0.055	ns
Professional (0, 1)	–	–	–	–	–	–	0.009	0.201	ns
Teamwork (0, 1)	–	–	–	–	–	–	0.204	0.230	ns
Sociotechnic (0, 1)	–	–	–	–	–	–	−0.222	0.334	ns
Size of workplace (0–10)	–	–	–	–	–	–	0.069	0.038	ns
Constant	−1.219	0.481	*	−1.025	0.561	ns	−1.015	0.667	ns
N	790			790			790		
Chi2 (df)	72.452	(3)		73.435	(5)		128.322	(16)	

Source: AIAS/EUR, 2002.

Notes
Significant at 5% (*), 1% (**) and 0.1% (***) level, ns = not significant.

Table 16.4 Explaining the diversity in ICT use with three clusters of factors (OLS regression)

	B	Standard error	Significance	B	Standard error	Significance	B	Standard error	Significance
Constant	2.665	0.649	***	2.390	0.765	**	0.573	0.803	ns
Individual characteristics									
Age	−0.009	0.011	ns	−0.009	0.011	ns	−0.002	0.011	ns
Gender (0 = male, 1 = female)	−1.485	0.223	***	−1.396	0.225	***	−0.912	0.225	***
Education (1–5)	1.141	0.109	***	1.130	0.109	***	0.944	0.111	***
Job-related characteristics									
Permanent contract (0, 1)	–	–	–	0.071	0.465	ns	−0.226	0.434	ns
Supervisory position (0, 1)	–	–	–	0.562	0.223	*	0.495	0.214	*
Workplace-related characteristics									
HRM practices (0–5)	–	–	–	–	–	–	0.364	0.065	***
Professional (0, 1)	–	–	–	–	–	–	1.326	0.244	***
Teamwork (0, 1)	–	–	–	–	–	–	0.701	0.281	*
Sociotechnic (0, 1)	–	–	–	–	–	–	−0.240	0.388	ns
Size of workplace (0–10)	–	–	–	–	–	–	0.164	0.045	***
N weighted	790			790			790		
Adjusted R^2	0.153			0.157			0.278		

Source: AIAS/EUR 2002.

Notes
Significant at 5% (*), 1% (**) and 0.1% (***) level, ns = not significant.

Table 16.5 Explaining the intensity in ICT use with three clusters of factors (OLS regression)

	B	Standard error	Significance	B	Standard error	Significance	B	Standard error	Significance
Constant	0.706	0.070	***	0.687	0.083	***	0.453	0.086	***
Individual characteristics									
Age	−0.002	0.001	ns	−0.002	0.001	ns	0.001	0.001	ns
Gender (0 = male, 1 = female)	0.072	0.024	**	0.063	0.024	*	0.135	0.024	***
Education (1–5)	0.011	0.012	ns	0.011	0.012	ns	0.032	0.012	**
Job-related characteristics									
Permanent contract (0, 1)	—	—	—	0.047	0.050	ns	0.013	0.046	ns
Supervisory position (0, 1)	—	—	—	−0.057	0.024	*	−0.051	0.023	*
Workplace-related characteristics									
HRM practices (0–5)	—	—	—	—	—	—	0.016	0.007	*
Professional (0, 1)	—	—	—	—	—	—	−0.056	0.026	*
Teamwork (0, 1)	—	—	—	—	—	—	−0.022	0.030	ns
Sociotechnic (0, 1)	—	—	—	—	—	—	0.010	0.041	ns
Size of workplace (0–10)	—	—	—	—	—	—	0.014	0.005	**
N weighted	790			790			790		
Adjusted R^2	0.014			0.019			0.187		

Source: AIAS/EUR, 2002.

Notes
Significant at 5% (*), 1% (**) and 0.1% (***) level, ns = not significant.

workplaces with more HRM practices. Overall, therefore, analysis of intensive usage of computers produces some unexpected findings which suggest that the welfare implications of this usage are not straightforward.

Conclusions

Table 16.6 summarises the results of the analyses on pages 214–218 for the three dimensions chosen to describe ICT use at work for the variables of most interest, and taking into account only the results of the third model in each case. In Table 16.6, a (0) indicates the absence of an effect, (+) indicates a positive effect and (−) a negative effect.

With respect to the three hypotheses formulated on page 210, we draw conclusions as follows. First, our major argument, that it makes sense to differentiate between the complexity, diversity and intensity of ICT use, is supported. It appears that these are not only distinct dimensions of ICT use, but the explanations for the differences in use are to be found in different sub-sets of variables.

With respect to the second hypothesis, that differences in ICT use can be explained by demographic, job and workplace characteristics, it is clear that significant variations exist in the strength of these explanations. Especially demographic variables such as gender and education are important factors in

Table 16.6 Summary of the factors affecting complexity, diversity and intensity of ICT use at work

	Complexity	*Diversity*	*Intensity*
Individual characteristics			
Age	0	0	0
Gender (0 = male, 1 = female)	−	−	+
Education (1−5)	+	+	+
Job-related characteristics			
Permanent contract (0, 1)	0	0	0
Supervisory position (0, 1)	0	+	−
Workplace-related characteristics			
HRM practices (0–5)	0	+	+
Production concept			
Professional (0, 1)	0	+	−
Teamwork (0, 1)	0	+	0
Sociotechnic (0, 1)	0	0	0
Size of workplace (0–10)	0	+	+

Source: AIAS/EUR, 2002.

Notes
− = negative effect; + = positive effect, 0 = no effect.

explaining differences in the complexity of ICT use. Job-related variables, on the other hand, do not play a role here at all. As with complexity, individual characteristics (again gender and education) are associated with diversity in ICT use. In contrast, however, job-related variables – such as supervisory level – also play a role (albeit limited), as do the workplace-related variables. A similar but more complex pattern was found with respect to the explanation for differences in the intensity of ICT use. Thus the profile for complex usage is relatively simple, but it gets more varied when we look at diverse usages and, surprisingly, even more so when we look at intensive usage.

Turning to the third hypothesis, that ICT usage is more favourable in less highly controlled set-ups, it is clear that the effect of HRM practices and type of workplace organisation, especially on the diversity of ICT usage, should be highlighted. The positive effect of increased HRM practices and appropriate style of workplace organisation supports our third hypothesis and, moreover, suggests that organisations are able to influence the ICT usage of their workers. If our original assumption, that a more diverse usage of ICT is related to a better quality of working life, is correct, this is an important finding as it indicates how organisations could positively influence the well-being of their workers.

Finally, let us return to two individual-level characteristics, age and gender. Contrary to what we had expected, there appears to be no relationship between age and the complexity, diversity and intensity of computer usage. This suggests that older workers – and perhaps older people in general – are able to use computers in a similar way to younger workers. In other words, it appears that the well-being of older workers is not negatively affected by their computer usage. More predictably, perhaps, but also possibly more importantly, regardless of the nature of work, ICT usage by men is more complex, more diverse and less intensive than that of women.

It would be even more interesting to investigate what the effect of this is on the *outcome* of ICT use. It is perhaps not too far-fetched to suspect that these differences might influence the quality of working life. They might possibly also explain some of the differences in wages between men and women. It seems to us that people who work with less complex and less diverse computer applications, but in a more intensive way – as women often appear to do – will have a less rewarding job, both with respect to the quality of their working life and to their financial returns.

Notes

1 This chapter is based on a paper presented at the ICT, the Knowledge Society and Changes in Work Conference, The Hague, 9 and 10 June, 2005.
2 We appreciate and thank them for having done this task.

References

Andries, F., Smulders, P.G.W. and Dhondt, S. (2002) The use of computers among the workers in the European Union and its impact on the quality of work, *Behaviour & Information Technology*, 21(6), 441–447.

Dolton, P. and Makepeace, G. (2004) Computer use and earnings in Britain. *Economic Journal*, 114(494), C117–C129.

Felstead, A. and Gallie, D. (2004) For better or worse? Non-standard jobs and high involvement work systems. *International Journal of Human Resource Management*, 15(7), 1293–1316.

Felstead, A., Gallie, D. and Green, F. (2002) *Work Skills in Britain 1986–2001*, Nottingham, DfES.

Guest, D.E. (2000) Human resource management – the workers' verdict. *Human Resource Management Journal*, 9(3), 5–25.

Steijn, B. (2001b) Work systems, quality of working life and attitudes of workers: an empirical study towards the effects of team and non-team work. *New Technology, Work and Employment*, 16(3), 191–203.

Steijn, B. and Tijdens, K.G. (2005) Workers and their willingness to learn: will ICT-implementation strategies and HRM practices contribute to innovation? *Creativity and Innovation Management*, 14(2), 151–159.

Tijdens, K. and Steijn, B. (2002) *Competenties van werknemers in de informatiemaatschappij. Een survey over ICT-gebruik*, Amsterdam, AIAS research report 11. Online, available at: www.uva-aias.net/files/aias/RR11.pdf.

Tijdens, K.G. and Steijn, B. (2005) The determinants of ICT competencies among employees. *New Technology, Work and Employment*, 20(1), 60–73.

17 What does telework tell us about teleworkers?

Leslie Haddon and Malcolm Brynin

Introduction

Interest in telework has many sources and involves a number of perspectives (some of which we briefly review in Haddon and Brynin, 2005). Yet running through these diverse approaches and accounts it is possible to discern two opposed discourses. An optimistic version sees the potential of new technologies to change the way we work through its ability to shift work over time and over space. This implies benefits both for the employer, who gains a productivity boost from the extra flexibility, and for employees or the self-employed, who acquire more control over their work. Set against this is a body of research that stresses social rather than technological change. The work and familial commitments of the individual place major constraints on the use of new technologies and the adoption of new working practices. Indeed, the technology might be seen as a tool to gain more output from the worker rather than being of universal benefit.

Whatever the balance of advantage from the changes, we support the view that technology is a social phenomenon in the sense that it is made by people, owned by people, and operated by people (Grint and Woolgar, 1997). All of these are in some way affected by a specific technology have a specific social location in terms of class, gender, ethnicity and so on, which inevitably influences the experience of technology and of telework. For example, in the analysis we present below we show that modes of telework are strongly associated with different types of occupation. This leads us to the conclusion that, to some extent, telework is less a re-organisation of work than an expression of occupational differences.

This does not mean we write off technology as merely a symbol of occupational prestige, like (in former times) the bowler hat of the 'City' financier. Rather, whatever the origins and intended purposes of telework, in the end they become part of the many facets of work which distinguish one type of occupation from another. The new ICTs were not developed in order to support telework (a process which has been quite limited anyway). They have instead been bolted on to old forms of work. As a result, new forms evolve.

The social effects of telework

The topic of telework started to gain publicity in academic circles in the early 1970s, when the energy crisis led researchers to consider telecommuting as an alternative to commuting physically. While that environmental interest has remained, in the 1980s a strand of analysis emerged from managerial and business schools, in particular from schools of personnel management, with a more complex assessment of the potential effects (Gillespie *et al.*, 1995; Anderson, 2001: 23–30). Telework was seen as a form of flexible labour derived from an apparent need for firms to adapt to market change. Teleworking could lower the unit costs of labour by reducing overheads. The employee (or, of course, the self-employed) might also gain from the extra freedom over their own time, for instance to combine work with home care – even if there is little evidence that teleworkers actually do this very much (Bailey and Kurland, 2002). Telework could even be seen as the basis for a transformation of homework from domestic drudgery to lifestyle choice (Hakim, 1987). Finally, the need to have computer equipment, Internet services or mobile communications raises the demand for new ICTs, which has important economic consequences. In sum, a radically enlarged teleworkforce could be viewed as part of a general modernisation characterised by new and cleaner technologies, flexible employment, lifestyle choices and both increased consumption and economic growth.

Many have been the critics of this rather benign vision. In terms of welfare, teleworking might include a resurgence of routine work from home, such as telephone sales or data entry, and could be exploitative. There might therefore be negative social effects, especially for women (Webster, 1996), for whom telework could be an extension of traditional, poorly paid work at home (Pennington and Westover, 1989; Rowbotham, 1993; Phizacklea and Wolkowitz, 1995; Felstead and Jewson, 2000). Another view is that telework is exploitative because it imposes upon the family. Clearly, some people might select telework because it makes family life easier, but often it is by no means the ideal solution (Olsen and Primps, 1984; Christensen, 1987). There has been a feminist undercurrent in much research that draws parallels with women's negative experience of traditional homework.

There is no unequivocal answer to whether telework is good or bad for the worker, or indeed the employer. Its social and economic effects are, in aggregate, very difficult to quantify. On balance, it is perhaps best to see telework as an organisationally neutral form of work. However, this does not mean it is unimportant. Telework takes several forms, and in respect of work shifted over time or place, is only distinguished from other forms of work, in particular from any work undertaken at home, by the use of technology. Whether this work is undertaken at all, and how it is undertaken, tells us a lot about the people who do this and the types of occupation in which they work. It is to how best to describe these technology-based differences that we now turn.

What is telework?

Telework is not easy to define. Indeed, any definition depends on the starting point of the analyst. Even the decision of what to include in its measurement depends on the interests of the researchers (Sullivan, 2003). It is therefore not always helpful to define clear-cut boundaries of who is and is not a teleworker (Huws, 1995; Gareis, 2002). A flexible approach is needed which is potentially useful for a variety of research interests. We have reviewed the definitional issue in detail elsewhere (Haddon and Brynin, 2005). Here we summarise its main aspects, which are in fact quite straightforward. Our main argument is that no a priori definition of telework is required if survey results or qualitative research produce the necessary information in the first place. What is important is how different aspects of this information are combined; this is up to the researcher. We therefore cite the usual elements – location, time, technology and contractual arrangements – though we do not necessarily agree with how these have often been approached.

Location is always a central element. Different analysts have sought to clarify how the concept of mobile work relates to telework (e.g. Gillespie *et al.*, 1995; Julsrud, 1998; Gareis, 2002) and there is a growing preference for concepts such as eWork or distributed work. In our view, a specific locus for work where ICTs are used does not tell us whether telework is taking place but *how* it might be taking place. The locational variations in the work process, for instance including 'hot desking', are quite extensive (Felstead *et al.*, 2005). Below, however, although we recognise that the concept of mobility is important, we choose the home as the chief 'non-standard' location.

Some people work at home in the evenings or at weekends as well as normal hours. Where these forms of 'overspill' or 'supplementary' work entail the use of ICTs they can be counted as telework (even, therefore, if this is not full-time). We do not feel that it makes sense to establish a definitional threshold for the amount of time spent in such activities, as this then becomes quite arbitrary. It makes little difference how much people telework, or when they telework; they are still teleworking. Nevertheless, we still need to take some account of time as a secondary characteristic. Someone waiting for a gas fitter at home, and who at the same time does some paid work at home using an online connection, would not necessarily be a teleworker, yet the activity taking place during that time would clearly be telework. Our emphasis below is therefore on the activity rather than on the person, and time is a significant element of this.

As regards technology, a minimalist definition could consider voice telephony to be sufficient, but the use of computers or sometimes of the Internet are now often regarded as central (eWork, 2000). However, people might make incidental use of ICTs in the course of their work (Haddon and Silverstone, 1993; Huws, 1995; Baines and Gelder, 2003). The Office of National Statistics (ONS) definition used in the British Labour Force survey distinguishes between teleworkers who merely use a phone and a computer, and those for whom these are *essential* for their work. Others have also recommended measuring the *level* of ICT use (Sullivan, 2003). Our own approach is to acknowledge technology as shaping part of the contours of teleworking practices, and then to differentiate users of different types of ICT. This takes the view that no specific technology defines a teleworker. Specific technologies define different forms of telework.

Taking these elements into account, we can derive a number of forms of telework. Initially we focus on the home and we find here two types of telework:

1 *Any* work at home entailing use of the Internet (*Net homework*).
2 *Any* work at home entailing use of a PC, but not the Internet (*PC homework*).

Adding an element of locational flexibility, we include a category based on the use of mobile telephony, although this is not usually included in standard definitions of telework.

3 Work where use of a mobile phone (or other mobile technology) is important for work but where neither the Internet nor a PC are used (*Mobile work*).

There are forms of work at home to which telework is closely related. We can therefore contrast telework to other homework, which we might consider to be 'potential' telework, as it only requires a limited use of technology at home to convert this work to telework. This gives us:

4 *Homework:* People who do any work at home during normal work hours but who do not use a PC or the Internet to do so and do not view the mobile phone as important for work (*Day homeworkers*), or who work at home in the evenings or at weekends (*Overtime workers*).

It is possible to treat the above as two separate categories but, in practice, the distinction is often not useful. Finally, we have the 'residual' but also obviously the largest category of work in a standard workplace.

5 Work at one or more workplaces, excluding the home (*Standard work*).

We have little to add as regards contractual arrangements, with the exception of how this might relate to self-employment. Some researchers do not like to include the self-employed in the same research as employed teleworkers (Pyöriä, 2003). However, self-employment is a distinct and important form of work outside a standard workplace, and on this basis its telework component is very important (Gillespie *et al.*, 1995; Baines, 2002; Hotopp,

2002). In the research reported below, we treat employment status as a variable in samples combining both the self-employed and employees. However, it is perfectly reasonable, again depending on the nature of the research focus, to make a distinction between employed and self-employed teleworkers on the one hand, and employed and self-employed homeworkers on the other.

The research reported below uses the above classification scheme to see whether it is possible to discern differences between its categories in terms of gender, education, occupational groupings and pay.

The analysis

The data derive from the e-Living project, funded by the EU's IST Programme. The project is based on a household survey of 1,750 homes in six countries – Britain, Bulgaria, Germany, Israel, Italy and Norway, undertaken towards the end of 2001.

The classification scheme is shown in Figure 17.1 for all six countries. However, the only data in the survey that could describe mobile working was a question (and then, for wave one only) on the importance of the use of a mobile phone for the respondent's work. While a significant indicator, clearly it captures only a part of the mobile telework experience.

The figure shows that half or more of the workforce have non-standard modes of work if we (tentatively) include use of a mobile phone in this. It also shows that the variation between Britain, Germany and Italy is limited. Norway and Israel have the lowest proportions of people in the workplace. Israel and Norway have the largest proportions of their workforce who are 'PC homeworkers', Norway and Britain show the highest proportion of 'Net homeworkers'.

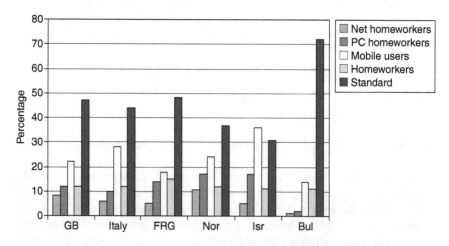

Figure 17.1 The incidence of telework, homeworking, and 'standard' work.

While telework appears to be undertaken by many workers, it generally takes only a small proportion of total work hours, which is not apparent in the graph. Moreover, only 50 per cent of teleworkers (Net plus PC) in Britain use a PC for their work at home for at least half of the time spent working. This suggests that while telework is fundamentally work at home for which the technology is important (by our definition), the technology is not always necessary. Finally, though we again do not show this graphically, the self-employed are over-represented in Net, PC and mobile work. Thus, self-employment is strongly associated with telework.

Are there differences between the type of people who are engaged in standard work, traditional homework, PC homework and net homework? Here we need to take into account the characteristics of different types of teleworker and of homeworker (Stanworth, 1997), including factors such as gender, age, education and occupation. The age distribution is, in fact, roughly equal across the various work categories defined above, but there are clear gender differentials. Net-based and mobile-phone-based telework are predominantly male, especially in Germany and Italy (the least so in Israel). PC homeworking is generally male, but less overwhelmingly. Homeworkers are more likely to be women, but not by much (and not at all in Germany). The gender divide for standard work is about equal. Thus homework has a slight female edge but its telework variant is far more male.

In all the countries, Net homeworking is very much a graduate activity, as is PC homeworking, if less so. Those using mobile phones for work have about the same chance of having a degree as people in the labour force as a whole (though not in Germany or Israel). However, homeworkers are also more highly educated than the labour force in general. Therefore, on the whole, non-ICT-based homeworking does not appear to be undertaken by people with low levels of education. (This need not apply, of course, to the much smaller groups of homeworkers who are dependent on this form of work rather than merely shifting some of their normal work to the home.)

Overall, the picture shows that Net homeworking is dominated by well-educated men, PC homework by somewhat less well-educated men, mobile-phone-based work by men who are educated to roughly the same level as the average for the labour force as a whole, and homework by the well-educated generally, with a slight preponderance of women. The different technological forms give a clear indication of the social characteristics of the users.

Is this reinforced by occupational differences? The ONS study in Britain found that teleworking is dominated by managerial, professional and associate professional/technical workers (Hotopp, 2002). Figure 17.2 shows the proportions in each of our forms of work comprising professional or managerial workers. (It excludes Bulgaria because of the small proportion in some categories. Also, for simplicity, it does not show the proportion of managerial and professional people in the labour force as a whole. However, this is similar to the proportion of mobile users who are from this occupational group.)

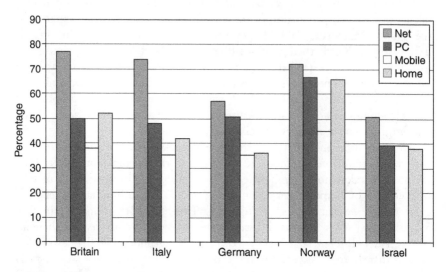

Figure 17.2 Percentage of teleworkers and homeworkers who are professional or managerial.

Between 50 and nearly 80 per cent of Net homeworkers are managers or professional workers, with the highest proportion occurring in Britain, Italy and Germany. In each country the proportion of PC homeworkers is less predominantly managerial and professional than this, but still well above average for the labour force as a whole. Homeworkers are generally similar to this. Thus, Net homeworkers are predominantly professional or managerial, while PC homeworkers and homeworkers generally are more likely than not to be in this group.

If we look at this from the point of view of the occupation (though we do not show the results here), only professional and managerial workers consistently have a higher proportion of net workers than in the labour force as a whole, as well as a higher proportion of homeworkers. Technicians have roughly the same proportion of Net or PC homeworkers as in the workforce. Clerical workers tend to be under-represented in all forms of telework and homework. The mobile phone is of some significance for craft workers.

In sum, Net-based teleworking is overwhelmingly a managerial and professional practice. However, the fact that homeworkers often have degrees and are also professional or managerial workers suggests that, on our definition, homeworkers are not very different from Net homeworkers. In fact, work on transitions between these groups over the two waves of e-Living shows that there is considerable movement between these two forms of work over time by the same individuals. The technology might therefore be marginal. Yet there is some social and occupational difference between the two groups, and even more so between Net homeworkers, PC homeworkers and mobile workers.

Are these differences reflected in pay differences? Hartman *et al.* demonstrate in their study of telecommuting productivity a 'lack of significant relationships between demographic and occupational variables and telecommuting productivity' (1991: 224). However, the e-Living study shows that the differences between the forms of work we have reviewed thus far, which appear to reinforce background and occupational differences, will also be matched by similar differences in pay. We present this by showing in Table 17.1 the results of conducting ordinary least squares regression with gross hourly pay (logged) as the dependent variable, and where the key explanatory variables are the various forms of work discussed above. As the question on the importance of mobile phones for work was only asked in wave one, and this analysis pools both waves, mobile workers are included as standard workers. (This makes no noticeable difference to the results.) Standard work is the reference category, so the results for the three remaining categories are relative to the pay that people receive for working for their entire working time in a standard workplace. The results are shown separately for each of five occupational groups, as it seems likely that the relationship between pay and the tele/homework categories would work differently in each group. (The alternative of using interaction terms between occupation and the tele/homework categories is technically preferable but less straightforward to interpret.) Because of low numbers once we have split the sample by occupation, the countries are pooled. However, only the most industrially homogeneous countries (Britain, Germany, Italy and Norway) are included. Again, to ease interpretation, only a limited number of explanatory variables

Table 17.1 Regression of log of gross hourly pay (in euros) of teleworkers, homeworkers and standard workers by occupation (Britain, Germany, Italy and Norway pooled)

	Managers	*Technical*	*Clerical*	*Service*	*Craft*
Britain	0.18***	0.14**	−0.01	0.02	0.07
Italy	−0.26***	−0.40***	−0.29***	−0.58***	−0.39***
Germany	0.03	0.07	0.15*	−0.07	−0.01
Age	0.01***	0.01***	0.01***	0.00	0.01***
Male	0.18***	0.15***	0.18***	0.31***	0.16*
Has degree	0.25***	0.39***	0.27***	0.19	−0.14
Net-worker	0.26***	0.20*	0.24**	−0.04	0.10
PC-worker	0.09*	−0.01	0.14	−0.01	0.36*
Homeworker	0.14***	0.05	0.01	0.09	−0.04
Constant	2.35***	2.15***	2.17***	2.50***	2.08***
R^2	0.23	0.24	0.17	0.13	0.14
N	2,053	935	610	520	705

Note
* $p < 0.5$, ** $p < 0.01$, *** $p < 0.001$.

are used. The results exclude the self-employed as their pay data (like their tax returns) are generally unreliable.

Only the three variables of interest really need comment. In the professional and managerial group, net homeworkers are better paid than standard workers (the reference category), but so too are homeworkers who do not telework, though they are less well paid than Net homeworkers. PC homeworkers are paid less than these two groups but somewhat more than standard workers. Thus, even within a single occupational group, and controlling for age, gender and education, there is a clear hierarchy of financial returns to work on the basis of the classification scheme that we elaborated above. Of course it is possible that ICTs make those who use it more productive, but this is unlikely, especially as many are teleworking or homeworking only part-time. It is far more likely that Net homeworkers are an elite of managerial and professional employees, with other homeworkers not far behind, while PC homeworkers barely stand out at all.

The same ranking applies to technical staff, but only Net homeworking achieves statistical significance of any sort. In clerical work, Net homeworking is again ahead, though this time PC homeworking comes second, even if (at least with this sample size) it is not statistically significant. All the coefficients for service work are insignificant in both senses. However, PC homeworking comes into its own within craft work. Thus different occupations might be characterised not only by different forms of telework presumably appropriate to this work, but at the same time, workers who use the different forms are paid differently across occupations. Perhaps the clearest outcome is that, in all white-collar work, whatever its level, Net homeworking is associated with the highest pay. It seems to describe an 'elite'. However, this elite does not exist only in the professional and managerial group but is a distinct element in many occupationals.

One thing missing here is any sense of how the categories of the classification scheme compare regardless of occupation. Elsewhere (Haddon and Brynin, 2005) we have undertaken alternative analysis regressing pay on a variety of factors for the countries separately. Online teleworkers again earn much more – that is, regardless of their education and type of job. In most countries PC homeworkers earn less than homeworkers and Net homeworkers. It is not the case, therefore, that all forms of telework are associated with higher pay. PC homeworking is not that well paid relative to other categories of work once the background and other characteristics of the various workers are taken into account, and seems to be rewarded less even than plain homeworking; nevertheless, in some occupations, PC homeworking represents a relatively elite form of work.

Conclusion

This chapter has demonstrated how telework is not a homogeneous entity but can comprise various elements of technology and location, whose different combinations produce a range of types of work. The flexible classification utilised here shows how it might be more useful to think of a spectrum of telework practices, rather than argue from particular agendas about what should count or not as 'real' telework.

The research also shows that there are gender, educational, occupational and pay differences between the categories of the classification discussed in the beginning of the chapter. In other words, the categories are populated by different people with different personal or occupational characteristics. For instance, Net homeworkers are likely to be male, professional and relatively highly paid. PC homeworkers are of significantly lower social status, as measured by occupation, than Networkers. This suggests that at least some categories of home and telework reflect traditional categories of work associated with the social status of the job rather than a new determining role for technology in the organisation of work. By the same token, female homework is relatively high-status and not predominantly either routine or low-paid when compared to the traditional form that has been much discussed in the literature.

The variation shown in this chapter would make one wary of seeing telework as a unitary phenomenon with any unitary effects. Our analysis suggests that telework tells us more about the teleworker than about the nature of technology.

References

Anderson, B. (ed.) (2001) e-Living D3: State of the art review. *E-Living project deliverable*. Online, available at: www.eurescom.de/e-living.

Bailey, D. and Kurland, N. (2002) A review of telework research: findings, new directions, and lessons for the study of modern work. *Journal of Organizational Behaviour*, 23, 383–400.

Baines, S. (2002) New technologies and old ways of working in the home of the self-employed teleworker. *New Technology, Work and Employment* 17(2), 89–101.

Baines, S. and Gelder, U. (2003) What is family friendly about the workplace in the home? The case of self-employed parents and their children. *New Technology, Work and Employment*, 18(3), 223–234.

Christensen, K. (1987) Impacts of computer-mediated home-based work on women and their families. *Office: Technology and People*, 3, 211–230.

eWork 2000: Status Report on New Ways to Work in the Information Society, Brussels: European Commission.

Felstead, A. and Jewson, N. (2000) *In Work, At Home: Towards an Understanding of Homeworking*, London, Routledge.

Felstead, A., Jewson, N. and Walters, S. (2005) The shifting locations of work: new statistical evidence on the spaces and places of employment. *Work, Employment and Society*, 19(2), 415–431.

Gareis, K. (2002) *The Intensity of Telework in 2002 in the EU, Switzerland and the USA*, Bonn, Empirica.

Gillespie, A., Richardson, R. and Cornford, J. (1995) *Review of Telework in Britain: Implications for Public Policy*. A report for the Parliamentary Office of Science and Technology, Sheffield, Employment Department, February.

Grint, K. and Woolgar, S. (1997) *The Machine at Work: Technology, Work and Organization*, Cambridge, Polity Press.

Haddon, L. and Brynin, M. (2005) The character of telework and the characteristics of teleworkers. *New Technology, Work and Employment*, 20(1), 34–46.

Haddon, L and Silverstone, R. (1993) *Teleworking in the 1990s – a View from Home*. A report on the ESRC/PICT study of teleworking and information and communication technology, Science Policy Research Unit.

Hakim, C. (1987) *Home-based Work in Britain: a Report on the 1981 National Homeworking Survey and the DE Research Programme on Homework*, London, Department of Employment.

Hartman, R.I., Stoner, C.R. and Arora, R. (1991) An investigation of selected variables affecting telecommuting productivity and satisfaction. *Journal of Business and Psychology*, 6(2), 207–225.

Hotopp, U. (2002) *Labour Market Trends*, 11(6), Norwich, The Stationery Office.

Huws, U. (1995) *Social Europe: Follow Up to the White Paper – Teleworking*, European Commission DGV, Office for Official Publications of the European Commission.

Julsrud, T. (1998) Combinations and tracks: an investigation of the relationship between homework and mobile work, *Teleworking Environments. Proceedings of the Third International Workshop on Telework*, 1–4 September, Turku, Finland. TUCS General Publication No. 8.

OECD (2003) *ICT and Economic Growth: Evidence from OECD Countries, Industries and Firms*, Paris, Organisation for Economic Co-operation and Development.

Olsen, M. and Primps, S. (1984) Working at home with computers: work and nonwork issues. *Journal of Social Issues*, 40(3), 97–112.

Pennington, S. and Westover, B. (1989) *A Hidden Workforce: Homeworkers in England, 1850–1985*, Basingstoke, Macmillan Education.

Phizacklea, A. and Wolkowitz, C. (1995) *Homeworking Women: Gender, Racism and Class at Work*, London, Sage.

Pyöriä, P. (2003) Knowledge work in distributed environments: issues and visions. *New Technology, Work and Employment*, 18(3), 166–180.

Rowbotham, S. (1993) *Homeworkers Worldwide*, London, Merlin Press.

Stanworth, C. (1997) Telework and the information age. *New Technology, Work, and Employment*, 13(1), 51–62.

Sullivan, C. (2003) What's in a name? Definitions and conceptualisations of teleworking and homeworking. *New Technology, Work and Employment*, 18(3), 158–165.

Webster, J. (1996) *Shaping Women's Work: Gender, Employment and Information Technology*, London, Longman.

18 Have information and communication technologies changed the patterns of high-skilled migration?

Michael Rothgang and Christoph M. Schmidt

Background

It is often asserted that international migration of high-skilled workers has accelerated during the 1990s (e.g. OECD, 2002). At the same time, policies to attract high-skilled migrants have received the support of many policy-makers in developed economies. Not only has the publicly perceived importance of high-skilled migration changed, but also the patterns of high-skilled migration (Straubhaar and Wolter, 1997; Mahroum, 1999). In particular, short-term migration has become more important and the international mobility of students, researchers and also entrepreneurs has increased. Today, firm-internal migration within multinational enterprises makes up an important share of high-skilled migration, and the professions of high-skilled migrants have also been changing over time. In the period from 1960 to 1980, university teachers and health professionals captured a large share of overall high-skilled migration. Since then, the international migration of ICT professionals has gained particular importance.

Of course, many different factors have influenced these recent patterns of high-skilled migration. In particular, migration policies that try to attract professionals to industrialised countries have apparently contributed to the recent increase in high-skilled migration. However, technological factors seem to have been of similar importance. Specifically, the available evidence suggests that information and communication technologies have influenced high-skilled migration in several ways (Rothgang and Schmidt, 2003). The most direct effect results from the increasing demand for high-skilled IT professionals in the industrial countries during the 1990s. Since the development of ICT is closely related to the increasing demand for high-skilled employees. More generally, technological progress has been an important element in the overall increase in the demand of high-qualified employees (Acemoglu, 2002a, b). In addition, ICTs have changed the balance between the costs and benefits of migration for potential migrants by making access to information about candidate destinations and contact to other migrants easier.

It is very difficult – if not impossible – to estimate to what extent increases in aggregate high-skilled migration are a consequence of technological change.

Yet, more informative data have become available recently and they shed some light on the changing patterns of high-skilled migration and, specifically, on the effects of ICT diffusion on high-skilled migration and on other determinants of migration. In this chapter, we analyse changes in the effect of both standard determinants of high-skilled migration such as population size and home-country GDP, and of the availability of highly skilled persons in the countries of emigration. Using a comparison of two samples (from 1990 and 2000) which span a period in which the 'new economy boom' took place, we scrutinise three central questions:

- How did the patterns of high-skilled migration change in the 1990s?
- What factors are responsible for these changes in general, and specifically what role did the diffusion of ICT play?
- To what extent are the negative consequences of the brain drain for emigration countries compensated for by a brain gain in the form of higher rates of human capital accumulation?

The first of these questions provides the context of the discussion of high-skilled migration. Regarding the second question, we focus primarily on ICT skills. The third question concerns the welfare balance from the point of view of the countries from which skilled people emigrate. The argument here is that the demand for skills in the richer countries encourages education in the poorer countries. This, while it leads to a loss of skills through migration, in the long term also leads to more skill aquisition as some trained workers are retained while the infrastructure overall improves. While it is not possible to examine the contribution of ICT skills to this development, there is no reason to think that the role of these skills differs much from the role of other high-level skills.

Patterns of high-skilled migration

Migration statistics, especially those regarding international emigration from less developed economies have always been scarce. In 1998, however, Carrington and Detragiache (CD) (1998) published estimates of emigration rates for sixty-one developing countries to the OECD. With this data, it became possible to analyse determinants and effects of high-skilled migration on a cross-country basis for the year 1990 (Rothgang and Schmidt, 2003; Faini, 2005).

Recently, a new dataset on high-skilled migration has been made available by Docquier and Marfouk (DM) (2004). They estimate skilled workers' emigration rates to OECD countries for 170 countries in the year 1990, and 190 countries in 2000, covering more than 90 per cent of the stock of immigrants to the OECD in these years. In addition to providing estimates for the year 2000 and to extending the number of countries for which emigration rates are made available, the DM dataset increases the accuracy of the estimated migration rates.[1]

Although many contributions discuss the increasing importance of high-skilled migration over time, we still lack precise quantitative accounts of these changes. Obviously, the importance of high-skilled migration has increased during the later years. Haque and Jahangir (1999) estimate that the yearly number of high-skilled migrants from Africa increased from 1,800 in the period from 1960 to 1975, to 23,000 in 1984 to 1987. Correspondingly, Docquier and Marfouk estimate that the share of high-skilled immigrants in the OECD immigration stock has increased from 33 per cent in 1990 to 37 per cent in 2000 (Docquier and Marfouk, 2004: 22). Thus, during the 1990s, the importance of high-skilled migration as part as overall migration has apparently increased. New OECD estimates (OECD, 2005: 116–149) allow us to assess more precisely the volume of high-skilled emigration from OECD-countries as well as high-skilled immigration to the OECD, both from OECD and non-OECD countries.

Based on these estimates, Table 18.1 provides an overview of important patterns of high-skilled migration for a range of OECD countries. The table documents that the overall proportion of residents in European countries who are foreign-born appears to be higher than is often assumed. With the exception of Norway, the population share of foreign-born residents in the European countries shown is higher than the OECD average of 7.7 per cent. For Germany, Europe's major immigration country, the share of foreign-born (12.5 per cent) is about the same as for the USA (12.3 per cent).

For most of the countries displayed, the proportion of immigrants who are highly skilled is smaller than for the native-born populations, while the share of expatriates (the workers 'exported' by OECD countries) who are highly skilled expatriates is greater. Notable exceptions are Norway and Great Britain, where over 30 per cent of foreign-born residents are highly skilled. Thus, overall migration tends to decrease the skill intensities of most European countries. Yet, considering the varying magnitudes of the overall inflow of migrants to the countries shown, immigration increases the number of highly skilled residents in their overall population by between 1.5 and 15 per cent. In the USA, this 'net' increase amounts to 7.8 million people, or 15.3 per cent of the native-born highly skilled. The increase of the high-skilled population due to migration is smallest in the United Kingdom (1.5 per cent) because of the high share of expatriates.

Which countries are mostly affected by high-skilled emigration? All three available sources (CD, DM and the OECD calculations) document a high variability across non-OECD countries and fairly high emigration rates for some of them. Emigration rates, calculated as the share of high-skilled expatriates in the sum of high-skilled expatriates and high-skilled resident native-born taken together, range from 1.2 per cent for Brazil and 1.4 per cent for Thailand to 76.9 per cent for Guyana and 72.6 per cent for Jamaica (OECD, 2005: 129).[2] Notably, many small countries display rather high emigration rates.

Table 18.2 reports our estimates for the determinants of high-skilled

Table 18.1 High-skilled foreign-born and expatriates from selected OECD countries, people aged fifteen and over, individual numbers for 1999 to 2003

	Belgium	France	Germany	Norway	UK	USA
Overall migrants						
Foreign-born (millions)	1.1	5.9	10.3	3.3	4.9	34.6
Share of population (%)	10.7	10.0	12.5	7.3	8.3	12.3
Expatriates (millions)	0.3	1.0	2.9	0.1	3.2	0.8
Share of population (%)	3.1	1.7	3.6	2.7	5.5	0.3
Highly skilled persons (native-born)						
Individuals (millions)	1.6	7.2	10.7	0.7	7.2	51.0
Share of native-born population (%)	22.9	16.9	19.5	23.2	20.1	26.9
Highly skilled persons (foreign-born)						
Individuals (millions)	0.2	1.0	1.4	0.7	1.4	8.2
Share of foreign-born (%)	21.6	18.1	15.5	31.1	34.8	25.9
Highly skilled expatriates						
Persons (millions)	0.1	0.3	0.9	0.05	1.3	0.4
Share of all expatriates (%)	34.6	36.2	30.4	33.9	41.2	49.9
Highly skilled migrants: share of highly skilled native-born						
Foreign-born (%)	11.3	14.1	12.9	8.9	19.0	16.1
Expatriates (%)	6.9	4.9	8.1	5.3	17.5	0.8
Highly skilled: net immigration						
Difference: immigrants – expatriates (millions)	0.1	0.1	0.1	0.05	0.1	7.8
Share of native-born highly skilled (%)	4.3	9.3	4.7	3.6	1.5	15.3

Source: OECD 2005, own calculations.

emmigration in a country cross-section regression that allows us to separate the common patterns from individual country-to-country differences in emmigration. In addition to emigration data, we use data from the Barro and Lee dataset on educational attainment (1993, 2001) and further economic indicators from the Penn world tables (Heston and Summers, 1991). Regression 1 displays estimates for the factors influencing high-skilled migration for 1990 (based on CD data). Carrington and Detragiache (1998) estimate high-skilled migration as the ratio of the stock of the foreign-born living in the USA with tertiary education to the population of those with the same education in their country of origin. The results show a clear negative relationship between emigration rates and population size, while the origin-country GDP per capita has no discernable effect on emigration behaviour. Thus, it is not so much the very poor countries but the countries with a smaller population size that are mostly confronted with the effects of the migration brain drain. The regression also does not reveal any statistically significant relation between high-skilled emigration and the population share with a tertiary education. The point estimate is negative.

In both other regressions (columns two and three), we use the DM data. In this study, emigration rates are estimated more accurately. In the second column, the DM data are used for the same year (1990) and the same set of countries as in column one. In addition to the clear negative relation between high-skilled emigration and population size, this regression indicates both a positive and statistically significant effect of origin-country GDP per capita and, again, a negative effect of the population share with tertiary education. These results suggest that small, though not the poorest, countries are prone to high-skilled emigration. However, economies with a small

Table 18.2 Determinants of high-skilled migration to OECD countries

	(1)	*(2)*	*(3)*
Constant	31.40	32.94	54.12***
	(25.79)	(29.34)	(13.26)
Log population	−4.80***	−6.86***	−4.96***
	(1.20)	(1.37)	(0.70)
Log GDP (origin country)	3.44	7.36**	1.72
	(3.07)	(3.50)	(1.40)
Population share with tertiary education	−94.71	−234.0***	−120.5***
	(69.15)	(78.67)	(30.79)
Year 2000			2.40
			(2.22)
Number of observations	60	60	197
Adjusted R^2	0.22	0.37	0.28

Notes
***Significant at the 1 per cent level. **Significant at the 5 per cent level. *Significant at the 10 per cent level. Standard errors are reported in parentheses.

share of highly skilled people are also likely to contribute heavily to emigration flows. Thus, those countries with limited skill resources are most likely to suffer losses.

This is further confirmed by the third regression where we pool all available country variables for 1990 and 2000. As before, high-skilled migration proves to be negatively related with population size in the country of origin. While the coefficient for GDP per capita is statistically insignificant, high-skilled migration is again negatively related with the population share with tertiary education. Thus, smaller countries as well as countries with a small share of highly skilled workers obviously suffer most from the brain drain. Finally, the coefficient for the difference between 1990 and 2000 is positive, but insignificant.

Determinants of high-skilled migration: the role of ICT

Which factors are likely to influence high-skilled migration?

The determinants of high-skilled migration can be discussed from different perspectives. The traditional economic approach (Sjaastad, 1962) views the migration decision as a cost–benefit consideration from the perspective of the individual. In deciding to move, the migrant weighs monetary and non-monetary benefits against the costs associated with the migration decision. The benefits include future earnings streams but also non-monetary amenities. Costs of migration comprise travel expenses, foregone earnings, but also loss of social contacts in the origin country. Thus, aggregate migrant flows between countries constitute the cumulative expression of these individual decisions.

Based on this fundamental insight, modern economic analyses on (i) the migration decision, (ii) the economic performance of immigrants and (iii) the impact of migration on the indigenous populations in the countries of origin and destination, all emphasise the heterogeneity of individual migrants. Regarding the migration decision, potential migrants who will be able to realise higher gains in income through migration than others, tend to be more prevalent among actual migrants. Borjas (1991) argues that the migration incentive for individuals with different skills is strongly influenced by the wage structure. When the potential destination wage differentials for high-skilled workers increase, the economic incentive for the highly skilled to move to developed countries grows in comparison to that for low-skilled workers.

These considerations point to the role of changing demand and supply for different qualifications as important determinants of changes in the wage structure and, therefore, alterations in the skill structure of migration (Table 18.3). What factors influence demand and supply for different qualifications in different countries? Demand for different qualifications is strongly determined by production requirements and, consequently, technical progress. Supply of workers with different qualifications first of all depends on demo-

Table 18.3 Sources for the changing nature of migration

Migrants	Demand	Supply	Policy
Low-skilled	High low-skilled unemployment in wealthy economies (−)	Demographic changes (+)	Stop of guest worker programmes (−)
High-skilled	Technical progress; scarcity of human capital/qualifications (+)	Demographic changes; increasing endowment of human capital (+)	Promotion of high-skilled immigration (+)

graphic factors and the educational system. Of course, policy decisions play a crucial role for the migration streams at all times, as international migration is strongly regulated. In striving for long-term growth effects, many industrialised countries have relaxed their immigration laws for high-skilled persons, especially during the 1990s.

Current trends are not without historical precedent. Technical progress has shaped the incentive structure for migrants since at least the Industrial Revolution in the eighteenth century. Prominent examples were European workers who were attracted by the industry in the United States in the eighteenth and nineteenth century (Chiswick and Hatton, 2002). Skilled migrants have always been part of these migration streams, but this skill was often characterised by tacit knowledge. The current importance of codified knowledge means that qualifications are what counts, and these are internationally increasingly transferable. The following section looks more closely at the channels by which information and communication technologies influence the incentives for international migration.

ICT and high-skilled migration

ICT influences the migration decision by changing employment opportunities, and at the same time, altering the direct costs and benefits of migration for the individual in several ways (Table 18.4). First, the availability of better information through the Internet and the standardisation of workplaces reduce the costs for the individual migrant. However, these cost reductions might be rather small in the whole migration context. Second, technical progress driven through ICT increases the demand for highly skilled workers, especially for IT experts. Third, policy reacts to the increasing demand for highly skilled workers and facilitates migration to industrialised countries.

To judge the effects of ICT on high-skilled migration would mean that all the channels captured by Table 18.4 should be analysed. Obviously, though, this would be a rather difficult exercise. However, there are some general trends that show the close relationship between ICT and high-skilled

Table 18.4 ICT and determinants of the migration decision

What are the relevant general trends in the context of ICT?	How do these trends influence the migration decision?	What are the effects on costs and returns of high skilled migration?
Reduced costs of information transfer and adoption to new work environments		
Standardisation of IT applications leads to increased share of general, in relation to specific, knowledge	Increasing transferability of knowledge between firms, sectors, economies	Higher personal returns to human capital, reduced costs of changing employment (national and international); erosion of specific knowledge that ensures 'quasi-rents'
Diffusion of ICT	Availability and use of the Internet as medium for information and communication	Reduced costs of communication and information
Increasing international demand for high-skilled IT experts and entrepreneurs		
Boom of ICT production industry and organisational changes in ICT using industries	International labour demand for ICT experts due to the Internet and new economy boom	Employment and income opportunities
Standardisation of ICT goods and services	Increased trade of standardised ICT goods and services	Increased employment and income opportunities within the home country
Profit incentives for ICT entrepreneurs	Availability of VC capital accompanied by growing markets for ICT goods and services	Expected profit opportunities; reduced cost of capital supply and low cost of becoming self-employed

Technical progress and internationalisation of labour markets for the highly skilled

Skill bias of technical change	Increased demand for qualified labour	Increased employment and income opportunities
Migration as one aspect of the knowledge management of multinationals which is assisted by the use of ICT technologies	Growing importance of internal and external labour markets of multinational enterprises	Reduced cost and increased income opportunities of migrants within the firm-internal labour market; partly substituted by information flows
Internationalisation of the academic and scientific world, facilitated by the availability of ICT technologies	Growing importance of international careers, increased diffusion of scientific knowledge	Attraction of places with high scientific reputation; future academic career chances, increased reputation; increased local supply of high-level education

Policy changes

Increasing awareness of the importance of tacit and human-embodied knowledge in relation to codified knowledge (brain drain/gain)	International policy aiming at the attraction of skills and the diffusion of knowledge	Opening of legal migration channels Reduction of the cost of migration

migration. During the last decades, skill-biased technological change has constantly increased the employment opportunities for high-skilled employees in the industrialised countries. This trend has caused wage distributions to become wider in many industrialised countries, while increasing the unemployment of unskilled workers. Many observers argue that the rising demand for skills is due to the complementarity of ICT with skills (Autor *et al.*, 1998). However, the question of whether the increasing demand for higher skills is due to the diffusion of ICT is still disputed (Acemoglu, 2002b: 32–35).

The most direct effect of ICTs on international migration can be observed when IT specialists migrate to industrialised countries – either to set up their own businesses or to work as an employee in the country of destination. According to OECD estimates, 6.6 million foreign ICT professionals and specialists worked in the six countries – Belgium, France, Germany, Norway, the United Kingdom and the United States – in 2001 (OECD, 2003: 66). This number amounts to 52 per cent among the 1.3 million foreign employees in the three sectors with the highest number of foreign high-skilled workers – university teachers, health professionals and ICT specialists. As Figure 18.1 shows, the share of foreign ICT specialists is comparable to the share that foreign employees have in the other two sectors.

Of the countries shown, this share is highest in the USA with 18.3 per cent. In the European countries, the share of foreign professionals is between 4.2 per cent for France and 6.4 per cent for the United Kingdom, and there are notable differences in the relative share of professionals in the three most

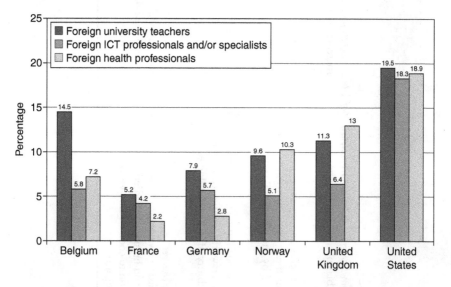

Figure 18.1 Foreign employment in university education, ICT and health (shares in per cent, 2001).

important professions. In the USA, the share of foreign professionals in ICT is about the same as the share in university teachers and health professionals, but among the European countries, the UK shows a notably higher share of professionals in university teaching and health. Altogether, foreign ICT professionals are obviously important in many industrialised countries, but by far the most important in the USA.

There is, however, not only a tendency for ICT professionals to move to the location in the industrialised countries where the demand for their professions is high and earnings opportunities are excellent. At the same time, firms locate some offshore production and service activities to countries where the wage for high-skilled labour is low (Read, 2001). New technologies like the Internet render the coordination between different firm divisions easier. In particular, the relocation of ICT-related activities (like software development) has recently accelerated. This movement of capital may substitute high-skilled migration.

To conclude, it is not clear whether new jobs for high-skilled employees will lead to the relocation of people (migration) or of production of goods and services. Therefore, the development of international high-skilled migration is by no means automatic. New employment opportunities could alternatively be created in the developing countries. Furthermore, as has already been argued above, the traditional pattern of a one-time migration to a destination country is increasingly substituted by more heterogeneous migration patterns. The highly skilled move to another country for their studies and – later on – go back to their country of origin or move to a third country. Whether this increase in migrant flows ultimately also increases the stock of highly skilled migration is therefore not clear.

The effects of high-skilled migration: brain drain and brain gain

The export of skilled workers from developing economies to OECD countries raises concerns about the detrimental consequences of this transfer of skills for those left behind. Historically, the first wave of discussions about the brain drain as a problem for less-developed countries arose in the 1960s, when increasing migration from developing to developed countries was observed. At the time, the rich countries' policies to attract migrants were criticised heavily, because the exodus of skilled workers threatened to deprive developing countries of their best talents. Today, the discussion is quite similar, as the international poaching of talent through active recruitment policies has intensified. In particular, temporary visas for skilled migrants reflect the rapidly rising relative demand for skills.

Economic theory is ambivalent about the effects on the sending countries of international high-skilled migration. A first generation of contributions entertained static models with perfectly competitive labour markets.

In the basic framework, only negligible adverse welfare implications arise for the non-migrants left behind (Grubel and Scott, 1966). This result leads to the principal policy prescription to advocate the free mobility of labour. However, with internationally mobile capital, this clear-cut conclusion can be questioned (Johnson, 1967; Barry and Soligo, 1969). In addition, when there are distortions in wage setting (Bhagwati and Hamada, 1974; Schmidt et al., 1994), international migration of skilled workers might even imply negative welfare effects for unskilled workers in the sending country.

Yet, a complete account of the welfare effects involved needs to address the cost of education as well as economic activity foregone. If education is subsidised in the country of origin, international mobility of skilled labour imposes a cost on the sending country. Indeed, since developed economies are the recipients of these skills, they could compensate the sending countries by way of a brain drain tax (Bhagwati and Hamada, 1974; but also McCulloch and Yellen, 1975). However, the welfare effects are more complex than this. The possibility of later emigration might encourage young individuals in the sending regions to invest in their own human capital in the first place. Since not all plans for later migration are realised, there might even be an excess of skill formation over the loss of emigrating skills (Mountford, 1997; Stark et al., 1997, 1998; Vidal, 1998). Thus, the imbalance in the international wage structure encourages the growth of education in the poorer countries where the incentive to gain an education might otherwise be limited.

In empirical work, it is certainly difficult to collect evidence for or against these arguments, due to the simultaneous nature of education, migration and economic activity. The contributions by Beine et al. (2001, 2002) analyse the impact of migration on the education level in a cross-country regression, while Faini (2005) and Rothgang and Schmidt (2003) investigate the effect of migration on secondary and tertiary educational enrolments. In this chapter we compare the empirical results of the effect of migration on education enrolment using the CD and the DM data. We analyse the impact of high-skilled migration on tertiary and secondary level enrolment, holding economic activity per capita and the educational level constant across countries.

Table 18.5 indicates a positive effect of GDP per capita on tertiary enrolment for both 1990 and 2000. For the 1990 data, the effect of high-skilled migration on tertiary enrolments is not significant. Yet a numerically small negative effect is revealed in the pooled sample, together with a trend towards higher tertiary enrolment rates. Moreover, as the share of the working-age population with post-secondary education aggregates all factors that influenced education enrolment in the past, it is not too surprising to find a significant and strong positive influence of the share of the high-skilled in the working-age population on the tertiary-level enrolment rate. Overall, this evidence does not lend support to the revisionist hypothesis

Table 18.5 Tertiary level enrolment in higher education and high-skilled migration

	(1)	*(2)*	*(3)*
Constant	−0.252**	−0.473***	−0.621***
	(0.079)	(0.088)	(0.077)
Log GDP	0.036**	0.067***	0.084***
	(0.011)	(0.012)	(0.010)
Tertiary migration rate	−0.001	−0.001	−0.001**
	(0.001)	(0.001)	(0.001)
Post-second-level school completed total	2.184***	1.786***	1.876***
	(0.232)	(0.286)	(0.223)
Year 2000			0.060***
			(0.016)
Number of observations	51	94	165
Adjusted R^2	0.80	0.72	0.78

Notes
Standard errors are reported in parentheses. ***Significant at the 1 per cent level. **Significant at the 5 per cent level. *Significant at the 10 per cent level.

that the opportunity for future emigration fuels the demand for skills acquisition in the origin countries. Similar results apply to the relationship between migration and secondary-school enrolments.

Table 18.6 comprises the same specifications as Table 18.5, but with secondary level enrolments as the dependent variable. In this case, though not in the pooled regressions for 1990 and 2000 in column three, we find a small but significant impact of future high-skilled migration on secondary enrolments. Thus, overall, our statistical analysis lends some, but only weak, support to the brain-gain hypothesis that higher income opportunities abroad increase the incentives for obtaining more education. There is some evidence of a positive effect of high-skilled migration on secondary-level education. This investment perhaps seems a prerequisite for going abroad to pursue advanced university studies.

Conclusions

The development and diffusion of ICT has definitely been one outstanding factor that has influenced the growth and structure of high-skilled migration in recent decades. Foreign IT professionals are now as important in the IT sector in industrial countries as in healthcare and university teaching. The notion that a shortage of IT workers could hamper economic growth has certainly been crucial in the liberalisation of high-skilled migration flows that has taken place in many industrialised countries. In addition, ICTs have – together with the factors that have driven the internationalisation of scientific research and economic activity – fostered the internationalisation of labour markets.

Table 18.6 Secondary level enrolment and high-skilled migration

	(1)	(2)	(3)
Constant	−1.087***	−1.44***	−1.512***
	(0.248)	(0.149)	(0.115)
Log GDP	0.179***	0.229***	0.239***
	(0.033)	(0.020)	(0.015)
Tertiary migration rate	0.003***	0.015**	−0.001
	(0.001)	(0.001)	(0.001)
Post-second-level school completed total	1.636**	1.040***	0.990***
	(0.734)	(4.89)	(0.338)
Year 2000			0.083***
			(0.024)
Number of observations	58	100	183
Adjusted R^2	0.57	0.78	0.80

Notes
Standard errors are reported in parentheses. ***Significant at the 1 per cent level. **Significant at the 5 per cent level. *Significant at the 10 per cent level.

Our results demonstrate that there has been a moderate increase in the intensity of high-skilled migration over the course of the last decade and that it is particularly the smaller countries which export a large share of their best talents to the more advanced economies. Moreover, we find only weak evidence for a compensating brain-gain effect of future migration opportunities on current education enrolments for these smaller countries. Of course, this analysis can only lay a basis for further research to go deeper into the relationship between the information society and high-skilled migration.

Acknowledgements

We thank Birgit Petter and Marlies Tepaß for their assistance.

Notes

1 This is due to the use of census, register and survey data for the OECD countries. The Carrington and Detragiache estimates had relied on OECD immigration statistics which do not provide data for small sending countries (Docquier and Marfouk, 2004: 26). In addition, Carrington and Detragiache had to assume that distribution of immigrants across attainment groups to be the same for other OECD countries as for the USA (1998: 26).
2 OECD calculations are based on data for educational attainment from Barro and Lee (2001).

References

Acemoglu, D. (2002a) Directed technical change. *Review of Economic Studies*, 69, 781–809.

Acemoglu, D. (2002b) Technical change, inequality, and the labor market. *Journal of Economic Literature*, XL, 7–72.

Autor, D., Katz, L. and Krueger, A. (1998) Computing inequality: have computers changed the labor market? *Quarterly Journal of Economics*, 113(4), 1169–1213.

Barro, R.J. and Lee, J.-W. (1993) International comparisons of educational attainment. *Journal of Monetary Economics*, 32, 363–394.

Barro, R.J. and Lee, J.-W. (2001) International data on educational attainment: updates and implications. *Oxford Economic Papers*, 53(3), 541–563.

Barry, R.A. and Soligo, R. (1969) Some welfare aspects of international migration. *Journal of Political Economy*, 77, 778–794.

Beine, M., Docquier, F. and Rapoport, H. (2001) Brain drain and economic growth: theory and evidence. *Journal of Development Economics*, 64, 275–289.

Beine, M., Docquier, F. and Rapoport, H. (2002) *Brain Drain and LDCs' Growth: Winners and Losers*, Working Paper. Online, available at: www.biu.ac.il/soc/ec/toolbar/main/wp/8-02/8-02.pdf.

Bhagwati, J. and Hamada, K. (1974) The brain drain, international integration of markets for professionals and unemployment, a theoretical analysis. *Journal of Development Economics*, 1, 19–42.

Borjas, G.J. (1991) Immigration and self-selection. In Abowd, J.M. and Freeman, R.B. (eds) *Immigration, Trade and the Labor Market*, Chicago, University of Chicago Press, pp. 29–76.

Carrington, W.J. and Detragiache, E. (1998) *How Big is the Brain Drain?* IMF Working Paper WP/98/102.

Chiswick, B.R. and Hatton, T.J. (2002) International migration and the integration of labor markets. *IZA Discussion Paper*, 559.

Docquier, F. and Marfouk, A. (2004) *Measuring the International Mobility of Skilled Workers (1990–2000): Release 1.0*. Policy Research Working Paper No. 3381, The World Bank.

Faini, R. (2005) *Migration, Remittances and Growth*. In Borjas, G.J. and Grisp, J. (eds) Poverty, international migration and asylum, World Institute for Development Economics Research. Studies in Development Economics and Policy. Basingstoke, Hampshire, Palgrave Macmillan.

Haque, H. and Jahangir, A. (1999) The quality of governance: second generation civil reform in Africa. *Journal of African Economies*, 8, 65–106.

Heston, A. and Summers, R. (1991) The Penn World Table (Mark 5): an expanded set of international comparisons, 1950–1988. *Quarterly Journal of Economics*, 327–368.

International Monetary Fund (2004) *International Financial Statistics Yearbook*, Washington, DC, International Monetary Fund.

Johnson, H.G. (1967) Some economic aspects of the brain drain. *Pakistan Development Review*, 7, 379–411.

McCulloch, R. and Yellen, J.L. (1975) Consequences of a tax on the brain drain for unemployment and income inequality in less developed countries. *Journal of Development Economics*, 2, 249–264.

Mahroum, S. (1999) *Highly Skilled Globetrotters: the International Migration of Human Capital*. OECD Working Paper DSTI/STP/TIP (99)/2.

Mountford, A. (1997) Can a brain drain be good for growth in the source economy? *Journal of Development Economics*, 53, 287–303.

OECD (2002) International mobility of the highly skilled. *OECD Observer*, Policy Brief, Paris, OECD.

OECD (2003) *Trends in International Migration*, Annual Report, 2002 Edition, Paris, OECD.

OECD (2005) *Trends in International Migration*, Annual Report, 2004 Edition, Paris, OECD.

Read, B.B. (2001) *Is India Viable for Call Centers?* Online, available at: www.commweb.com/article/COM20010321S0001 (accessed 25 March, 2003).

Rothgang, M. and Schmidt, C.M. (2003) The new economy and the impact of immigration and the brain drain. In Jones, D.C. (ed.) *New Economy Handbook*, San Diego, Elsevier.

Schmidt, C.M., Stiltz, A. and Zimmermann, K.F. (1994) Mass migration, unions, and government intervention. *Journal of Public Economics*, 55, 185–201.

Sjaastad, L.A. (1962) The costs and returns of human migration. *Journal of Political Economy*, 70, S80–S93.

Stark, O., Helmenstein, C. and Prskawetz, A. (1997) A brain gain with a brain drain. *Economic Letters*, 55, 227–234.

Stark, O., Helmenstein, C. and Prskawetz, A. (1998) Human capital depletion, human capital formation, and migration: a blessing or a 'curse'? *Economic Letters*, 60, 363–367.

Straubhaar, T. and Wolter, A. (1997) Globalisation, international labour markets and the migration of the highly skilled. *Intereconomics*, 174–180.

UNESCO (2000) *World Education Report, The Right to Education: Towards Education for All Throughout Life*, Paris, UNESCO.

UNESCO (2004) *Gross Enrolment Data*, November. Online, available at: www.uis.unesco.org/ev.php? URL_ID=5187&URL_DO=DO_TOPIC&URL_SECTION=201.

Vidal, J.-P. (1998) The effect of emigration on human capital formation, *Journal of Population Economics*, 11(4), 589–600.

World Bank (1999) *World Development Indicators 1999*, Washington, DC, World Bank.

19 Electronic waste and dematerialisation

Alberto Pasquini and Lorenzo Vicario

Introduction

There is clear evidence that information and communication technology (ICT) is transforming our society into an information society. That is, a society where the access to information and information services, accumulated knowledge and learning opportunities is fast, cheap and efficient, and can be done without any significant spatial and temporal constraints (Castells, 2000). This modification is having a strong influence on human behaviour, and the changes induced can have a significant effect on the environment (Jokinen *et al.*, 1998). Since the environmental issues are one of the central aspects in our future, we need a better understanding of this relationship between the development of the ICT and the environment.

This chapter is based on the e-Living surveys and illustrates two of the influences that the ICT diffusion within households is having on the environment. The first is an example of direct influence; that is, a type of influence that is present even if the households do not change their lifestyle or intentionally modify their environmental impact. Direct influences, also called effects of ICT usage (Dompke *et al.*, 2004), are just consequences of buying, using and disposing ICT products, and they include, for example, the increase in electric power consumption due to the use of ICT devices. The example we analyse in the following is the disposal of ICT devices.

The second is a case of indirect influence on the environment. Indirect influences, also called systemic effects of ICT (Dompke *et al.*, 2004), are the results of changes in behaviour, such as when adopting a more environmental friendly lifestyle, either intentionally or unintentionally. Several applications of ICT can have an influence on the behaviour and attitudes of household members, as in the case of online shopping, teleworking and dematerialisation. We analyse an example of dematerialisation by studying the adoption of digital music.

'Electronic waste'

The disposal of ICT devices is becoming a major problem because of the volume of the waste produced and, even more, because of the possible presence of hazardous substances such as lead, mercury, flame retardants and plastic softeners (Kiuchi *et al.,* 2001). The problem is made worse by the continuous reduction of the lifespan of computers. Some authors claim that because of the advances in chip technology, this lifespan has been reduced from perhaps four-to-five years to approaching two years or less (Kiuchi *et al.*, 2001). However, other authors (Cooper, 2000) have shown that the real lifecycle of computers can be much longer than expected because computers are recycled through commercial channels, donated to less-demanding users or kept as possible back-up for the new systems. An indication of this is that, since 1996, the market for refurbished computers in the UK has increased by 500 per cent, although still less than 20 per cent of all redundant computers are being recovered.

e-Living results

Our data, shown in Table 19.1, shows how the computers in use in the six countries of the e-Living survey are of relatively recent production, with a mean age ranging from 2.6 years in Bulgaria to nearly four years in Germany, with the low mean age in Bulgaria probably due to the recent growth of PC penetration in this country (Raban *et al.*, 2002).

Our previous work (Pasquini *et al.*, 2002) shows how the number of computers that have been thrown away by household members is very low compared to the take up and diffusion of PCs over time (as described in Raban, 2002). This does not match with the short lifecycle one would expect from the literature, or from the data shown in Table 19.1. According to some authors (Kiuchi *et al.*, 2001) the discrepancy between data concerning acquisition, lifecycle duration and the number of computers thrown away might be due to the attitudes of people to storing computers in back rooms and offices. People are unwilling or reluctant to throw away computers because these are perceived as still valuable goods.

These findings are confirmed by our data reported in Figure 19.1, showing, for the six countries of the survey, the average age of computers when these are thrown away and definitively enter the waste stream. Charting this against the respondent's PC skills, we can detect signs of 'higher

Table 19.1 Mean age of computers in use

Country	Mean age
UK	3.06
Italy	3.89
Germany	3.98
Norway	3.52
Bulgaria	2.62
Israel	2.67

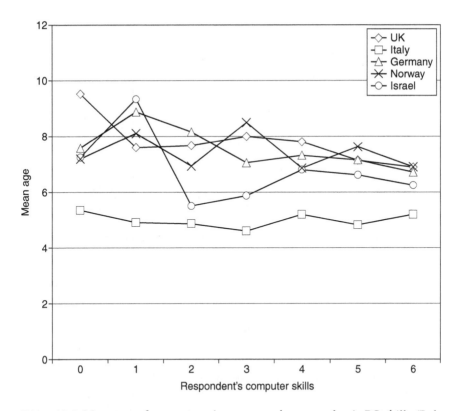

Figure 19.1 Mean age of computers thrown away by respondent's PC skills (Bulgaria excluded due to small *n*, base = all who have ever been PC owners).

waste' in potentially more demanding users. With the exception of Italy, there is a clear downward trend such that those with greater skills are likely to throw away younger PCs. As PC skills and experience increase, this trend may intensify, or at the least affect a wider proportion of the population. In addition, the mean figure for the UK is in agreement with the survey conducted by the E-Scope project (Cooper, 2000) that reports an average age of six-to-eight years for computers discarded in the UK.

Figure 19.2 shows the percentage of computers that have been thrown away, by computer age and by country. The distribution of this percentage is rather uniform across the countries, with the only exception of Italy, which has a slightly higher percentage of computers disposed of in the age groups 'three-to-five years' and 'two years or less'. However, even in this country of excessive waste, as well as in a country of 'early adopters' like Norway, the percentage of computer owners who have never thrown away a computer is very high at more than 60 per cent. This reinforces the hypothesis that old, out of use computers are not thrown away but temporarily

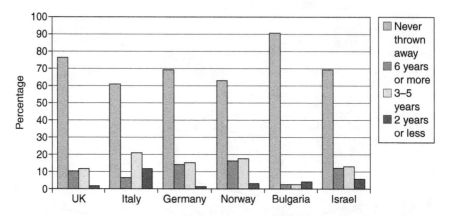

Figure 19.2 Percentage of computers thrown away, by age group and by country (base = PC owners).

stored in the owner's house. However, the storage capacity of attics, garages and warehouses is not infinite. We can expect that an increasing number of these items will soon enter the waste stream, thereby accelerating dramatically the problem of electronic waste.

In addition, if the reason for not throwing away computers is that people perceive even old computers as valuable goods, this situation is likely to change. As soon as people start to be more familiar with computers, using them for leisure or work in their everyday life, their perception as a valuable good will be replaced with a perception as a tool, useful as long as it is updated. This phenomenon has already started and can be clearly seen in Figure 19.1.

It is not clear from these charts how important these factors are relative to each other. We have examined this using a simple logistic regression model which predicts the probability of discarding a computer, based on the level of the respondent's computer skills, the number of rooms in the home, the number of children, whether or not the respondents are a member of an environmental group, and their family status.

The results of this simple model are given in Table 19.2. This shows the odds ratios: a value of 1 would mean no effect, a value less than 1 indicates a negative effect, a value greater than 1 indicates a positive effect. In fact, having higher computer skills slightly reduces the likelihood of throwing away a computer when other factors are controlled. Having more children in the household also reduces the likelihood, as one might expect, since older PCs can be redistributed to children. Compared to the UK, Italians are more likely to throw away a PC, as are Germans and Bulgarians, although we should beware the magnitude of this last result as it is almost certainly an artefact of there having been historically fewer PC owners in Bulgaria in any case. Of the household groups, compared to young childless couples, those

Table 19.2 Factors affecting the probability of throwing away a computer

Variable	Odds ratio	z
Sum of computer skills	0.87***	−12.13
Number of rooms in house	1.02	1.20
Number of children	0.92**	−3.14
Member of environmental group	1.17	1.90
Household type (contrast = couple, no children, aged <36)		
Unrelated	0.87	−0.55
Mixed relatives	2.22*	2.38
Alone <56	1.26	1.58
Alone >55	3.68***	7.62
Lone parent, children aged <16	0.90	−0.61
Other lone parent	1.17	0.95
Couple, no children, aged <56	1.15	0.88
Couple, no children, aged >55	1.81***	4.03
Couple, children <16	0.91	−0.69
Couple, children >16	1.03	0.12
Country (UK = contrast)		
Italy	1.26**	2.90
Norway	1.07	0.87
Germany	1.27**	2.99
Bulgaria	9.52***	16.44
Israel	1.09	1.03

Notes
All countries pooled, logistic regression model, pseudo $R^2 = 0.12$, * $= p < 0.05$, ** $= p < 0.01$, *** $= p < 0.005$.

with mixed relatives, those alone over fifty-five, and couples aged over fifty-five with no children, were all more likely to have discarded a PC. The age component of this effect should be read in relation to Figure 19.1, which implies that people with higher computer skills (who are also likely to be younger) have newer computers. One might expect on this basis that younger people would be more likely than older people to dispose of a computer. However, it could be that older people have retained their computers for less time simply because the machines tend to be old. Perhaps in time these processes will cancel out.

Modelling future computer waste rates

In the next few years we are likely to see the joint entrance of old and relatively new computers into the waste stream. The old computers are those that cannot be stored any longer or in which people have lost interest. The relatively new computers are those that are thrown away because they are considered as a useless or out-dated tool. This is the probable consequence of people becoming more familiar with the technology and no longer perceiving computers as valuable goods but as expendable commodities.

We have estimated the absolute numbers of computers that will be thrown away in the six countries of the survey in the years from 2004 to 2010. The sources of data and the assumptions for this estimate are shown in Table 19.3. We considered the number of computers bought in the past years, the current average age of computers when thrown away and the trend towards a reduction of this age.

The results are presented in two figures, because of the different scales required by the two groups of the three most populated countries (Germany, Italy and the UK) and of the three less populated (Bulgaria, Israel and Norway). The former are presented in Figure 19.3, the latter in Figure 19.4. The two figures show the upper and lower limits of the estimates based on upper and lower estimates of overall PC penetration derived from Raban (2004).

In our estimation, the increased penetration of computers and the decrease in the average age of the computers disposed of leads to a dramatic rise in the number of PCs in the waste stream, with a yearly increase at a much higher rate than the current 3–5 per cent that is currently considered the more realistic estimate (European Union, 2003). The only exception to this is Norway.

In Europe, the whole problem should now be regulated by Directive 2002/96/EC on waste electrical and electronic equipment, as amended by Directive 2003/108/EC (also known as the WEEE Directive) adopted by the Council and European Parliament in 2002. This deals with electronic equipment design, recycling and the presence of hazardous materials such as mercury and flame retardants. The Directive requires member states to ensure the establishment of systems for the collection of e-waste (by August 2005). Furthermore, they have to ensure its re-use, recovery and recycling, and the sound disposal of the remaining waste. When the collection systems

Table 19.3 Data used for the estimate of computers thrown away

Data	Source
Population 2004–2010	ONU estimate
Average household size 2003	Data from the National Statistical Institutes of the six countries
Average household size 2004–2010	Assumed to be equal to 2003
Future diffusion of computers	As in (Raban, 2002)
Current mean age of computers when thrown away	As in Table 19.1
Mean age of computers when thrown away 2004–2010	Estimate based on current values and on the influence of familiarity shown in Figure 19.2

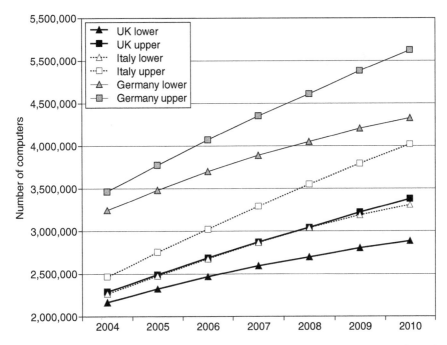

Figure 19.3 Number of computers that will be thrown away in Germany, Italy and UK in the coming years (upper and lower estimates in absolute numbers).

are in place, consumers will be able to take these products back to shops and collection points for free. The Directive also sets re-use and recycling targets of 75 and 65 per cent of all e-waste material respectively.

In addition to the WEEE Directive, the Council and European Parliament also adopted the Directive on the Restriction of the Use of Hazardous Substances (Directive 2002/95/EC of the European Parliament and of the Council of 27 January 2003 on the restriction of the use of certain hazardous substances in electrical and electronic equipment, also known as the RoHS Directive). This Directive bans certain hazardous substances from electronic equipment from 1 July 2006 onward to facilitate recycling, and to reduce emissions when the remaining e-waste is landfilled or incinerated.

Taken together, these actions could significantly influence the projections presented here. However the implementation of the WEEE Directive is facing significant resistance, as shown by the legal action taken by the Commission against eight member states because of the delays in transposing the WEEE Directive into their national laws.

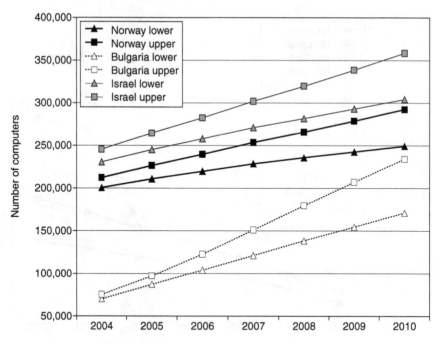

Figure 19.4 Number of computers that will be thrown away in Bulgaria, Israel and
Norway in the coming years (upper and lower estimates in absolute
numbers).

Dematerialisation

Dematerialisation is the use of new services and goods to perform the same
functions as the old ones, but with a reduced use of material and energy.
Examples are new personal computers needing fewer material than the old
mainframe or the use of electronic services (such as telephone directories via
the Internet) instead of physical objects offering the same services (such as
the hard copies of the telephone directories). The main functions of the telephone directory (data storage and retrieval) are performed far more efficiently online than on paper. Telephone books go out of date each year,
while electronic versions can be up-dated continuously, offer various search
capabilities and have no associated printing and distributing costs.

However, innovations introduced by the technology are mainly directed
towards increasing total production and thus total profits rather than saving
material and energy. Thus, the total use of material resources may increase
more than the savings because of the rebound effect. The rebound effect is an
economic and social phenomenon reducing the potential environmental
benefits of innovation. The resource savings from innovations of specific
products and services are eaten up by extending the consumption of the

new, resource effective, products and services, usually because of their lower price and hence greater demand. For example, it is true that personal computers cost much less and need fewer material than the old mainframe, but there is a much wider diffusion of personal computers if compared with mainframes. Another reason for the rebound effect is the diffusion of other patterns of resource consumption that originate mainly in a change in consumer behaviour. The increase in paper use due to the ease and low costs of processing, storing and printing texts with the support of personal computers is a good example of this. In addition, quite often the new services do not completely replace the old ones, but are used additionally, helping to extend the limits that the old technology would have eventually hit.

The degree of replacement depends on several social and economical factors, including the ability of the new services to offer all the features provided by the old one, the usability of the related instrument and of the service itself, and the cost.

We report one example of ICT and Internet-enabled services that could replace tangible good and services: the use of digital music (e.g. MP3) with the related substitution of conventional disks and tapes. This example was chosen because the adoption of the new service/technology is significant in all the countries of the e-Living survey, excluding Bulgaria. The data show very well how the degree of replacement is influenced by several factors, including the functionality, usability and the familiarity with the new service/technology, and finally it is extremely topical with respect to current debates about online piracy and copyright issues.

Dematerialisation and digital music

Figure 19.5 shows the percentage of Internet users who downloaded music at least once in the three months prior to interview (excluding Bulgaria) for the two waves of the survey. At the country level (not shown) there is a slight increase in the percentage for all countries, except Norway, perhaps due to a greater familiarity with the service/technology and with the use of the Internet (although the low number of new users does not allow a better analysis of the causes).

The adoption of this new service/technology is correlated to the age of the users, as shown in Figure 19.5. The slight increase in usage is common to all the age categories except forty-five-to-sixty-five and is noticeably higher for the oldest and youngest groups.

Figure 19.6 shows, for the two waves of the survey, the percentage of those downloading music divided into three classes: those who said they did not replace disks or tapes with digital music in the last three months and continued to buy the same number as before; those who said they replaced from one-to-four disks or tapes with digital music; and those who said they replaced five or more disks. The adoption of digital music brings several new possibilities, such as transferring to other devices or sharing

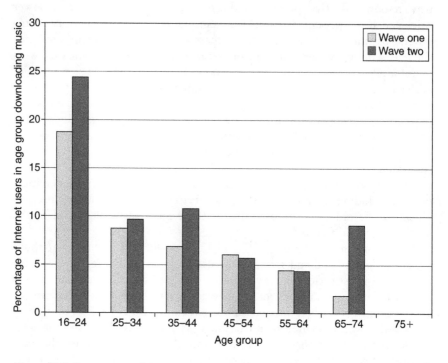

Figure 19.5 Percentage of Internet users who reported downloading music in the last three months, by age group (UK, Italy, Germany, Israel and Norway, pooled).

pieces through the Internet, but has also some negative points including lower quality and some usability problems. Figure 19.6 shows how the different, non-overlapping features of the two services/technologies (music on conventional support and digital music) do not favour a complete replacement of the first with the second.

The comparison between the first and the second wave of the e-Living survey in Figure 19.6 could lead to the assumption that the increased familiarity with the new service/technology leads to a growing replacement of music on conventional supports (disks or tapes) with digital music. However, using the longitudinal data, we can see that there is not a simple increase in the number of those downloading digital music. In fact, there is considerable churn. Figure 19.7 shows the percentage of Internet users in each age group who have stopped, started or continued to download music. The percentage of those who stopped downloading is quite high in all the countries, and in most of the cases this is comparable to the other two classes.

There are apparently almost as many music downloaders who are abandoning the practice as are starting it, and whilst there is a clear churn for the

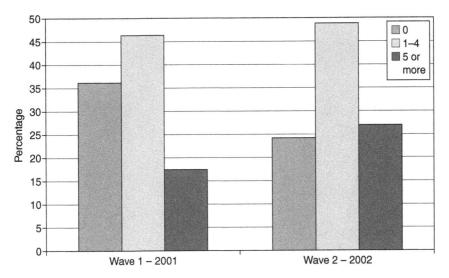

Figure 19.6 Percentage of Internet users by number of disks or tapes not bought in the last three months, because replaced with music downloaded through the Internet, for the two waves of the survey (UK, Italy, Germany, Israel, Norway, pooled).

youngest users, it is interesting to see that there are peaks in other age groups. The question is, to what extent these are related to skills, age or simply to changes in Internet access.

To test this we have conducted a similar regression analysis to that reported above, but this time analysing the factors effecting stopping downloading music compared to continuing to download. The results are shown in Table 19.4. We can see that there are predominantly age and computer skills (negative) effects, but none for level of education. Whilst there are no effects for mode of Internet access (PSTN or ISDN+, which includes broadband), there were in an earlier form of the model which excluded computer skills, showing how the two correlate. We can also see that Internet experience is not significant. Compared to being aged sixteen-to-twenty-four, older Internet users are much more likely to stop downloading and the oldest are the most likely, in contrast to the bivariate results shown in Figure 19.7.

There could be several possible reasons for this strong tendency to stop downloading music with age. The most important is probably the difficulty in using the new technology and this is supported by the results for computer skills, even when age is controlled. The e-Living survey could not investigate in-depth other possible causes for stopping downloading, such as excessive downloading time, or legal constraints, although in the case of the former the lack of an effect for broadband as opposed to PSTN access suggests that mode of access may not be as important as the other

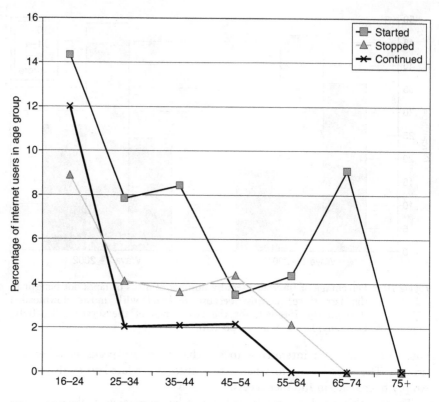

Figure 19.7 Percentage of Internet users who have stopped, started, or are continuing to download music going from the first to the second wave, by age group.

factors we have discussed. However, our data are an additional example of how replacement is not automatic, but depends on several social, economic and technological factors.

Conclusions

The interaction of human activity with the environment is a compound process based on a complex of pressures. ICTs can greatly influence most of the elements of this process. A detailed analysis of the process and of the ICT influence on it appears in Marletta *et al.* (2004). In this work we have focused only on two aspects: electronic waste and dematerialisation.

Electronic waste is a major problem for waste disposal, because of the volume of the waste produced and, even more, because of the possible presence of hazardous substances such as lead, mercury, flame retardants and plastic softeners. We expect that the number of computers thrown away will rise dramatically in the coming year, as soon as the large numbers of old, out-of-use computers start to emerge into the waste stream. These comput-

Table 19.4 Factors affecting the probability of stopping downloading music

Variable	Odds ratio	z
Education (none)		
GCSE or equivalent	0.51	−1.58
A-levels or equivalent	0.63	−1.08
First or higher degree	0.45	−1.73
Sum of computer skills	0.71***	−4.10
Years of Internet use	0.96	−0.70
PSTN Internet access	0.65	−0.61
ISDN+ Internet access	0.43	−1.21
Age (16–24)		
25–34	2.21***	3.34
35–44	2.18***	3.03
45–54	2.79***	3.03
55–64	5.64***	2.99
Country (UK)		
Italy	0.95	−0.16
Norway	0.91	−0.30
Germany	1.77	1.77
Bulgaria	0.64	−0.50
Israel	0.52*	−2.04

Notes
All countries pooled, logistic regression model, pseudo $R^2 = 0.12$, $* = p < 0.05$, $** = p < 0.01$, $*** = p < 0.005$.

ers are currently stored within households and have not yet been thrown away because they are still perceived by the owners as valuable goods. We also expect that this tendency to store computers will be reduced in the coming years as long as people become more familiar with the technology and start to consider computers as a tool of day-by-day use rather than as a valuable good to be conserved. This will worsen the problem because more and more newer computers will be disposed of, thus joining the others in the waste stream. It is therefore essential that the European Directives concerning the Waste Electrical and Electronic Equipment are transposed into national laws without further delays.

The influence of ICT on human activity that could generate pressures on the environment was investigated by considering dematerialisation. Dematerialisation has much potential for reducing environmental pressure due to human activity. However, this good potential for energy and material saving is not automatic. The survey has confirmed that the degree of replacement with new services and goods depends on several social and economical factors, including the ability of the new service or good to offer all the features provided by the old one, the usability of the related instrument and of the service itself, the age of the users, competition with other technologies and cost.

Innovations introduced by the technology are mainly directed towards increasing total production rather than saving material and energy. Thus, the total use of material resources may increase more than the savings because of the rebound effect. The potential for a reduction of environmental pressure, which would be possible with dematerialisation, will only be exploited, in a commercial market, if we are able to consider the real costs of services and goods. That is, if we are able to account for the hidden environmental and social costs of services and goods, such as the cost of pollution or the costs implied in the consumption of non-renewable resources, or any other cost that, at the moment, is paid by the whole society and by future generations (see also Alakeson and Goodman, this volume, Chapter 20). An effort in this direction is represented by the recent White Paper on the Integrated Product Policy and the new draft Framework Directive on the Eco-Design of Energy-Using Products of the European Union, both promoting whole-lifecycle thinking. One of the desired outcomes of these initiatives is to enable consumers to consider not only the technical function and purchase price of goods and services, but also their environmental burdens. Until this whole cost approach can be implemented, increasing ICT penetration and the waste this causes are likely to outweigh any environmental benefits that the information society may bring.

Bibliography

Castells, M. (2000) *The Rise of The Network Society, The Information Age – Economy Society and Culture, Vol. 1*, London, Blackwells.

Cooper, T. (2000) *Prospects for Household Appliances, Final Technical Report*, E-scope project, UK.

Dompke, M., von Geibler, J., Gøhring, W. *et al.* (2004) *Memorandum Nachhaltige Informationsgesellschaft*, Stuttgart, Fraunhofer IRB Verlag. Online, available at: www.giani-memorandum.de/.

European Union (2003) *Directive 2002/96/EC on Waste Electrical and Electronic Equipment*, Official Journal of the European Union L37, Brussels.

Jokinen, P., Malaska, P. and Kaivo-oja, J. (1998) The environment in an information society. *Futures*, 30(6), Finland.

Kiuchi, T., Gable, C., Cassel, S. and Shirman, B. (2001) *Computers, E-Waste, and Product Stewardship: Is California Ready for the Challenge?* Technical Report of the Global Futures Foundation, San Francisco, USA.

Marletta, P., Pasquini, A., Stacey, G. and Vicario, L. (2004) *e-living D11 Environmental Impact of ICT: a Cross-Sectional Analysis*. Public e-Living Project Deliverable. Online, available at: www.eurescom.de/e-living/.

Pasquini, A., Velardo, M. and Vicario, L. (2002) *e-living D7.1 Environmental Impact of ICT: a Cross-Sectional Analysis*. Public e-Living Project Deliverable. Online, available at: www.eurescom.de/e-living.

Raban, Y. (2004) ICT uptake and usage: panel data analysis. *e-Living Project Report*. Tel Aviv, ICTAF, University of Tel Aviv.

Raban, Y., Soffer, T., Mihnev, P. and Ganev, K. (2002) *e-living D7.1 ICT Uptake and Usage: a Cross-Sectional Analysis*. Public e-Living Project Deliverable. Online, available at: www.eurescom.de/e-living/.

20 Sustainable business in the digital society

Vidhya Alakeson and James Goodman

Introduction

Corporate social responsibility (CSR) is an attempt by companies to ensure that their day-to-day business operates in a responsible manner involving the management of wider social and environmental risks and opportunities. This can include labour standards in the supply chain, the design of products, and transparency and consistency in government lobbying.

The 'CSR industry' may be relatively new, but CSR itself is not. There have long been more and less ethical ways of doing business, with companies like Rowntree investing in their local communities and boosting civic pride, or socially progressive business models like that of the John Lewis Partnership, owned entirely by its staff, who have an equal share in profits. But perhaps the new emphasis on CSR, which is associated most with shareholder-owned companies, can be attributed to the increasing privatisation of the public sector, or with a perception that companies, especially larger companies trading globally, are accruing increasing amounts of power.

In many cases, there is a clear, short-term business case for embracing CSR. For example, energy-efficiency measures cut corporate electricity bills as well as reducing their contribution to climate change. However, the business case for CSR is often less clear-cut, and sometimes companies pursue ethical policies simply because it appears to be the right thing to do. In the long run, however, the global economy needs to become more sustainable. The private sector is far larger than the public sector globally, and so the necessity for business to take its social, environmental and wider economic impacts seriously is clear.

The emergence of the Internet and mobile telephony has generated excitement in corporate responsibility circles and has promised to extend the business case for CSR. The ability to transfer information huge distances at the click of a mouse, for example, was thought to offer the same kind of win–win opportunity as energy efficiency: financial savings for the company and environmental savings in equal measure. Mobile phones would make flexible working for staff easier and so usher in a range of social benefits. But few things are that simple. Just as ICT has transformed business in far more subtle ways than the initial hype suggested, its impact on the environmental, social and wider economic impacts of business are complex because many factors are beyond the control of businesses themselves.

The impact of digital technologies on CSR was investigated in detail as part of the Digital Europe project between 2001 and 2003 (Alakeson *et al.*, 2003). This chapter draws on research conducted for the project and we look at three areas where the digital society is, or may be, changing CSR: first, the effect for some companies on the social or environmental impacts of their products; second, the tendency for companies to become – of their own volition or under pressure from external forces – more transparent to the outside world; and third, how the strategic response to CSR may be affected by the tools that digital technology gives companies. Finally, we arrive at a concluding summary with a number of recommendations for policy and research action and consider briefly some of the opportunities that this new landscape provides for companies in the ICT sector.

CSR and products

New types of product have become possible in the digital society. Does the shift from physical products to virtual products, which is transforming certain sectors such as music and banking, create products that do less environmental harm? Is there any truth in the assumption that the digital revolution will inevitably benefit sustainable development by replacing the physical manufacture and transportation of products with the electronic transfer of data? This was a question that was explored extensively in the Digital Europe project using the Wuppertal Institute's 'material input per service unit' (MIPS) methodology[1] to calculate the environmental impact of a product or service. MIPS involves collecting detailed information on all raw materials and energy used in the manufacture, transport, retailing and purchasing of the product. All material that does not end up in the final product goes into a metaphorical 'ecological backpack' and the results can be surprising: the 'ecological backpack' of a 10 g wedding ring is more than 5 tonnes.

According to the calculations conducted by the Wuppertal Institute in collaboration with EMI, downloading fifty-six minutes of music is twice as resource efficient as buying a CD online and more than two-and-a-half times as resource efficient as going to a shop to buy a CD. The savings come from every stage of the transaction (Tuerk *et al.*, 2003a).

The resources needed to make a physical CD give it an ecological backpack seven times its actual weight. Delivering music via the Internet eliminates the transport and infrastructure needed to get a CD from the factory to the consumer. In the case of EMI in Europe, CDs are taken by road from the factory to national distribution centres and on to the retailer. Finally, the consumer makes a journey to the retailer to make a purchase. The average CD travels well over 1,000 kilometres before it reaches the consumer and, in this time, its environmental backpack has increased to as much as fifteen times its weight.

Similarly paying a bill online is two-and-a-quarter times more resource efficient than paying the same bill at a branch if we allow for all required infrastructure and journeys (Tuerk *et al.*, 2003b). Not only has the individual to get to the branch, then, whilst the data on the payment slip is entered into the bank's electronic system at the branch and transferred to a clearing house for payment, the slip itself needs to be transported to the clearing house and stored. Even if one driver collects from fifteen branches at once, because Barclays only has one clearing house in the country, the average round trip is still 500 kilometres.

E-banking and digital music downloads are only two examples drawn from a plethora of products and services with the potential for virtualisation. However, if these results for music and banking hold true in general – which might be expected given that they are products whose economic justification is one of efficiency – virtualisation could represent a real opportunity to reduce the environmental impact of products and services. However, consumer behaviour could entirely change the picture, wiping out any environmental savings or even going the other way, making virtual products less resource efficient than their physical equivalents (see also Pasquini and Vicario, this volume, Chapter 19). Unlike physical products where material intensity tends to be influenced most by the production phase, with virtual products and services, consumers have far greater influence, because material intensity is no longer concentrated in the production and delivery phase of the product lifecycle. Figure 20.1 shows how overall material intensity is distributed between producer, retailer and consumer when a CD is purchased in a music store, online, and when a CD's worth of music is downloaded over the Internet. There is a marked downward shift in the distribution of material intensity across the value chain, making consumers as much the guardians of the environmental potential of virtual products as producers.

There are a number of aspects of consumer behaviour that could influence overall material intensity. Most of the material impacts of virtual products and services come from the electricity used by the technology needed to

Figure 20.1 The distribution of material intensity for CDs for different dematerialisation methods (source: Alakeson *et al.*, 2003, reproduced with permission).

deliver them. According to the Wuppertal Institute's calculations, the consumer's computer and Internet connections account for one-fifth of this. This is based on the assumption that the average consumer PC has a life span of four years (Geibler *et al.*, 2003). If the rate at which consumers upgrade their technology continues to increase, the average life span of the PC will decrease, and the overall material intensity of virtual products and services will rise. On current form, this seems likely (see Pasquini and Vicario, this volume, Chapter 19). In the USA, forty million computers became obsolete in 2001 alone (Goodman, 2003). In the UK, the average mobile phone is replaced after only eighteen months, although it has a life span of up to seven years.[2] And as electronic devices continue to get smaller, consumers are more likely to view them as disposable products and throw them away.

The speed with which consumers connect to the Internet has the potential to influence the material intensity of virtual products and services simply because it may affect the amount of time spent online. Downloading 56 MB of music (the average size of an album) takes four hours with a standard 56k modem, but just over a minute with a 10 MB connection. With every minute spent online waiting for a file to download, electricity is being used, making a 10 MB connection in theory considerably more resource efficient than a 56k modem. But of course faster download speeds do not benefit the environment if they encourage consumers to buy more online than they would have done offline, or to leave their computers on and connected to the Internet thus pushing up electricity usage. Indeed, as Anderson and Raban (this volume, Chapter 4) show, current evidence suggests that switching to broadband increases time spent online.

The potential environmental savings from virtualisation can also be lost if consumers choose to rematerialise virtual products, for example by printing out emails or burning digital music files on to CDs. Virtual products are relatively new and, as a result, we tend to want to consume them in the same way as their physical equivalents, rather than adapting to the virtual environment. The Digital Europe project calculated that if a blank CD is used to store fifty-six minutes' worth of downloaded music, the ecological backpack more than doubles and only a minor resource saving is made compared to a CD bought in a music store.

Even where virtual products and services remain virtual, people are unlikely to completely abandon the old way of doing things. The majority of e-banking customers tend to use all the channels available to them – the Internet, the telephone and the local branch – rather than using e-banking exclusively. Since much of the environmental and profitable potential of e-banking derives from having no high-street branch to support, it is clear immediately that realising this potential is not a straightforward task. Digital downloads exist alongside CDs, e-books have not closed down book shops and retailers offer online shopping as well as high-street shopping.

Virtual products and services need to be considered not in isolation but as part of the full 'product ecology' if we are to get a full picture of the material intensity of consumption in the digital society.

If consumer behaviour has a major part to play in realising the environmental potential of virtual products and services, producers must also play an important role in promoting consumer responsibility. BT has recently taken this step in some of its marketing material, drawing the attention of its customers to the fact that the 'always-on' benefits of broadband Internet access have an environmental downside, and asking them to make use of standby modes, or to turn the technology off when not in use.[3]

However, in general, producers unsurprisingly use their marketing muscle to influence consumer attitudes and beliefs for profit first and sustainable development second. When Apple added CD burners to their line of iMacs in 2001, they chose the marketing slogan, 'Rip, Mix, Burn' – the process of collecting the best tracks from several different albums and transferring them on to a CD using a computer. Rather than using its marketing campaign to encourage consumers to adapt to the virtual environment and keep products virtual, Apple effectively encouraged the re-materialisation of virtual products, and thus inadvertently promoted behaviour that increased the environmental burden. Too often, marketing sits with one part of the company, while commitments to sustainable development (as far as they go) sit with another.

CSR and transparency

Perhaps the greatest impact of ICT on CSR has been in the management of information, relationships and processes, often under pressure from outsiders who have been quick to spot the potential of these new technologies to reveal the inner workings of the corporate world. The Internet gives users much easier access to information about companies, their activities and their effects. Most company websites contain information that was available before the Internet but much less accessible. Annual reports, press releases, financial statements, and the names and contact details of key staff are all easily accessed, whilst even information that companies try to hide frequently finds its way out.

Levine and Locke (2000) have argued that widespread access to information is giving civil society greater control over corporations. They suggest that political and environmental activists are increasingly exploiting the abundance of information, often made available by companies themselves, to maintain pressure on companies to improve their social and environmental performance. Indeed, Henderson argues that the Internet has caused a step-change in the ability of non-governmental organisations (NGOs) to organise and mount effective campaigns against businesses, and laments that this has been one of the primary causes of the rise of CSR (2001).

Certain pressure groups, whose members may never even have met face to face, have set up websites specifically to target particular companies or malpractice, presenting information on activities that would have struggled to see the light of day before the Internet. Shell has been a victim of the activist group RTMark (now archived at www.rtmark.com/shell) while, during the controversy over genetically modified crops, Monsanto fell foul of a cyber-activist group called the Decepticons who set up www.monsantos.org (Taylor, 2001). Protest using the Internet has grown in sophistication, as activists have learned the skills of computer hackers to harass companies through their websites, or even disrupt internal systems, in a phenomenon referred to as 'hacktivism' (Miller, 2002; Wishart and Bochsler, 2002), an online version of civil disobedience. Virtual blockades and virtual sit-ins can be thought of as the equivalents of physical blockades and trespass and, inevitably, the mainstream pressure groups, such as Greenpeace or Friends of the Earth, now do a lot of their campaigning online.

The rate at which that information can diffuse also seems qualitatively different from previous waves of ICT. The Internet allows social networks to transmit information rapidly across the globe, often with unexpected consequences including greater transparency and accountability.

In 2001 sportswear manufacturer Nike was running a promotion in which individuals could customise their trainers with a slogan of their choice. MIT student and activist Jonah Peretti asked for the word 'sweatshop', but Nike refused (Peretti, 2001). There ensued a prolonged debate between Peretti and Nike which he saved and forwarded to a few well-connected friends, knowing that they would pass it on to others and that eventually the story would get out. But Peretti was stunned by the speed that this happened. Within days his email reached millions and soon he was getting calls from journalists and TV producers asking him for interviews. NBC's Today programme even flew him to New York to appear live in front of millions of viewers. Nike, of course, had to respond in real time.

CSR and e-business practices in Europe in 2002

The fate of Jonah Peretti's email suggests the potential power that information and speedy communication could bring to bear on companies. Few have fallen victim so far. There have been no high-profile cases to rival earlier campaigns such as Greenpeace's campaign against Shell's dumping of the Brent Spar oil platform in the North Atlantic in 1995. But wouldn't companies that are serious about sustainable development already be exploiting the unique properties of ICT to enhance their social and environmental track record?

As part of the Digital Europe project we conducted a survey of businesses in order to investigate whether there was a link between the use of e-business applications within companies and their CSR performance for those already active in this area.

Fieldwork was conducted in July 2002, with fifty-nine UK companies, eleven from Denmark, ten from the Netherlands, ten from Norway, eight from

Sweden and two from Ireland. Companies ranged from under 100 employees (six) to over 5,000 employees (fifteen). Roughly half of the companies in the survey had 1,000 employees or fewer, and half had more than 1,000 employees. One-quarter (25 per cent) of the companies contacted were in the manufacturing sector. Just under one-fifth (18 per cent) were services or retailing companies and 14 per cent were in the financial sector. The rest (43 per cent) were split between ICT/media (9 per cent), transport (9 per cent), mining (8 per cent), utilities (6 per cent) and construction (3 per cent). A further eight companies fell into the 'other' category (Goodman and Dawkins, 2004).

To qualify for the survey, companies had to be addressing four or more specific CSR-related issues, such as energy use, material use, employee diversity or supply-chain performance. Of the 100 companies in the survey, a total of eighteen of the companies interviewed were in one or more of the major sustainability/CSR indices. Nine were listed in the Dow Jones sustainability index, ten in the FTSE4Good Global Index, thirteen in the FTSE4Good Europe Index and nine in the FTSE4Good UK Index.

Two interviews were conducted per company, one initially with a CSR practitioner who had detailed knowledge of their company's sustainable development performance. They were then asked to refer the interviewer to an IT practitioner who had detailed knowledge of their company's use of e-business applications. Respondents were asked detailed questions about:

- what sustainable development issues they monitored or measured;
- whether performance on the issues they measured was thought to be improving or worsening;
- how e-business applications were used directly as tools to aid with sustainable development performance;
- what specific areas of e-business applications were used in the company;
- whether e-business had enabled geographic decentralisation of company activities;
- company profiling information.

The research was not designed to gather a representative sample of businesses in the six countries mentioned, and so it is not possible to draw conclusions about the general state of either e-business or CSR on the basis of its results. The survey aimed to investigate a link between levels of e-business application and levels of CSR performance within the non-random sample.

There were wide variations in the extent to which companies in the sample had adopted different e-business applications. The most popular applications were intranets (with 92 per cent of companies having one), online product information (used by 81 per cent of the companies) and platforms for electronic payments to suppliers (used by 78 per cent of the companies contacted). Factor and cluster analysis allowed us to separate the companies into four different groups, according to how they used e-business. The 'communications laggards' (16 per cent of the companies) had an average use of many e-business applications, but were less likely to use electronic payments, staff remote working, intranets and video-conferencing. The 'process laggards' (27 per cent) had an average score on most applications but were less likely to use process-orientated applications such as e-procurement, production management, inventory management, order tracking, energy management and project management. The 'mainstreamers' (46 per cent) had average use of all of the applications. The 'leaders' (11 per cent) had average use of many applications but were more likely to be using process applications such as e-procurement, production management, inventory management, order tracking, energy management and project management, and were more likely to use e-business in staff facilities, such as expenses, payroll and car sharing.

Having profiled corporate e-business use, we developed two indices of social and environmental performance. The sustainability measurement index showed how many of the social and environmental indicators companies were measuring, such as electricity use, water use, paper use, business travel or employee diversity. In the index, a score of 100 meant that all the companies measured all the indicators, and a score of 0 meant than none measured any indicators. Second, the sustainability performance index showed how many of the social and environmental indicators were reported by companies as improving. A score of 100 meant that all the companies were improving on all the indicators, and a score of 0 meant that all were worsening on all indicators. As Table 20.1 shows, 'e-business leaders' scored higher on both the sustainability measurement index and the sustainability performance index.

The difference between 'e-business leaders' and the rest of the companies in measuring social and environmental issues was statistically significant, but the difference in performance on those issues was not statistically significant.

The research did not investigate the direction of causality in this relationship, but it seems likely that progressive companies within the sample were more likely both to adopt e-business and to engage with social and environmental issues. This would support the idea that addressing sustainable

Table 20.1 Sustainability measurement and performance indices across organisational group

	Index score out of 100				
	Comms laggards	Process laggards	Mainstream	Leaders	Average
Sustainability measurement index	71	64	75	77	71
Sustainability performance index	78	72	78	83	77

Base: 100 companies

Source: Goodman and Dawkins, 2004, reproduced with permission.

development issues is a demonstration of good, enlightened management practice which is particularly important for companies wishing to prove to investors the importance of their sustainable development policies to the health of their company. Our survey showed no conclusive evidence that companies that used a lot of e-business actually performed better than other companies on sustainable development when other aspects were controlled. There may be a relationship here – which could become more obvious as e-business applications are more fully integrated into companies' operations – but more detailed research would be needed to assess any such link.

The worst performers in both indices were the 'process laggards'. The main difference in e-business use between the 'process laggards' and the 'leaders' was for applications such as e-procurement, production and inventory management, order tracking, energy management and project management. This could mean that, if there are automatic benefits to sustainable development to be realised through the use of e-business applications, it is these applications where benefits are most likely to accrue. There is also the possibility that these are the kind of applications that are more likely to be adopted by progressive companies, which in turn are more likely to address the social and environmental impacts of their operations.

The survey revealed a rather low awareness of the potential of ICT for better CSR among the companies tested. This is perhaps not surprising given the relatively low status of social and environmental issues in most companies' priorities. E-business tools are normally sold on the basis of cost savings and efficiencies, with little mention of the environmental efficiencies or improved stakeholder relationships that might result. This may represent a business opportunity for progressive ICT companies to market their products, as long as those products are designed with high social or environmental performance in mind.

Conclusion

We have discussed how increasing penetration of ICT and ICT-related innovations present a changing environment for companies' CSR activities. The research presented here looked at three areas where this was happening: with products, with the transparency with which companies operate and with the internal use of e-business applications to improve CSR performance.

There are various opportunities available here to improve the sustainability of business by improving CSR. For example, the virtualisation of music and banking products could lead to an overall reduction of the resources required to deliver those products. This could be seen as a catalyst for a wider shift away from product delivery towards service delivery.

But opportunities such as this will only be realised given the right policy from businesses and governments, and behavioural response by consumers. The businesses that deliver products that could be virtualised need to investigate that possibility and then develop business models that will be profitable and environmentally sound. Embedding the principles of sustainable development into the research, development and product innovation processes within companies is the only way to make this happen. Similarly, companies should communicate to their customers about socially and environmentally responsible use of products.

Businesses that use ICTs extensively can make social and environmental capital out of applications that may have an initial economic justification, while the companies delivering such applications could make more of their social and environmental benefits when marketing them. So far, the evidence base for the social and environmental benefits of various ICT products is quite weak. More research is certainly needed, in particular to look at how behaviour changes as a direct and indirect result of consumption of ICT products and services.

Ultimately, however, the potential for ICT to contribute to a more sustainable economy will not be realised until macro-level policy is changed. For example, a number of studies have shown how companies that encourage their staff to work at home a few days a week can save money on office space and reduce carbon dioxide emissions from commuting travel (see, for example Arnfalk, 1999; Sustel, 2002). Whilst this has localised benefits, freeing up office space and road capacity may not have aggregate-level effects since this capacity is then filled by others. Thus transport and consumption growth continue to correlate with GDP growth, despite the fact that telework in one form or another is no longer a minority pursuit in many countries in Europe as Haddon and Brynin (this volume, Chapter 17) show. What is needed is macro-level policy to consolidate the opportunities that individual companies are taking by, for example, making it more expensive to demand workstyles that cause their employees to emit carbon. Transport, energy and planning policy has also yet to respond significantly to new patterns of working and living so towns and suburbs continue to be built around the mass commuting model. In a market framed by policies that favour sustainable development, ICT is more likely to fulfil its socially and environmentally transformative potential.

Acknowledgements

This work was partially funded by the European Commission funded Framework 5 project Digital Europe.

Notes

1 See www.wupperinst.org/Projekte/mipsonline/.
2 Data from Fonebak. See www.fonbebak.co.uk.
3 Although this is also a strategy for reducing contention in the local loop so that more households can be supported by a small number of digital subscriber line (DSL) installations, thus reducing infrastructure set-up and maintenance costs.

References

Alakeson, V., Aldrich, T., Goodman, J. and Jorgensen, B. (2003) *Making the Net Work: Sustainable Development in a Digital Society*, London, Xeris.

Arnfalk, P. (1999) *Information Technology in Pollution Prevention: Teleconferencing and Telework Used as Tools in the Reduction of Work Related Travel*, Lund, Lund University.

Geibler, J.V., Ritthoff, M. and Kuhndt, M. (2003) The environmental impacts of mobile computing: a case study with HP. *Digital Europe Project Report*, Digital Europe Project.

Goodman, J. and Dawkins, J. (2004) Is e-business good business? *Survey Key Findings*, 2003 Digital Europe Project.

Goodman, P.S. (2003) China serves as dump site for computers: unsafe recycling practice grows despite import ban. *Washington Post*. Online, available at: www.ban.org/ban_news/china_serves.htm.

Henderson, D. (2001) Misguided virtue: false notions of corporate responsibility. *Hobart Paper 142*, London, Institute of Economic Affairs.

Levine, R. and Locke, C. (2000) *The Cluetrain Manifesto: the End of Business as Usual*, London, FT.COM.

Miller, P. (2002) *Open Policy*, London, Forum for the Future.

Peretti, J. (2001) My Nike media adventure. *The Nation*, 9 April.

SusTel (2002) An overview of the case study (and survey) findings. *SusTel Project Report*, SusTel Project.

Taylor, P. (2001) Hacktivism: in search of lost ethics? In Wall, D. (ed.) *Crime and the Internet*, London, Brunner-Routledge.

Tuerk, V., Alakeson, V., Kuhndt, M. and Ritthoff, M. (2003a) The social and environmental impacts of digital music: a case study with EMI. *Digital Europe Project Report*, Digital Europe Project.

Tuerk, V., Kuhndt, M., Alakeson, V., Aldrich, T. and Geibler, J.V. (2003b) The social and environmental impacts of ebanking: a case study with Barclays Bank. *Digital Europe Project Report*, Digital Europe Project.

Wishart, A. and Bochsler, R. (2002) *Leaving Reality Behind: Inside the Battles for the Soul of the Internet*, London, Fourth Estate.

21 Conclusion

A slow start?

Jonathan Gershuny

Most of the chapters in this book, and especially the introduction, imply that the new ICTs have socially had little transformative value. This is an important assessment, but what is its long-term significance? Are things changing so fast that almost any evaluation quickly becomes nugatory? It is hard to say, and the main reason is that there is no counter-factual. How fast *should* things change? When does a rate of change become an *event*, a defining time in history?

We think of the nineteenth and twentieth centuries as times of fundamental and rapid technological transformation, and of course communications and transport technologies in particular have had a powerfully transformative role. The cities of Europe and America were transformed twice within 100 years, first by railways, then by the motor car. The telegraph and then the telephone had less-obvious effects on the built environment, but even more on the organisation and coordination of production.

Yet the timescales were substantial. Rail-based transport was certainly a fact of life in a few parts of the UK in the 1780s.[1] There were demonstrations of steam-powered railways in the UK early in the nineteenth century, a first regular steam-powered service in 1827, huge railway building booms before 1850, but mass effects of railways on urban settlement patterns continued for at least a further century.

The motor car, requiring vast collective infrastructural investment, considerable private wealth and, initially at least, considerable skill from its owner/operator, was particularly slow to catch on. Otto Benz's first motor car was built in the 1880s, but thirty years later, the car was still an exotic item reserved for the rich. Indeed, the eventual social implications of the car were for many decades quite unclear. Forty years after Benz, when Shaw's *Man and Superman* sought to explore the twentieth-century socio-technical revolution, the superman of the title was in fact an educated motor mechanic, a graduate of the Regent Street Polytechnic in London, who was employed as a superior kind of servant by a grand family – hardly representative of the eventual impact of the motor car! Fewer than 50 per cent of households in the UK had a car by 1960.

The computer has been similarly slow to emerge as an object of mass consumption. The elements of a fully-fledged computing technology have been gradually accumulating since the eighteenth century, with Descarte's differencing machines, Babbage's analytic engines in the nineteenth century, Herman Hollerith's use of nineteenth-century Jacquard loom punch-card technology to automate the 1900 US census, and the Second World War electromechanical devices for code-breaking. However, the first commercial (if not commercially *successful*) electronic computer, essentially borne out of the boredom of an executive of a UK tea-shop chain, was the Leo computer, which provided automated stock control for Lyon's tea shops in the early 1950s.[2] Its technology was to some degree immature, with its main calculating storage device a mercury delay tube – an eight-foot mercury bath buried beneath the floor of its control room. Yet it worked successfully, as did the other ten original Leo machines ever sold (one of which ran a steel mill throughout a working life of some fifteen years, ending in the late 1960s). Several years later, Thomas J. Watson Jnr, Chief Executive of IBM, the inheritor of the Hollerith technology, allegedly underestimated demand for the IBM 370 by several thousand per cent.[3] Slow to develop, by 1969, more than fifteen years after the first commercial applications of the Leo computer, a leading science-fiction writer still found it necessary to explain the principles of multiple access 'time sharing' of computer facilities.[4]

Certainly, some saw the future relatively clearly: the eminent political scientist Norman Nie in 1971 was speaking publicly about a by-then-just-imaginable, but still quite distant, future in which every social scientist would have a computer console and instant access to a library of survey materials, but nevertheless at the time this prediction had an element of science fiction about it.

The diffusion of remote voice telecommunications was similarly slow. The telephone was first publicly deployed in 1880s, but its household penetration had not hit 50 per cent in many countries before the end of the 1950s. Television was first publicly broadcast by the BBC in 1936[5] – but it was subject to very little development until 1953, and had still not fully diffused by the early 1960s, mirroring the situation in many of the richer countries. The origin of the Internet can be traced to the 1960s' US Defense Advanced Research Projects Agency Network (DARPANET), which pioneered emails from around 1967, electronic packet switching technology in the 1970s, but the World Wide Web emerged more than twenty years later.

In 2006 we should still think of ourselves as being in the very early years of diffusion of computing. Serious home or personal computers have been around for more than a quarter-of-a-century. I will suggest that we might interpret where we are now as having very low levels of diffusion of the converged computing–telecommunication technologies which are also still quite a way off a stable developed form. Let us therefore try to get a picture of where we are now with some empirical data.

Twenty years' diffusion of home-computing in the UK

We use the British Household Panel study to estimate the diffusion of access to domestic computing equipment in Britain. This was available to just about one-quarter of the population in 1991, and by 2004/2005 this proportion had risen beyond two-thirds of the (sixteen-plus) population. In 1996 just under half of those with home computers, or 16 per cent of the population, had Internet access, whereas by 2004/2005 more than 80 per cent of those with access to home computers (56 per cent of the population) had home Web access. Clearly there has been a rapid diffusion of domestic access to computing services over this period, and access to personal computer equipment in particular might be interpreted as approaching saturation. This is shown in Figure 21.1.

But this information does not tell us to what extent the equipment is *used* – and certainly it gives us no clue as to the remaining potential of the technology for social transformation. To get a picture of this potential, we must use direct evidence of home-computing activity. For this purpose, we can deploy diary-derived time-use evidence to illustrate various features of

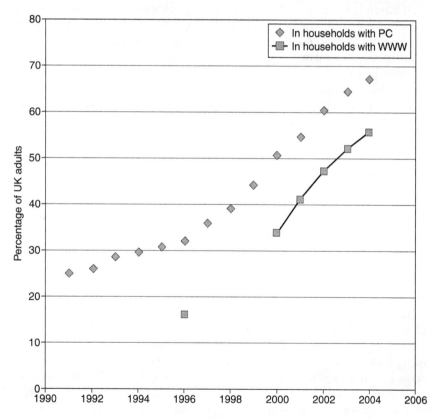

Figure 21.1 UK diffusion of PC and Web access (source: BHPS 1991–2004).

computer usage. All of the evidence that follows is drawn from large nationally-representative samples of randomly selected diary days.[6]

In all cases, respondents to these surveys were asked to describe their activity sequences (outside the workplace, but including work time as a whole) throughout the sampled day. The most straightforward statistic that we can derive from this material is the proportion using domestic computers (Table 21.1). In the 1980s just under one of every 100 men aged eighteen-to-sixty-four, and one in 500 women used home computers on a given day. In 2000, 15 per cent of men and 9 per cent of women did so; by 2005, 22 per cent of men and 13 per cent of women.

Table 21.2, constructed from a smaller-scale cross-national comparative study, shows approximately similar levels of daily computer usage in northern European countries (but unsurprisingly at a much lower level in Bulgaria). Essentially, one in four or five European men and one in ten women used their home computers on a given day.

However, while there has plainly been some very considerable historical growth in daily participation in domestic computing activity over the last twenty years, the amount of daily time spent using the home PC *by those who do use it on that day* has been relatively stable. Table 21.3 shows us, for example, that men using a PC, on a given day, spent two hours and seven minutes in 1985, one hour and forty-five minutes in 2000, and two hours and eleven minutes in 2005.

Table 21.1 Percentage using home computer on a random day, UK

	Whole sample			*Sample aged 18–64*		
	1985	*2000*	*2005*	*1985*	*2000*	*2005*
All	0.5	12.3	15.0	0.5	11.7	16.9
Men	0.8	17.2	20.3	0.8	15.4	22.2
Women	0.2	8.2	10.7	0.2	8.6	12.6

Sources: ESRC diary studies 1984–1987; ONS Time Use Study 2000; ONS Omnibus Time Use Study 2005.

Table 21.2 Percentage using home computer on a random day, 2003

	UK	*Italy*	*Germany*	*Norway*	*Bulgaria*
Whole sample	14.2	9.2	15.1	13.1	2.6
Men	20.3	14.9	22.3	20.1	3.3
Women	9.6	5.3	8.6	7.0	2.0
Sample aged 18–64	15.5	10.0	16.7	14.2	3.7
Men	21.7	15.9	24.5	21.4	4.5
Women	10.4	5.8	9.3	8.0	2.9

Source: e-Living survey.

Table 21.3 Computing time in the UK

	All	Users	Men		Women	
			All	Users	All	Users
1985	1	113	1	127	0	75
2000	11	91	16	105	6	70
2005	20	120	29	131	13	104

Sources: ESRC diary studies 1984–1987; ONS Time Use Study 2000; ONS Omnibus Time Use Study 2005.

The cross-national comparative materials in Table 21.4 show somewhat larger amounts of time devoted by users to domestic computing – but a quite remarkable cross-national similarity, varying by hardly more than five minutes around the mean of two hours and twenty minutes.

We might suspect that this virtual cross-national constancy reflects a similar pattern of applications of the technology – and we do in fact have some reasonably direct evidence, in the most recent UK survey, of what the computer is used *for*. These results are shown in Table 21.5. Computers are, generally speaking, a means of achieving some further purpose, whether work or leisure, along the lines of the 'service functions' discussed in Chapter 9. Respondents to the 2005 UK survey were asked to link domestic

Table 21.4 Time spent using home computer on random day, 2003

	All	Users	Men		Women	
			All	Users	All	Users
UK	22	139	33	154	12	114
Italy	14	139	26	164	5	91
Germany	23	136	33	134	13	144
Norway	20	140	30	138	11	143
Bulgaria	5	145	7	157	4	129

Table 21.5 Uses of home computer, UK 2005

% of time with allocated purpose	All	Men	Women
Paid work, study	40.5	37	44
Unpaid work, personal	16.5	14	19
Shopping	4	3	5
Leisure	39	46	32
	100	100	100
% of all PC time with allocated purpose	49	47	51

computer use to some other activity or purpose, though not all did. Around half of all the time spent using computers can, as a result, be classified as a means to some other purpose (and indeed, since computer use in the home is only rarely an end in itself, it may be appropriate to assume that the half of time for which respondents failed to assign a purpose is in fact distributed in a roughly similar manner). Table 21.5 shows that around 40 per cent of (allocated) domestic computing time is related to paid work, a similar proportion to leisure activities, 16 per cent to unpaid work and just 4 per cent to shopping.

The future and the home computer

It is implicit in this evidence that the process diffusion of domestic computing activities is hardly to be considered as complete. It is likely to be a long time until we reach the end of the spread of computing and telecommunications equipment. Nevertheless, falling costs, together with continuing growth in the range of home-computer-based applications, mean that eventual Web penetration is likely to approach that of the telephone – a saturation level approaching 100 per cent.

If we predicted the growth of personal computing and telecommunications use only on the basis of the diffusion of the equipment, we might infer a relatively trivial increase in time spent using a home computer, perhaps a 35 per cent to 45 per cent increase from the current twenty minutes per day over the next ten-to-twenty years in the UK for instance. But there is scope for a much more substantial change. At present just 20 per cent of the adult population use a personal computer on any given day, yet we might expect this to increase substantially. The use of computers is related to the availability of applications, and the range of these is growing. There are three particular examples in which considerable increase in activity might be expected.

- Video-on-demand or similar systems: the average adult in the UK spends around two hours per day watching television, and video-on-demand enables greatly increased choice in material.
- Home shopping: conventional shopping takes the average UK adult around forty minutes per day, and most adults shop twice or more per week. Again, home shopping is likely to provide a considerable market for home-computing activity, particularly with appropriate solutions to problems of home delivery.
- Paid work-related applications: it is difficult to judge the likely scale of the effect, but just-in-time production plus growth in managerial jobs make it likely that this sort of activity will increase markedly over coming years.

It is not implausible that these, combined with the equipment saturation levels discussed previously, might lead to a three- or four-fold increase in the daily participation rate – to 70 per cent or even to 80 per cent. It is difficult to explain the evidence of historical and cross-national stability of time devoted to computer use by users, but if we assume that this will rise even quite slowly, the implication is 100 or so minutes per day of home-computing-type activity – approaching the scale of present-day television and video in our daily lives now ... and implying changes at least as far reaching as those of the transport technologies mentioned in the opening paragraphs of this conclusion.

Notes

1 For example, the horse-drawn tram from Croydon to Central London.
2 Georgina Ferry, *A Computer Called Leo*, London: HarperPerennial, 2003.
3 This is apparently a misattribution: the honour of the 'half a dozen computers administered by skilled mathematicians' prediction belongs to Douglas Hartree of Cambridge University (Ferry, 2003: 138).

4   as many as two hundred people had been able to use the same computer at once; the principle was that computers acted very swiftly – in fractions of a second – while people operated slowly. . . . One person using a computer was inefficient, because it took several minutes to punch in instructions, while the computer sat around idle...
                (Michael Crichton, *The Andromeda Strain*, Jonathan Cape 1969: 119)

5 With a first-night maximum audience of less than 400 receivers, and a second-night potential audience of around 200 other receivers, since two incompatible systems – the Marconi electronic and the Baird electromechanical – had been selected.
6 The UK materials from ESRC surveys in mid-1980s (N of days = 16,413, Gershuny *et al.*, 1986), ONS (2000 N = 12,603, 2005 N = 2,506), cross-national evidence from e-Living survey wave two (Brynin, this volume, Chapter 15): samples reweighted to represent national populations.

Index

Page numbers in *italic* represent tables and in **bold** represent figures.

For Product Safety Concerns and Information please contact our EU
representative GPSR@taylorandfrancis.com
Taylor & Francis Verlag GmbH, Kaufingerstraße 24, 80331 München, Germany